Children's Services at the Crossroads

A Critical Evaluation of Contemporary Policy for Practice

Edited by
**Patrick Ayre and
Michael Preston-Shoot**

RHP

Russell House Publishing

Russell House Publishing
First published in 2010 by:
Russell House Publishing Ltd.
4 St. George's House
Uplyme Road
Lyme Regis
Dorset DT7 3LS
Tel: 01297-443948
Fax: 01297-442722
e-mail: help@russellhouse.co.uk
www.russellhouse.co.uk

British Library Cataloguing-in-publication Data:
A catalogue record for this book is available from the British Library.

ISBN: 978-1-905541-64-5

Typeset by TW Typesetting, Plymouth, Devon

Printed by Bell & Bain, Glasgow

Russell House Publishing

Russell House Publishing aims to publish innovative and valuable materials to help managers, practitioners, trainers, educators and students.

Our full catalogue covers: social policy, working with young people, helping children and families, care of older people, social care, combating social exclusion, revitalising communities and working with offenders.

Full details can be found at www.russellhouse.co.uk and we are pleased to send out information to you by post. Our contact details are on this page.

We are always keen to receive feedback on publications and new ideas for future projects.

Contents

Conclusion

About the Contributors

Patrick Ayre is a Senior Lecturer at the University of Bedfordshire where he teaches and researches in the fields of social work and child safeguarding. He has worked in the field of child protection and child welfare for over 30 years and was a social worker and manager of child protection services for some 17 years before taking up his present post. In recent years, he has been heavily engaged in the preparation of Serious Case Reviews, and is active as an expert witness in children's services' negligence cases.

Norma Baldwin BA (Hons) M.Phil., trained as a Probation Officer and worked in Greater Manchester and Salford Probation Service before moving to training and personnel in Warwickshire Social Services. She then moved to Warwick University where she taught and researched in child care and residential care. She moved to Dundee University as Professor of Child Care and Protection and Head of Social Work. She was later appointed Associate Dean (Research) for the Faculty of Education and Social Work. She is currently an Emeritus Professor at Dundee and Hon. Prof. at Warwick. Her research interests are in the links between poverty and harm to children and in the assessment of need and risk in families and communities. She continues her research at the Social Dimensions of Health Institute, Universities of Dundee and St. Andrews. She was Chair of the working group on Assessment on which the Scottish Assessment Framework in GIRFEC is based. She is Convenor of the Board of Trustees of the Scottish charity Circle (formerly FSU Scotland).

Tim Bateman has recently joined the University of Bedfordshire as a Reader in Youth justice, having previously been employed as a senior policy development officer for Nacro youth crime section. He has extensive experience of work in youth justice social work and residential child care. Tim has written widely on youth crime policy and practice. He is news editor of the journal *Youth Justice*, an associate editor of *Safer Communities*, and secretary of the *London Association for Youth Justice*.

Isabelle Brodie is Senior Research Fellow at the University of Bedfordshire. She has some 16 years experience as a researcher, working principally in the area of looked after children and specialising in their educational experiences.

Ian Butler is a qualified social worker with considerable practice and managerial experience in both the statutory and voluntary sectors. He is Professor of Social Work at Bath University. In 2005, he was seconded to the Welsh Assembly Government in Cardiff where he is a Special Advisor to the First Minister. He was joint Editor of the *British Journal of Social Work* between 1999 and 2004 (with Mark Drakeford). He was elected as a member of the Academy of Social Sciences in 2004. In 2009, he was appointed to the Board of Cafcass (England). He has published widely on social work policy and practice with children and families.

Martin C. Calder has specialised in the field of child protection for 25 years – establishing Calder Training and Consultancy in 2005. He is driven to provide robust and practical systems for child protection policy and practice but notes that 'this task has been made more difficult given the raft of government initiatives detracting from these goals'. He has written over 20 books addressing policy flaws and developing and disseminating assessment frameworks for frontline staff. He is currently Honorary Research Fellow at Durham University.

Alex Chard MSc is a Director of YCTCS Ltd and has worked for the last 18 years as an organisational consultant within children's services. Recent consultancy projects have included reviewing the strategic role of local children's trusts. He regularly works with management teams in order to enhance collaborative management practice. Alex is currently completing a Professional Doctorate in Systemic Practice. His MSc was on the impact of inspection on a management team. He is co-author of *Defending Young People*, a comprehensive guide to the law on young offenders. He recently wrote *Creating a Sense of Belonging*, national guidance on Positive Activities for Young People and he is a member of the Editorial Board of Community Care Inform.

Brigid Daniel MA (Hons) PhD, CQSW, originally studied psychology and carried out research in infant perceptuo-motor development. Following qualification as a social worker she practised in Edinburgh in Intake and then in a Children and Families team. She then worked at Dundee University on post-qualifying courses in child care and protection, at Stirling University as Senior Lecturer in Social Work and returned to Dundee as the Professor of Child Care and Protection and Director of Studies of Child Care and Protection. She is currently Professor of Social Work at Stirling University in the Department of Applied Social Science and is head of the Social Work section which delivers undergraduate and post-graduate qualifying social work programmes as well as a range of continuing professional development courses. Brigid was a member of the team that undertook the multi-disciplinary audit and review of child protection in Scotland that reported in '*It's everyone's job to make sure I'm alright*'. Her research interests and publications are in the areas of child development, children's resilience, work with fathers and child neglect.

Mark Drakeford has worked as a probation officer, community worker and in youth justice. He is currently Professor of Social Policy and Applied Social Sciences at the University of Cardiff. Since 2000 he has been the Cabinet's health and social policy adviser at the Welsh Assembly Government. He has published extensively on the development of devolution and social welfare services for young people.

Harry Ferguson is Professor of Social Work and Director of the Centre for Social Work, University of Nottingham. He has taught, researched and published widely in the areas of child abuse/protection, domestic violence, fatherhood, men's sexuality and masculinities, best practice, and the social science of social work. His books include, *Protecting Children in Time: Child Abuse, Child Protection and the Consequences of Modernity*, Palgrave, 2004; and *Best Practice in Social Work*, Palgrave, 2008.

Donald Forrester was a child care social worker in inner London from 1991 to 1999. During this time he worked continuously with families in which there was parental substance misuse, and the challenges and opportunities involved in such work have become a central interest since he became an academic. Professor Forrester is a consultant for the Welsh Assembly Government who are radically reconfiguring services to address parental substance misuse. In 2009 he obtained a grant of £1.1 million to set up the Tilda Goldberg Centre at the University of Bedfordshire. The centre is focused on developing the evidence base in social work with an initial focus on substance misuse issues.

Kate Morris is Associate Professor of Social Work at the University of Nottingham; prior to this she was Head of Social Work at the University of Birmingham. She is a qualified social worker with extensive practice and management experience. She has a longstanding interest in family inclusion strategies in social work, and in preventative services and practices. She has researched and published in both these areas and she managed the National Evaluation of the Children's Fund from 2003-2006. More recently she led on the literature review that informed the Cabinet Office 'Think Family' policy stream.

John Pitts is Vauxhall Professor of Socio-Legal Studies at the University of Bedfordshire. He has worked in printing and publishing; as a school teacher; a street and club-based youth worker; a group worker in a Young Offender Institution and as a consultant to workers in youth justice and youth social work, legal professionals and the police in the UK, mainland Europe, the Russian Federation and China. More recently he has acted as a consultant on violent youth gangs to local authorities, police forces and 'think tanks'. His research includes studies of the differential treatment of black and white young offenders; Anglo-French responses to youth crime and disorder; the violent victimisation of school students; inter-racial youth violence; the impact of youth work on the life chances of socially excluded young people in five European cities; the contribution of detached and outreach youth work to the life chances of socially excluded young people in the UK and violent youth gangs in three London boroughs. His publications include: *The Politics of Juvenile Crime*, Sage Publications (1988); *Working With Young Offenders*, BASW/Macmillan (1990 & 1999); *The New Politics of Youth Crime: Discipline or Solidarity*, Macmillan (2001); *Crime Disorder and Community Safety* (with R. Matthews [Eds.]) Routledge (2001); *The Russell House Companion to Working with Young People* (with F. Factor & V. Chauchun [Eds.]) Russell House Publishing (2001); *Reaching Socially Excluded Young People* (with D. Crimmens, F. Factor T. Jeffs, C. Pugh, J. Spence & P. Turner) National Youth Agency (2004); *The Russell House Companion to Youth Justice* (with T. Bateman [Eds.]) Russell House (2005); *Reluctant Gangsters: The Changing Face of Youth Crime*, Willan Publishing (2008). He is editor of *Safer Communities*, associate editor of *Youth and Policy* and an editorial board member of *Youth Justice* and *Juvenile Justice Worldwide* (UNESCO).

Michael Preston-Shoot is Professor of Social Work and Dean of the Faculty of Health and Social Sciences at the University of Bedfordshire, England. He has held posts in universities since 1988 following a career in local authorities and voluntary organisations as a social worker, groupworker and team leader. He has also practised as a family therapist and psychotherapist. He is an elected Academician of the Academy of Social Sciences. He was Chair of the Joint University Council Social Work Education, which represents the perspectives of United Kingdom social work education in higher education institutions, between 2005 and 2009. He was editor of *Social Work Education: The International Journal* between 1993 and 2006 and was managing editor of the *European Journal of Social Work* between 2003 and 2007. He is one of the founding editors of the journal *Ethics and Social Welfare*. He was awarded a National Teaching Fellowship by the Higher Education Academy in 2005. His research and writing has concentrated on the interface between law and social work practice, on which in 2005 he co-authored a systematic review on teaching, learning and assessment of law in social work education for the Social Care Institute for Excellence (SCIE). He has subsequently co-authored a resource guide and ten e-learning objects on the subject of law and social work, also published by SCIE. He has also undertaken research and published in the areas of social work education, group work, the involvement of service users in social work education and research, and on the needs and service outcomes for young people in public care and older people requiring care in the community. He is the Independent Chair of a Local Safeguarding Children Board and of a Safeguarding Vulnerable Adults Board.

David Wastell is Professor of Information Systems at Nottingham University Business School. He began his academic career as a psycho-physiologist, carrying out research on stress and technological innovation in collaboration with British Telecom. His interests in technology developed during an extended period at

Manchester and Salford Universities, before moving to Nottingham in 2005. Dave's current interests are in public sector reform, innovation and design, and cognitive ergonomics. He has extensive public sector consultancy experience and was co-author of the SPRINT design methodology, which is widely used in the local government community.

Sue White is Professor of Social Work at the University of Lancaster. She qualified in social work at the University of Leeds in 1983 and was employed as a practitioner and manager in statutory children's services until 1995 when she took up an academic post at the University of Manchester. Her research has focused principally on the analysis of professional decision-making in child welfare, with a particular emphasis on safeguarding. She has recently completed two influential Research Council funded studies, the first focusing on electronic information sharing in multi-disciplinary child welfare practice and the second on the relationship between performance management of public services responsible for safeguarding children, and the impact of anticipated blame within the decision-making practices of those providing, supervising and managing these services. During 2009, Sue served on the Social Work Task Force, charged with undertaking a comprehensive review of frontline social work practice in England. She is currently Chair of the Association of Professors of Social Work and editor in chief of *Child and Family Social Work*.

Introduction

CHAPTER 1

Children's Services: Reversing the Vicious Spiral

Patrick Ayre and Michael Preston-Shoot

Failing services and failed reforms

In response to widespread and persistent concern over the ability of social services for children and families to safeguard and promote the wellbeing of the most vulnerable children, the UK government has in the last decade introduced some of the most far reaching changes ever encountered in this field. However, the evidence as to whether these changes are in every case yielding improved results is at very best equivocal. Indeed, it may be argued that, in England at least, despite the best intentions of those driving these changes forward, the outcome of the particular approaches to reform which have been adopted has been to substantially diminish the capability of children's social services to respond effectively to the complex challenges they face and there is a danger that these services are becoming locked into a vicious spiral of decline from which it will be hard to recover.

The failure of the government's preferred approaches to quality improvement may be seen clearly reflected in key reports presented to the government in 2008 and 2009. Lord Laming (2009) has commented trenchantly on the apparent intractability of many of the problems identified by him in his earlier report (Laming, 2003) noting with some surprise that, though existing law and procedures were repeatedly and determinedly asserted to be adequate, safeguarding performance continued to display persistent serious flaws. The recent summaries of the findings of Serious Case Reviews produced by Ofsted (2008; 2009) have raised again for our attention a host of failings first identified in similar digests dating back as far as 1994 (Brandon et al., 2008; Brandon, Owers and Black, 1999; Falkov, 1996; James, 1994; Sinclair and Bullock, 2002). Tony Blair, in his foreword to *Every Child Matters* (Boateng, 2003: 1) mourned Victoria Climbié as the latest addition to a litany of names of the victims of child safeguarding tragedies, which 'echoing down the years, are a standing shame to us all' and inquiries into the death of Peter Connolly suggest that many of the same grave causes for concern remain.

The contributors to this book recognise that child and family social work represents only one element in the complex web of interagency activity which forms the 'team around the child' in modern child welfare practice. It is, however, our view that social workers can and should play a key role within this team, but that their ability to do so has been substantially degraded. If social work is to fulfil its potential within a multi-agency context, significant systemic change will be required and it is on this change which this book focuses. In seeking to outline and address the challenges which we face, this book examines the impact of a number of linked strands of the reform agenda on key areas of children's services practice including child safeguarding, youth offending, children in care, child and family support and child welfare law. It also draws on more general reflections on the nature of social work with children and families and on how it should be organised and delivered. Each contributor offers a range of original insights, but a number of common cross-cutting themes may be seen to emerge.

The obstacles to better services

Read as a whole, this book suggests that many of the obstacles which we face in rebuilding our profession have their origins in profound changes which have taken place within the environment within which child care social work is conducted. The following are some of the key propositions which are offered:

- The predominant position accorded to managerialist approaches has, overall, had a profoundly undermining effect on performance (see chapters by Ayre and Calder; Chard and Ayre; Ferguson; Pitts and Bateman; Preston-Shoot)
- In consequence of this approach, social work is being transformed from a professional activity

to a technical one. Within this new environment, process and procedures are prioritised over objectives and outcomes (Ayre and Calder; Butler and Drakeford; Pitts and Bateman), targets and indicators over values and professional standards (Butler and Drakeford; Preston-Shoot) and compliance and completion over analysis and reflection (Ayre and Calder; Ferguson; Forrester)

- There has been an irrational faith in improvement strategies which have proved unsuccessful and inappropriate (Chard and Ayre; Wastell and White)
- We are in danger of forgetting that the essence of social work lies in what happens between the social worker and the service user when they meet. Real change in the wellbeing of the children and families with whom we work is more likely to derive from the effectiveness of our interaction with them and with our professional environment than from our attainment of statistical targets (Ayre and Calder; Butler and Drakeford; Fergusson; Forrester; Pitts and Bateman; Preston-Shoot)
- Research evidence has been used as a prop for policy, rather than a foundation (Brodie; Forester; Morris; Pitts and Bateman)
- Substantial investment has been devoted to addressing a number of key factors contributing to social exclusion. However, the effectiveness of the social care response has often been undermined by undue haste and a failure fully to analyse the challenges before rolling out solutions intended to resolve them (Brodie; Morris) In some instances, services have been configured as short term initiatives outside the social care mainstream. As a result of their position on the fringes, they all too readily disappear when their funding ceases, leaving only a limited legacy of learning or experience (Morris).

It may be tempting to dismiss these concerns as the musings of social work academics remote from the realities of service delivery, but it must be recognised that those selected by the government to report on the state of practice are offering many of the same messages. Whilst Lord Laming seems on occasion to be suggesting that what we need is 'more of the same' and that significant improvements might be brought about by tinkering with targets (2009: 16) he has nonetheless described clearly some of the systemic weaknesses underpinning existing provision. He notes, 'concern that the tradition of deliberate, reflective social work practice is being put in danger because of an overemphasis on process and targets, resulting in a loss of confidence amongst social workers' (p 32), adding that 'supervision should be open and supportive, focusing on the quality of decisions, good risk analysis, and improving outcomes for children rather than meeting targets' (p 32). He reports anxieties that professional practice and judgment are being compromised by process-driven assessment and recording systems (p 44) and uses two helpful quotes to illustrate how children's services social workers may be losing their sense of what really matters about what they do:

It seems like they have to do all this form filling, their bosses' bosses make them do it, but it makes them forget about us.

Boy, 16

She does things by textbook, she doesn't know me as a person.

Girl, 16

At the same time, the social workers who spoke to the Social Work Task Force (Social Work Task Force, 2009b: 6) told them that they were 'tied up in bureaucracy' and did not have enough time to devote to the people they wanted to help. Systems for managing performance were not driving quality and they were frustrated with the tools and support they received. The Task Force 'found evidence of some social workers feeling overloaded, unsupported and de-skilled by some of the resources and systems designed to support their effectiveness' (p 19) and frontline workers reported widely that 'supervision tends to be process driven and dominated by case management' (p 20) at the expense of its supportive, analytical and evaluative functions. Overall, the Task Force gained 'a sense of a profession that is, in places, at risk of becoming too mechanised and of being "de-skilled" through an over emphasis on compliance rather than judgement' (p 32). They noted that 'many of these weaknesses can end up compounding one another, causing a vicious circle in which service improvement becomes hard to achieve' (p 35).

Analysis at three levels

Both Lord Laming and the Social Work Task Force (Social Work Task Force, 2009a) have offered a range of important recommendations aimed at improving the effectiveness of social work services. However, it is a commonplace in the field of service evaluation and improvement that recommendations are only as good as the analysis on which they are based. The Social Work Task Force and Lord Laming note with some concern that social workers' skills in analysis and interpretation are generally in need of improvement, but it may be argued that similar frailties are demonstrated in their own reports, which may be felt to be very strong on the 'what?' questions, but rather weaker on the 'why?' questions. A clear and cogent account is given of what is wrong with existing patterns of provision, but the analysis of why these problems have arisen may be felt sometimes to lack the requisite depth.

One of the authors of this introductory chapter (Ayre) has a particular interest in the effectiveness of Serious Case Reviews, which are conducted when a child has been killed or seriously injured, and abuse or neglect are felt to be causal factors. He has identified three levels of analysis to be found in such reports, each with an associated type of recommendation. At the first and crudest level, which we may refer to as *injunctive* or *Level 1* analysis, the problem is simply reformulated as an instruction. For example, the conclusion that 'this child was injured because we did not do X' is associated with a recommendation stating simply that 'we must do X in the future'. Many Serious Case Review recommendations have, unfortunately, tended to follow this unreflective and essentially unhelpful format, which clearly ignores the fact that we need to concern ourselves less with *the fact that X did not happen*, and more with *why X did not happen*.

At the second and slightly more analytical level, which we may refer to as *procedural* or *Level 2*, the problem is addressed by suggesting change to, or enhanced promotion of, approved processes for managing the issue in question. We should write more procedures, provide more training or, very often, do both of these things. This approach assumes that failures have arisen because those involved did not understand what they should be doing, either because essential guidance did not exist, or because they were insufficiently familiar with the guidance which was available. Such a response, though limited, may have utility in some circumstances. However, it does not recognise that if we

consider the most infamous recent child abuse scandals, we may observe clearly that tragic consequences arose because key participants failed to take in practice actions which they must certainly have known in principle were the right things to do. The central question, which so often goes unanswered, is 'why, then, despite adequate training and guidance, did they still fail to take the action required?'

The answer to this question requires analysis at a third level. Such *Level 3* analysis is *systemic* and involves seeking out and describing the fundamental organisational and relational weaknesses which underpin and encourage failures in performance (see Fish, Munro and Bairstow, 2009). The Social Work Task Force report (2009a) and to a lesser extent that of Lord Laming (2009) are notably lacking in analysis at this level, and one of the main contributions of this book to the change debate may be felt to rest on its ability to fill this glaring gap. Unless we truly understand the cause of the illness which we seek to cure, the remedies which we prescribe are likely to be at best ineffective and at worst positively harmful.

By way of illustration, we may note that the Social Work Task Force and the contributors to this book agree that weaknesses in supervision are currently a significant factor in the social work profession's ills. The Task Force report offers a Level 2 analysis of this, suggesting that this deficiency may be addressed by changing procedures to define a minimum frequency for supervision, and by enhancing the training provided to managers (2009a: 28). Ayre and Calder, however, adopting a Level 3 analysis, suggest that the managerialist culture which holds sway in social care inevitably conditions managers to undertake supervision which focuses on procedure and process at the expense of analysis and evaluation. Indeed, it may be argued that, given that resources of time are limited and that the measures of effectiveness currently in place focus on quantity not quality, managers are acting entirely rationally in providing supervision which is almost entirely managerial, and that to offer supervision of the analytical and evaluative type recommended by the Task Force would, however praiseworthy in professional and ethical terms, be irrational in these circumstances.

Here we come across something which we might describe as the *Mission Statement fallacy*, under which it is assumed that if one asserts an objective with which all relevant stakeholders agree strongly in principle, this objective will be realised in practice. In fact, we know that you could train managers in good supervision practice from now until eternity, but if the environment in which they are working in practical reality emphasises the importance of only one aspect of supervision, it is that aspect which will, by and large, be delivered, and other aspects, however worthy, admirable and 'right' will receive less attention. A similar argument may be applied to the emphasis on early engagement asserted as a commitment within the *Every Child Matters* agenda. We may be able to agree that every children's services worker, whether manager or practitioner, values prevention and would like to be doing it, but asserting the rightness of a preventive approach does not mean that such an approach will thrive in the longer term if, in reality, this approach is marginalised and its resourcing rendered insecure by powerful systemic drivers which remain unchanged by the underlying Mission Statement (see Morris in this book).

Change at three levels

Whilst the summary of Serious Case Reviews produced by Ofsted in 2008 (Ofsted, 2008: 24) seems to suggest that, in evaluating the reasons for failures of performance, we have tended to pay insufficient attention to the individual shortcomings of the staff involved, the authors of this book are unanimous in regarding the most crucial failings of children's social care as being institutional rather than personal, and in seeing the staff involved as, in most cases, 'inheritors rather than instigators' (Reason, 1995: 1711) of the performance deficiencies which arise. The problems are thus not technical ones, requiring a Level 1 or 2 tweak to existing patterns, but fundamental, requiring radical systemic transformation which must take place at each of three levels: central government, service management and frontline practice.

The process must start with central government. This book argues that the approaches to service development and performance management adopted by central government in recent decades have created a framework for practice which is undermining rather than promoting the effectiveness of children's services and of their practitioners. This framework must be reconfigured to value quality

as well as quantity and to appreciate and facilitate those aspects of social work practice most closely related to improving outcomes for children, rather than those which it is most easy to measure. It will be essential that ministers come to understand that it is through their deeds, not their words, that they convey to service providers where their priorities should lie.

Change is required at managerial level as well as governmental, but we may promote this change most effectively if we recognise that service managers may not be falling short because they are ignorant or incompetent, as a Level 1 or 2 analysis may suggest, but on the contrary, their behaviour may be a rational response to the environment in which they find themselves. Rational managers, senior or junior, will seek to ensure that the services which they offer are judged effective by those above them in the chain of responsibility. They will, in short, seek to give us what we ask for. If we ask for evidence based services which emphasise analysis and transformational relationships and if we confirm our wishes by providing a framework of resources and regulation which supports this, they will attempt to comply. On the other hand, if we make it clear through our evaluative frameworks that our primary concern centres on compliance with process and procedure, we may expect them to configure their services accordingly. Certainly, some retraining may be required by managers whose professional style has been shaped by the audit culture which has dominated recent years, but without a change in the demands placed on them by the environment in which they work, such training may be expected to have little impact in practice. Wastell and White set out very compellingly in their chapter in this book how our requirements of managers should be reconfigured to recognise that performance is conditioned by systems:

> *Middle managers need to see it as their main business not to be the brutal enforcers of targets but to be the benign designers of the workplace ... In an organisational context, this means the design of systems made up of people, processes and technology in order to achieve the best possible performance. Finding the best way of organising the workplace, in more prosaic terms. If this is not the primary business of management, then what on earth is?*

Reconfiguration at governmental and managerial levels of the environment within which social work with children is conducted will open up opportunities for social workers in the frontline to rediscover their identity and efficacy. If the processes of deprofesionalisation described in this book (Ayre and Calder; Chard and Ayre; Pitts and Bateman; Ferguson; Preston-Shoot) can be halted, the enhanced supervision, training and career structure recommended by the Social Work Task Force (2009a) may be expected to yield good results, If, however, we fail to acknowledge and address the systemic failings identified by contributors to this book, we must expect to find it hard to escape from the vicious spiral of decline into which children's services seem currently to be locked.

References

Boateng, P. (2003) *Every Child Matters*. Cm 5860. London: Stationery Office.

Brandon, M. et al. (2008) *Analysing Child Deaths and Serious Injury Through Abuse and Neglect: What Can We Learn?* London: Department for Children, Schools and Families.

Brandon, M., Owers, M. and Black, J. (1999) *Learning How to Make Children Safer: An Analysis for the Welsh Office of Serious Child Abuse Cases in Wales*. Norwich: University of East Anglia/Welsh Office.

Falkov, A. (1996) A *Study of Working Together Part 8 Reports: Fatal Child Abuse and Parental Psychiatric Disorder*. London: DoH.

Fish, S., Munro, E. and Bairstow, S. (2009) *Learning Together to Safeguard Children: Developing a Multi-Agency Systems Approach for Case Reviews*. London: SCIE.

James, G. (1994) *Study of Working Together Part 8 Reports*. London: DoH.

Lord Laming (2003) *The Victoria Climbié Inquiry: Report of an Inquiry by Lord Laming*. Cmnd 5730. London: The Stationery Office.

Lord Laming (2009) *The Protection of Children in England: A Progress Report*. London: The Stationery Office.

Ofsted (2008) *Learning Lessons, Taking Action*. London: Ofsted.

Ofsted (2009) *Learning Lessons from Serious Case Reviews: Year 2*. London: Ofsted.

Reason, J. (1995) A Systems Approach to Organizational Error. *Ergonomics*, 38: 8, 1708–21.

Sinclair, R. and Bullock, R. (2002) *Learning from Past Experience: A Review of Serious Case Reviews*. London: DoH.

Social Work Task Force (2009a) *Building a Safe, Confident Future: The Final Report of the Social Work Task Force*. London: Department for Children, Schools and Families.

Social Work Task Force (2009b) *Facing up to the Task: The Interim Report of the Social Work Task Force*. London: Department for Children, Schools and Families.

Part One: The Policy Context

CHAPTER 2

Children and Young People's Policy in Wales

Ian Butler and Mark Drakeford

Introduction

The Palais Wilson, on the shores of Lake Geneva, is the office of the United Nations High Commissioner for Human Rights. It is named after US President and Nobel Peace Prize laureate, Woodrow Wilson and was the first home of the League of Nations. Originally built as a hotel, it is referred to on the local tourist websites variously as 'majestic' and 'prestigious' and, elsewhere, as typical of Geneva's 'dull luxury'. It is also the place where the United Nations Convention on the Rights of the Child Committee holds its meetings.

It is the task of the Committee to periodically receive reports from signatories to the Convention [CRC] and to examine the so-called 'States Parties' on the 'measures they have adopted which give effect to the rights recognised (in the Convention) and on the progress made on the enjoyment of those rights' (Art. 44 (1)). The United Kingdom signed the CRC in 1990, ratified it in 1991 and submitted its first report to the Committee in 1994. The UK submitted its *Consolidated 3rd and 4th Periodic Report to the UN Committee on the Rights of the Child* in July 2007.

If the exterior of the Palais Wilson is nineteenth century 'grand style', the room in which the Committee undertakes its examinations is intimidating in a more modern way. Framed by a window giving an extensive view of Lake Geneva, the Chair of the Committee sits on a raised dais at one end of a room that spans the whole width of the building. In front of the top table are two concentric horseshoes of desks, with microphones and headsets. The outer horseshoe is occupied by the remaining 17 members of the Committee. The inner horseshoe is occupied by the States Party's delegates, there to answer the Committee's questions. This curious arrangement means that delegates rather uncomfortably have their backs to half of the members of the Committee and can see only those members of their delegation that happen to be sitting opposite them. Alongside the right hand wall of the room are the darkened cubicles occupied by the

translators. At the far end, opposite the top table, are several rows of seats set aside for the press and members of the public but, in reality, occupied by representatives of NGOs and other interested parties from the country whose turn it is to answer to the Committee.

It was in this room at one of those desks that one of us (Butler) found himself as part of the UK delegation to the 49th Session of the Committee on the 23 September 2008 (Meeting 1355) fully aware of the importance of the occasion and somewhat in awe of the event itself. The lengthy proceedings (the main examination started just after 10.00 a.m. and finished just after 6.00 p.m.) were rather formally conducted and the questioning, in the main, was close, intense and very well-informed. By general consensus, developed countries are not given an 'easy ride' by the Committee. This was certainly the case in this instance. It was, quite properly one might argue, a testing time.

However, it is not the purpose of this chapter to report in detail the conduct of the examination. The proceedings and much of the relevant documentation can be accessed through the Office of the United Nations High Commissioner for Human Rights' website and via the 'Strategy and Governance' section of the *Every Child Matters* website. What happened in the 10 minutes after the examination is arguably more telling.

Once the session was over, the 'Welsh members' of the delegation (all 3 of us) made our way to the back of the room as quickly as we could, pausing only to say hello and thanks to the Committee Rapporteur who had visited Wales and met the First Minister and the Children's Minister as part of the Committee's preparation for the UK's examination. We were keen to catch up with the Children's Commissioner for Wales and the small group of staff from Wales' NGOs that had attended the examination. We had flown over together and now we were anxious to find out how we had done and to make arrangements for where we could meet up that night to celebrate and plan our strategy for taking forward the Committee's 'concluding observations' once these were made known in a few weeks time.

Some delegates from the other devolved administrations (DAs) of the UK were doing the same. But not all. Some members of the delegation were quicker to leave than others. What became obvious in just a few minutes was how different in tone and content were the conversations that were taking place between delegates, Committee members and the various country representatives. There were clear differences in how well people knew each other and how much they had enjoyed the day's events. Those 10 minutes of conversation (and that evening in the bar afterwards) demonstrated as clearly as the evidence that we had given earlier in the day that devolution in the UK had produced real, substantial and important differences in policy and practice across the DAs. It demonstrated also how different the approaches that each DA had taken to the Geneva examination and how the idea of children and young people's rights are given differing degrees of priority in the various parts of the UK.

Over four years previously, on the 14 January 2004, the National Assembly for Wales had voted unanimously to reaffirm:

> ... *the priority which it attaches to safeguarding and promoting the rights and welfare of children and young people in Wales, particularly those who are vulnerable ...*

and

> *Formally adopt[ed] the United Nations convention on the rights of the child as the basis of policy making in this area ...*
>
> The National Assembly for Wales
> (The Official Record) 14/01/2004: 4)

It should be noted incidentally that this debate had taken place in the context of the post-Climbié period of high anxiety about children's services that was taking place throughout the UK. For us, if not for other members of the UK delegation, the CRC had been the organising principle behind much of what the Welsh Assembly Government has sought to do for children and young people since that time. This is what 'safeguarding' means in the Welsh context – an inseparable relationship between welfare and rights with rights being the guarantor of welfare, for everyone, including those who are vulnerable. While for some, scrutiny by the Committee might have

represented a challenge and the possibility for some embarrassment on an international scale, for those of us from Wales, Geneva was an opportunity to focus world attention, however briefly, on the progress that we had made in giving substance to the aims of the Convention and delivering on the Welsh 'safeguarding agenda'.

The purpose of this chapter is to articulate an account of the distinctive policy framework in place to safeguard children and young people in Wales that derives from the Welsh Assembly Government's commitment to the CRC. In providing the basis for a comparative account across the UK, it is important not to settle on England as the only and possibly invidious comparator. Each DA has developed its own distinctive approach. However, it probably is necessary to point out specifically that neither the *Every Child Matters* outcomes framework nor its associated apparatus and devices (for example, Children's Trusts; ContactPoint) have effect in Wales. Similarly, it should be noted that the 2004 Children Act is divided into those parts that apply to Wales and those that do not.

It is beyond the scope of this chapter to provide a broad account of Welsh political thinking over recent years by way of background (but see Jones and Scully, 2006; Davies and Williams, 2009; Birrell, 2009). I have described elsewhere (Butler, 2007) how children and young people's policy in Wales came to be founded on what is today called a 'rights perspective' but which actually has deeper roots in an established collectivist and non-conformist political tradition that is much more Welsh Labour than New Labour and which is embedded in a class and economic structure that is very different from England and Scotland (see also Drakeford, 2007a).

Instead, this chapter will concentrate on the proximate origins of Wales' rights based policy framework in the context of the devolution settlement for Wales and illustrate some of the policy processes and outcomes that we were happy to put before the CRC Committee.

The devolution settlement

The September 1997 referendum paved the way, by the narrowest of margins (50.3 per cent to 49.7 per cent of the vote) for the Government of Wales Act 1998. This, in turn, provided for an Assembly of 60 members, elected through a form of semi-proportional representation. The 1998 Act also established the 'functions' or policy areas over which the Assembly would have jurisdiction and, in so doing, perhaps inadvertently, settled on the Assembly the policy lead in relation to almost all of those 'traditional' areas that bear directly on children; namely education, social care and health. There were and remain (for now) some notable areas where responsibility for policy remains with the UK government (for example, youth justice and immigration) but, as far as our present purposes are concerned, almost all public policy explicitly directed towards Welsh children and young people that has emerged since the 1998 Act, is 'made in Wales'. This is not necessarily fully understood at either end of the M4.

The early years of the Assembly were difficult. The farce of Ron Davies' resignation as Secretary of State for Wales and the tragi-comic appointment of Alun Michael as the Assembly's very first First Secretary were followed by the epic romance of Rhodri Morgan's election to the leadership of the Labour Party in Wales and his confirmation as First Minister in October 2000. The First Assembly conducted its business through an effective Partnership Agreement between Welsh Labour and the Liberal Democrats which ran alongside the outbreak of foot and mouth disease, fuel protests and widespread flooding in parts of Wales. In the elections for the Second Assembly in May 2003, Welsh Labour won exactly half of the available seats and were provided with the slimmest of working majorities through the election of a Plaid Cymru member as Presiding Officer.

In July 2002, the Welsh Assembly Government established the Richard Commission to 'consider the sufficiency of the Assembly's current powers' and 'the adequacy of the Assembly's electoral arrangements' (Richard Commission, 2004: 265). It reported in March 2004 and broadly endorsed the success of the Assembly. The UK Government's *Better Government for Wales* White Paper, published in June 2005 did not meet many of the Richard Commission's recommendations but did pave the way for the Government of Wales Act 2006. This Act gave the Assembly the power to ask the UK Parliament for legislative competence to be transferred with respect to those functions already devolved. The Assembly would then be able to make 'Measures' in respect of those functions; in effect, to make Welsh law.

The Third Assembly Government, elected in May 2007, is a Labour-led coalition with Plaid Cymru and it has been the first to make use of these extended powers. Despite the fact that a final judgement remains to be made on the procedural and constitutional effectiveness of the LCO/Measure process, the legislative programme of the Third Assembly makes it clear that despite the fact of their demographic decline and the shift of political weight in favour of the older citizen, children would appear not to have lost the vanguard status as far as public policy in Wales is concerned. Of the first three LCOs to complete their progress through to Royal Assent for example, two related directly to children and young people. Similarly, four of the six government-introduced Measures and four of the Measures introduced by Assembly Members (broadly equivalent to a 'back bench bill' in Westminster) related directly to children and young people. We will return to some of these legislative outcomes below.

But behind these formal structures and processes, there lie deeper ideological and political currents that provide the immediate context for Wales' particular approach to policy for children and young people. As hinted earlier, the hegemonic New Labour, ratio-technical, modernising project; (that unique blend of social authoritarianism, scientism and piety that has been exemplified by the instruments and rhetoric of New Public Management, a low-trust relationship between central and local government and a valorisation of the individual over the social) has not penetrated as deeply in Wales as it has in England (see Butler and Pugh, 2004; Butler and Drakeford, 2005).

In part, this may be because of an historical legacy of collectivism and a cultural antipathy to the politics of 'choice', consumerism and self-enrichment (see Jordan, 2008). It may also be due to the fact that the voters of Wales feel closer to the 'traditions of Titmuss, Tawney, Beveridge and Bevan rather than those of Hayek and Friedman' (Morgan, 2002) as part of a political culture that has tended to be left of centre for the last 150 years. As Sullivan has noted (2007: 56):

. . . Labour. or Labour-led, administrations in Cardiff have retained old Labour's commitment to the welfare state as an engine of equality, social justice and social inclusion based on the political values of universality, social solidarity and free services.

More specifically, the majority Labour Welsh Assembly Government (WAG) at the commencement of the Second Assembly in 2003 made clear the principles on which it would operate in its 'strategic agenda', *Wales: A Better Country*. These included a commitment to partnership and participation with trade unions and the voluntary sector but emphasised (WAG, 2003:11):

> We will work together with local government not only to deliver national priorities and local solutions but also to embed these values in all levels of government in Wales.

It also included an explicit commitment to 'public services' designed in a way that suited Wales best (WAG, 2003:11):

> We will work across boundaries, communicate consistently and give responsibility to those who are best placed to take decisions . . . We will continue to develop a distinctively Welsh approach to improving the delivery of public services.

That 'distinctive Welsh approach to improving delivery of public services', included also a commitment to 'listening to people' (WAG, 2003:12):

> We want to ensure that the voices of children and young people, and of older people, are heard and valued in local decision-making. Our commitment to Funky Dragon (The Children's Parliament in Wales), to Young People's and Older People's Forums, to Community Health Councils at local level, and to a real engagement with the voluntary sector in planning, delivering and evaluating services, are central to realising this new approach.

It is this strong and continuing relationship with 'civil society', as the CRC Committee would term it (including NGOs) that lay behind the bonhomie that was evident in Geneva.

Making the Connections: Delivering Better Services for Wales (WAG, 2004) is even more definite about the role of government and its place in making public provision (WAG, 2004:1):

> We care deeply in Wales about our public services. We see them as belonging to our community, not just as providers to customers: people will speak of 'our school' and 'our' health centre.

The document goes further in endorsing a policy of collaboration and co-ordination and explicitly rejecting a culture of competition as far as the provision of public services is concerned. This kind of '21st century collectivism' (Sullivan, 2007: 56) is deeply antipathetic to the Blairite conception of the welfare state as a contributor to economic growth, a driver of responsibilisation and merely the guarantor rather than the provider of welfare services.

Moreover, *Making the Connections* also (see *Beyond Boundaries: Citizen Centred Local Services for Wales* published in June 2006, WAG) made explicit, using a language of citizenship rather than consumerism, that the purpose of the state in its provision of public services was to promote social justice (WAG, 2004: 3):

> Joint working is vital to deliver public services of top quality: they must be responsive to the needs of individuals and communities, delivered efficiently and driven by a commitment to equality and social justice.

A further recurring theme in the major policy statements of the Assembly Government since 2000 has been the commitment to 'openness' (WAG, 2003: 11) and 'democratic accountability'. This has been built into the very fabric of the home of the National Assembly, the Senedd. The original design brief for the project was to produce a building that generated 'a sense of open government and public accessibility'. The iconic building designed by Lord Rogers as a result has walls of glass.

More recent broad policy statements have been perhaps more cautious as befits the early days of a new and previously unimagined coalition but the direction of travel remains the same. *One Wales: A progressive agenda for the government of Wales*, the coalition agreement signed in June 2007, makes clear from the outset (WAG, 2007a: 5):

> Shared values, common goals and joint aspirations for the people of Wales will drive this four-year programme for government. It offers a progressive agenda for improving the quality of life of people in all of Wales's communities, from all walks of life, and especially the most vulnerable and disadvantaged.

Whilst rhetorically more restrained, *One Wales* captures what has come to be called the 'progressive universalism' of the Welsh welfare state no less accurately (see Drakeford, 2007b; Marquand, 2008; Stead, 2008).

It is in the context of a strong belief that government can be good for people; and that it must be accountable and collaborative rather than competitive; that the integrated, universal welfare state is critical to the pursuit of social justice; that citizenship is a desirable social and political end and that participation across the whole of civil society, including children and young people, is key to good governance that Wales' children's rights dynamic gathered its momentum.

Whilst the CRC mandates no particular political form nor service delivery framework, it does regard as axiomatic the central role of government in undertaking:

> ... all appropriate legislative, administrative, and other measures for the implementation of the rights recognized in the present Convention. With regard to economic, social and cultural rights, States Parties shall undertake such measures to the maximum extent of their available resources and, where needed, within the framework of international co-operation.
>
> CRC: Art. 4

As such, the potential congruence between the CRC and the expressed political will of the Welsh Assembly Government for much of the last decade should be self-evident.

If one adds to this a preparedness by Rhodri Morgan and many other Ministers to allow 'clear red water', a line in a now famous speech made by Morgan in December 2002, to separate New Labour from 'classic Labour', Cardiff from London and the Senedd from Westminster, in the pursuit of Welsh solutions to Welsh problems and reflecting Welsh political traditions then the differentiation in policy that became evident in Geneva is also more easily understood.

Rights to action to rights in action

I have described in more detail elsewhere (Butler, 2007) how one of the first major statements of children's policy made by the Assembly Government emerged in November 2000 in a rather 'technical' document concerned with improving local planning for children's services. Its endorsement of the UNCRC is unambiguous:

> Over the past 10 years [the UNCRC] has helped to establish an internationally accepted framework for the treatment of all children, encouraged a positive and optimistic image of children and young people as active holders of rights and stimulated a greater global commitment to safeguarding those rights. The Assembly believes

> that the Convention should provide a foundation of principle for dealings with children.
>
> WAG, 2000: 10

The expressed commitment to 'Welsh solutions to Welsh problems' during the Second Assembly ensured that the CRC was given a distinctively Welsh cast. This found expression in the publication, *Children and Young People: Rights to Action* (WAG, 2002). Here the Convention was translated into what the Government was to call its Seven Core Aims (7CA) which are designed to ensure that all children and young people:

- have a flying start in life
- have a comprehensive range of education and learning opportunities
- enjoy the best possible health and are free from abuse, victimisation and exploitation
- have access to play, leisure, sporting and cultural activities
- are listened to, treated with respect and have their race and cultural identity recognised
- have a safe home and a community which supports physical and emotional wellbeing
- are not disadvantaged by poverty.

Rights to Action went on to describe the programmes that had been put in place to deliver under these core aims and looks forward to the Assembly's second term.

A more comprehensive and detailed account of the Assembly's achievements in delivering its programme has been set out in *Rights in Action: Implementing Children and Young People's Rights in Wales* (WAG, 2007b). This document formed the basis of the WAG's submission to the CRC Committee in Geneva. Making this document available to the Committee was not achieved without some difficulty as there was considerable reluctance from the Department for Children, Schools and Family's officials in the first instance to have any of the DAs provide anything that looked like separate 'country reports'. Eventually insisted upon at Ministerial level, *Rights in Action* was a powerful introduction to what had been happening in Wales for many UK government departments and an important reminder to the CRC Committee.

Rights in Action describes dozens of initiatives operating across the full range of areas included within the CRC that seek to make 'the Convention Rights a reality for all children and young people' (WAG, 2007b: i) (see Butler, 2007:

175–7 for a summary of particular programmes and policies and also the Welsh Assembly Government website; *http://new.wales.gov.uk/topics/childrenyoungpeople*). The report highlights two areas in particular, however, that are understood as central to the rights project: participation and accountability. Only a cursory exploration of these two themes will have to be sufficient to illustrate what a rights based approach to policy making means on the front line.

Participation is described in *Rights in Action* as 'one of our greatest successes' (p i) and Wales can, with some justification, be said to have led the world in promoting children and young people's active citizenship. Defined by a young person as part of a national competition (WAG, 2007: 22):

> *Participation means that it is my right to be involved in making decisions, planning and reviewing action that might affect me. Having a voice, having a choice.*

This definition is the basis of national 'Participation Standards' that have been developed with young people by the Assembly Government funded Participation Unit (hosted by *Save the Children*) itself part of a Participation Consortium, a multi-agency, strategic body working across Wales 'to develop capacity and practice in terms of the participation of children and young people in decision making in Wales'. Work is underway to develop a national 'kite mark' system that will apply the standards to all aspects of services for children, including service planning and inspection.

The standards have been endorsed by the influential 'Funky Dragon', the children and young people's Assembly for Wales. Funky Dragon, substantially funded by the Assembly Government, is a young person led organisation which aims 'to give 0–25 year olds the opportunity to get their voices heard on issues that affect them' (Funky Dragon, 2003). Its role in preparing for Geneva is indicative of the status and capacity of the organisation. In a quite exceptional enterprise, a Steering Group of young people designed a survey that was completed by 14,000 young people across Wales aged from 7–18 that sought to answer a basic question: 'To what extent are you able to access your rights?' The two reports that resulted from the survey, *Our Rights, Our Story* (based on the survey of 11–18 year olds) and *Why do People's Ages go Up not Down?* (7–10 year olds) were presented, in person, by a delegation from Funky Dragon, to the CRC Committee in Geneva. Moreover, for the first time in the UK of which I am aware, the young people's delegation was invited to make their presentation to a cabinet committee meeting of the Assembly Government. Whilst the findings of both reports made uncomfortable reading in some respects, the process whereby young people were able to directly contribute to defining the policy agenda and to engage with government at the highest level offers the continuing prospect of being able to deliver our joint ambitions.

There are other examples of how participation is shaping the children's agenda in Wales: in schools, Wales is unique in the UK in having made school councils a statutory requirement in 2006; the Education (Wales) Measure currently before the Senedd will give young people a statutory right, in their own name, to make special educational needs appeals and claims of disability discrimination to the Special Educational Needs Tribunal for Wales. Even in academia, the 2009 ESRC Festival of Social Science included, in Cardiff, an event, 'By Us, For Us, About Us': A Children and Young People's Festival of Participation in Research' in which some 200 young people were able to 'learn about and participate in research and to express their views about research methods and findings'.

As far as accountability is concerned, almost one of the first acts of the National Assembly was to appoint a Commissioner for Children, via the *Care Standards Act 2000* (and later the Children's Commissioner for Wales Act, 2001). The Commissioner's primary functions are to safeguard and promote the rights and welfare of children in Wales and, in so doing, to have specific regard to the CRC. His annual reports are subject to plenary debates in the Senedd to which the government must publish a formal response.

As well as relying on institutional means of holding government and public services to account, the Assembly Government is committed to enabling young people to make their own representations and is in the process of establishing a national advocacy service, available to all young people and in relation to any issue. The service will be overseen by an independent National Advocacy Board, comprising equal numbers of adult and young person representatives.

Accountability means being able to demonstrate achievement as well as commitment and the CRC Committee's Concluding Observations on the UK's 2002 periodic report (CRC/C/15/Add.188) included a recommendation that (19) the UK:

> ... *establish a nation-wide system such that disaggregated data are collected on all persons under 18 years for all areas covered by the Convention, including the most vulnerable groups, and that these data are used to assess progress and design policies to implement the Convention.*

The Welsh Assembly Government published its first *Children and Young People's Well-being Monitor for Wales* in November 2008. Its purpose, as set out in the Foreword under the names of the First Minister and the Deputy First Minister, is (pp 3–4) to 'investigate the issues that affect the lives of all our children and young people . . . to measure progress . . . to raise awareness' and specifically to meet the CRC reporting requirements:

> *The Assembly Government's commitment to the Convention is paramount and we are pleased to deliver on this in Wales . . .*

Elsewhere in the UK, governments have been content to rely on international comparisons (for example, UNICEF, 2007) or accounts by third parties (such as Bradshaw and Mayhew, 2005) so the symbolic as well as practical effect of the government publishing its own 'warts and all' account of children's well being should not be overlooked. With data grouped under the 7CA, again, the Monitor (which also contains a very useful and accessible account of key Assembly Government policies) is far from all good news, not just in terms of the well-being of Wales' children and young people but also in identifying the significant gaps that exist in our knowledge of the lived experience of children and young people in Wales. In similar vein, and again ahead of the rest of the UK, the Assembly Government has now begun to publish regular statements of its spending on children. The data reveal that in 2006–07 the Welsh Assembly Government allocated an estimated £4.4 billion of its budget to children in Wales, equating to 28 per cent of its total expenditure. The data also show that annual expenditure per child is increasing:

- from £5,600 in 2005–06
- to £5,900 in 2006–07
- and £7,100 by 2010–11 (projection)

There is a great deal that is progressive in the ambitions and achievements of the rights project in Wales and the sense of the children's agenda in Wales being with and for children rather than about them is very close to the surface but it has been sustained by a relatively stable structure for delivering services that is not been the case elsewhere in the UK.

Translating the broad policy framework of the Assembly Government into direct services has relied, as already suggested, on a strong political investment in local government and, in particular, in social services departments. The vision for social services, expressed in *Fulfilled Lives, Supportive Communities: Improving Social Services in Wales from 2008–2018* (WAG, 2007c: 5) places local government in a 'central role' and in a 'strong position to lead change'. The overall vision is a familiar one; services must be (p 6):

- strong, accessible and accountable
- focused on citizen, family and community needs
- focused on social inclusion and the rights of individuals
- concerned with good outcomes
- delivered in a joined up, flexible and efficient way to consistently high standards and in partnership with service users.

This has resulted, in the main, in fully integrated social services departments; in essence, a 'family service' model that would have been familiar to Freddie Seebohm. This approach is strongly reflected in a major piece of Welsh law that is currently (June 2009) making its passage through the Senedd and the Welsh Affairs Committee. The Measure, *The Children and Families (Wales) Measure*, introduced by the Government on 2 March 2009, is centrally concerned with legislating for Wales' distinctive child poverty strategy (well ahead of broadly similar Westminster proposals) but includes the legislative framework for the introduction of 'Integrated Family Support Teams' (IFSTs) in every local authority in Wales, after a 'pioneer' phase in selected areas. As defined in the *Explanatory Memorandum* accompanying the Measure (p 4)

> *The IFST will be multi-agency teams whose function will be to deliver evidence-based interventions direct to families where children are at risk of developing long term difficulties or experiencing significant discontinuity in*

their upbringing that may result in the child entering care. The IFST will also support the reunification of children who are voluntarily accommodated. The IFST will have a training role in providing supervised training for wider staff working with families in local authorities and Local Health Boards on a range of techniques in engaging complex families and delivering evidenced based interventions.

As the *Explanatory Memorandum* also makes clear (p 21 ff.) the idea for the IFSTs arises from a concern with rising numbers entering care (and this preceded the 'Baby Peter' effect on the population of looked after children), especially from those families where the adults themselves are facing major challenges of their own through substance misuse or mental health problems, for example. The IFSTs are intended specifically to address the 'suggestion' that services in Wales may 'become preoccupied with identifying and managing risk rather than identifying protective factors that might avoid the development of problems' (p 21). The implied contrast with elsewhere in the UK is not unintentional.

At the risk of breaking our own injunction to avoid invidious comparisons, the fact that the 'safeguarding agenda' in Wales remains embedded in a holistic recognition of the place of children in their families is almost as critical to understanding the differences emerging across the UK as is Wales' rights-based approach to children and young people's policy. In England in particular, it would appear that it is those things that bind children to each other rather than that which binds them to their families and their communities have assumed precedence such that children's services, far from becoming increasingly 'integrated' look, from this side of the border, increasingly segregated.

The Welsh 'policy child'

Where children and young people are thought of in terms of their needs rather than their rights; their vulnerabilities rather than their strengths; the problems that they cause society rather than the problems that society causes for them; where policies are conceived and delivered reactively rather than in pursuit of an over-arching set of objectives (which are *not* the same as 'outcomes'); where services are delivered through a confused and constantly changing set of structures and professional networks; where there is a residualised model of the welfare state operating

and where a rhetoric of consumerism, competition and 'business' rather than justice, equality and participation makes little sense to front-line workers; where practice is subsumed into performativity, performance management and risk avoidance, it would suggest also that there exists, in Westminster at least, a dominant political vision of childhood that is anxious, uncertain, pessimistic and lacking in imagination.

In Wales, as we hope this chapter has begun to suggest, government sees children and young people differently. They are regarded as rights holders, citizens, expert on their own experience, articulate, capable and active members of families and communities. 'Safeguarding' is understood as a much broader concept than child protection and one that is best achieved by promoting self actualisation by children and young people, engagement in the democratic process and a strong public commitment by government to the pursuit of social justice.

Such a political programme does not deflect from a clear recognition of the unique experience of childhood, however, neither in terms of the particular vulnerabilities of children nor the special opportunities of childhood.

By way of final illustration and to understand fully the nature of the child as understood by policy makers in Wales, we return to the CRC reporting process. Once the concluding observations of the examination were published in October, back in the office, we looked carefully for specific mentions of Wales. There were two that were particularly gratifying to find.

Safeguarding should mean protecting every child from harm, not just those who have been identified as particularly vulnerable ('progressive universalism'). In the view of every Assembly Member who has spoken on this issue in the Senedd or elsewhere in public, it is impossible to talk sensibly of a 'safeguarding' agenda and to uphold a legal defence to an assault on a child by anyone, including a parent. At ¶40, the CRC Committee would seem to agree:

The Committee welcomes the commitment of the National Assembly in Wales to prohibiting all corporal punishment in the home, but notes that under the terms of devolution it is not possible for the Assembly to enact the necessary legislation. The Committee is concerned at the failure of State Party to explicitly prohibit all corporal punishment in the home and emphasises its view that the existence of any defence in cases of corporal punishment of children does not comply with the principles and provisions of the

Convention, since it would suggest that some forms of corporal punishment are acceptable.

It is a widely shared hope that Wales will be the first part of the UK to end corporal punishment in the home.

Secondly, safeguarding is a whole community obligation and it begins with a commitment to childhood itself. Central to the experience of childhood is play. This is recognised in the CRC (Art. 31) and by the Committee which, in its 2008 Concluding Observations (68) expressed itself concerned that:

> . . . *with the sole exception of Wales, the right to play and leisure is not fully enjoyed by all children in the State Party, especially due to poor play infrastructures, notably for those children with disabilities. The Committee is also concerned that the steady reduction in playgrounds occurred in recent years has the effect to push children into gathering in public open spaces, a behaviour that – however – may be seen as anti-social according to the ASBOs.*

Wales was amongst the first countries in the world to publish a play policy (October 2002). This was supplemented by an Action Plan in February 2006 and legislation currently making its way through the Senedd will impose a duty on local authorities to make and publish an assessment of 'play sufficiency' in their areas.

The choices facing government rarely resolve themselves into such stark alternatives; playgrounds or ASBOs? But such choices do have to be made at one level. The choice that has been made in Wales is one that suits its political traditions and political culture. It is one that reflects a particular sense of the nature and role of the welfare state and it is one that is progressive, optimistic and right for 'our' young people.

References

Birrell, D. (2009) *The Impact of Devolution on Social Policy.* Bristol: Policy Press.

Bradshaw, J. and Mayhew, E. (2005) *The Well-being of Children in the UK.* London: University of York/Save the Children.

Butler, I. and Drakeford, M. (2005) Trusting in Social Work. *British Journal of Social Work,* 35: 639–54.

Butler, I. and Pugh, R. (2004) The Politics of Social Work Research. In Lovelock, R, and Powell, J. (Eds.) *Reflecting on Social Work: Discipline and Profession.* Aldershot/Dartmouth: Ashgate.

Butler, I. (2007) Children's Policy in Wales. In Williams, C. (Ed.) *Social Policy for Social Welfare Practice in a Devolved Wales.* Birmingham: Venture Press.

Davies, N. and Williams, D. (2009) *Clear Red Water: Welsh Devolution and Socialist Politics.* London: Francis Boutle.

Drakeford, M. (2007a) Governance and Social Policy. In Williams, C. (Ed.) *Social Policy for Social Welfare Practice in a Devolved Wales.* Birmingham: Venture Press.

Drakeford, M. (2007b) Progressive Universalism. *Agenda* (Institute of Welsh Affairs) Winter 2007: 4–7.

Funky Dragon (2003) *Inventing the Wheel: Annual Report and Accounts 2002–03* Cardiff: Funky Dragon.

Funky Dragon (2007) *Our Rights, Our Story.* Cardiff: Funky Dragon.

Funky Dragon (2007) *Why do People's Ages go Up and not Down?* Cardiff: Funky Dragon.

HM Government (2007) *Consolidated 3rd and 4th Periodic Report to the UN Committee on the Rights of the Child.* London: DCSF Publications.

Jones, R.W. and Scully, R. (2006) Devolution and Electoral Politics in Scotland and in Wales. *Publius: The Journal of Federalism,* 36: 1 115–34.

Jordan, B. (2008) *Welfare and Well-being: Social Value in Public Policy.* Bristol: Policy Press.

Marquand, D. (2008) The Progressive Consensus: Hope for the Future or Fight to the Past? in Stead, P. *Unpacking the Progressive Consensus.* Cardiff: Cardiff University and The Institute of Welsh Affairs.

Morgan, R. (2002) National Centre for Public Policy Annual Lecture, Swansea, University of Wales.

Stead, P. (2008) *Unpacking the Progressive Consensus.* Cardiff: Cardiff University and The Institute of Welsh Affairs.

Sullivan, M. (2007) Post-devolution Health Policy. In Williams, C. (Ed.) *Social Policy for Social Welfare Practice in a Devolved Wales.* Birmingham: Venture Press.

The Richard Commission (2004) *Report of the Richard Commission: Commission on the Powers and Electoral Arrangements of the National Assembly for Wales.* Cardiff: TSO.

UNICEF (2007) *Child Poverty in Perspective: An Overview of Child Poverty in Rich Countries.* Florence: Innocenti Research Centre/UNICEF.

Welsh Assembly Government (2000) *Children and Young People: A Framework for Action.* Cardiff: WAG.

Welsh Assembly Government (2002) *Children and Young People: Rights to Action.* Cardiff: WAG.

Welsh Assembly Government (2003) *Wales: A Better Country: The Strategic Agenda of the Welsh Assembly Government.* Cardiff: WAG.

Welsh Assembly Government (2004) *Making the Connections: Delivering Better Services for Wales.* Cardiff: WAG.

Welsh Assembly Government (2006) *Beyond Boundaries: Citizen Centred Local Services for Wales.* Cardiff: WAG.

Welsh Assembly Government (2007a) *One Wales: A Progressive Agenda For The Government of Wales.* Cardiff: WAG.

Welsh Assembly Government (2007b) *Rights in Action: Implementing Children and Young People's Rights in Wales.* Cardiff: WAG.

Welsh Assembly Government (2007c) *Fulfilled Lives, Supportive Communities: Improving Social Services in Wales from 2008–2018.* Cardiff: WAG.

Welsh Assembly Government (2008) *Children and Young People's Well-being Monitor for Wales.* Cardiff: WAG.

CHAPTER 3

Safeguarding Children: The Scottish Perspective

Brigid Daniel and Norma Baldwin

Background context

There are 1,047,407 children under 16 living in Scotland. The *Growing up in Scotland* survey suggests that 4 per cent of very young children are from a non-white ethnic group, the majority being from Asian backgrounds (Scottish Government, 2007). It is estimated that one in 40 children has a learning disability. In 2007 10,926 school pupils were identified as being disabled (Action for Children, 2009).

Scotland has one of the highest rates of relative child poverty in the developed world; one third of households are in, or on the margins of, poverty. The rate of teenage conception is one of the highest in Europe. Between 40,800 and 58,700 children have a parent who is a problem drug user (Action for Children, 2009). In 2007/08, there were 12,382 child protection referrals to local authorities, which at 31 March 2008, had filtered down to 2,437 children on Child Protection Registers. 40,204 children were referred to the Reporter to the Children's Hearings on grounds unrelated to offending; and 13,219 were subject to supervision requirements. There is overlap between these two referral routes. Those providing services for children and their families, and especially social workers who retain the primary responsibility for formal 'child protection' activities, face significant challenges.

Scotland has a legal system separate from the rest of the UK, differing in its model, culture and traditions in small but important respects. A comprehensive overview of policy and legislative developments can be found in Stafford and Vincent (2008). Here we will summarise some key aspects that help to explain the current context.

Pre-1995

Kearney (2001: 38) shows how Scottish jurisprudence has for centuries emphasised principles which would be seen as central to modern commitments to the rights of children and to the responsibility of parents to act in the interests of their children's welfare. He argues that:

The concept of the importance, if not the paramountcy, of the interests of the child and the right of the mature child to express a view have long been recognised as principles which the courts would uphold, at least for those who could afford to go to law.

He draws on 17th, 18th and 19th century writers to demonstrate this and the link between the *powers* of parents and their *responsibilities*. He recognises that although the law refers to *parents*, greater emphasis was placed on the role of the father until the *UK Guardianship Act 1973* accorded formal parity. Parents' rights were clearly subordinated to consideration of the welfare and interests of the child.

The current law, policies and services for children in Scotland need also to be understood in relation to key debates pursued in the 1960s. *The Kilbrandon Report* (Scottish Office, 1964) provided the foundation for the current Children's Hearing system, which makes decisions about the needs for care or treatment of all children, whether they are in need, are vulnerable or abused, or have been involved in offending. The Hearing system came into operation in 1971 and remains at the core of children's services in Scotland. In the 1995 reprint (HMSO) of *The Kilbrandon Report*, Lord Carmyllie summarises the principles on which the system is based:

... separation between the establishment of issues of disputed fact and decisions on the treatment of the child; the use of a lay panel to reach decisions on treatment; the recognition of the needs of the child as being the first and primary consideration; the vital role of the family in tackling children's problems; and the adoption of a preventive and educational approach to these problems.

Fraser of Carmyllie, 1995: vii

The courts would only be involved if there was a dispute about or challenge to the grounds for referral.

The Kilbrandon Report, with its emphasis on the need to understand the causes of social problems and seek effective, integrated, local and national remedies, combined with a continuing tradition of communal responsibilities and public service, was influential beyond its original brief in relation to children. It led to a radical review of all social work services. As a result the *Social Work (Scotland) Act* was passed in 1968, with a strong emphasis on an integrated approach to services. This approach has continued and the *Social Work (Scotland) Act* has provided a strong foundation and philosophy, able to withstand numerous attacks on social work and continuing attempts to reorganise and restructure services to meet ever changing political priorities, often single issue and media driven. Tisdall discusses the progressive nature of the Act:

> Local authorities have the power to provide not only assistance in kind, but also in cash. To many early observers, this positive promotion of welfare in the 1968 Act was revolutionary and notably absent from parallel legislation in England and Wales.
>
> Tisdall, 1996: 25

In the 1980s Strathclyde, the largest local authority in Scotland, and the one with the most entrenched issues of poverty, had gone so far as to set up an initiative under the 1968 Act, using funding from its preventive section 12 budget, to try to prevent family breakdown by providing financial support to families in severe financial difficulties. It appears to have had some success in keeping children out of public care (Fowles, 1988). There followed major controversy and attempts to prevent local authorities from giving direct financial support. Such initiatives and approaches were in stark contrast with the political philosophy of the UK government and with the move to more target driven, managerial approaches in England.

In the Thatcher years – with policies attempting to roll back the reach of the state, where the emphasis was on individual and family responsibilities rather than societal factors – the culture and practice embedded in the *Social Work (Scotland) Act* continued, backed by strong socially aware local authorities and supported by traditions of community development. This alternative culture and political approach may have been a factor in the decision by the UK government in 1995 to go for a radical restructuring of the few large Scottish authorities into 32 much smaller ones. The effect of that reorganisation was felt strongly in social work services, in the decline and closure of some children's services, in financial crises, problems of

morale, loss of expertise and loss of longstanding partnerships (Craig and Manthorpe, 1999). At the same time, even with a system of social work and child care which could claim to be based on sound principles, there were still major problems in many areas of Scotland including numerous times when social work departments had insufficient social workers to allocate all cases.

There were also tragedies of children dying because of abuse; and traumatic consequences from ill thought through and inadequately prepared investigations. The most significant inquiry was that into the events in Orkney in 1991 when nine children were removed from home amidst allegations of sexual abuse with ritualistic elements (Clyde, 1992). The children were subsequently returned home, with the Sheriff ruling that procedures had been improperly conducted. The Inquiry report was highly influential in the drive towards the introduction of the *Children (Scotland) Act 1995* which remains the key child welfare and protection legislation and is underpinned by similar principles to the *Children Act 1989*. The act retained the thread of keeping a focus on the child's interests (Kearney, 2001). As well as formalising the process of child protection investigations and introducing a range of Orders, the Act also placed a duty on local authorities to safeguard and actively promote the welfare of children in need. However few extra resources were provided to do this:

> Forced to direct scarce resources to where they would be most effective, managers and practitioners have tended to focus attention on those children assessed to be at risk of 'significant harm', and hence towards investigation. This has meant that family support aspirations in the Act have not been fully realised.
>
> Stafford and Vincent, 2008: 41–2

Services in Scotland therefore face similar challenges to those in England, where, as Parton et al. (1997: 243) suggest, there is:

> . . . a failure to question the current structure of children's services and that exhortations to use a 'lighter touch' ignore the extent to which risk drives the current system and that simply 're-labelling . . . allegations and referrals as . . . 'children in need' does not overcome the issue.

The extensive guidance that accompanied the Act contributed to the development of a bureaucratic forensic investigative system, very similar to that of England, North America and Australia. At the same time, the holistic principles of the

Children's Hearing system in Scotland were more akin to systems in Continental Western Europe where there is 'a stronger emphasis on social solidarity and public provision' (Hill et al., 2002: 5). This has led to Scotland's child welfare and protection system being described as a 'hybrid' of the two models (Hill et al., 2002).

Post 1995 – a period of rapid reform

For many working in children's services and research there were major concerns about the future direction and quality of services partly because of the focus of resources on investigation. With devolution, however, in 1999 there was a resurgence of optimism and clear indications that the new Parliament was committed to the traditions of strong local government, including the integrated approaches built into the *Social Work (Scotland) Act*. Donald Dewar, giving one of the annual Kilbrandon lectures shortly before he became First Minister of Scotland following devolution in 1999, re-asserted the importance of the Children's Hearing system, and the underpinning principles (Dewar, 1998). He emphasised the importance of public and local involvement and the willingness to struggle with problems – including the problem of young offenders – and recognise complexity, when panels strive to achieve a 'balance between needs and deeds'. The need to understand personal needs and behaviour in the wider social context has remained a key strength of policy and services for children in Scotland.

The inquiries and reports prepared for the Scottish Executive (known since 2007 as Scottish Parliament) have generally followed the same analysis and philosophy as set out in *The Kilbrandon Report*. Many of the debates between agencies, academics and government advisers focused on the need to build on existing strengths, improving and developing what was there, rather than restructuring services. *For Scotland's Children* (Scottish Executive, 2001) set out again the links between poverty and inequalities and a range of harm to children. In particular the report pressed the case for continuing attention to integrated, child centred services.

In 1999 three-year-old Kennedy McFarlane was killed by her stepfather despite the fact that social work and health had been aware of concerns about Kennedy's well-being. The subsequent inquiry reiterated the findings of many other inquiries, and recommended that there be a review of child protection arrangements throughout Scotland (Hammond, 2001). The subsequent review was carried out by a multidisciplinary team, with a number of subprojects. The views of the general public, parents, children and professionals were obtained through consultation subprojects. A direct audit of the practice of all the key agencies was built around a set of individual, in-depth case studies. The cases were drawn from the whole spectrum of child care and protection, sampling cases known to health visitors, education departments, the police and social work. The audit considered compliance with guidance, but the key focus was on *outcomes* for children. The review report *It's Everyone's Job to Make Sure I'm Alright*, published in 2002, highlighted a number of weaknesses in the Scottish child protection system, suggesting that some children were not getting the help they needed because resources were being focused on acute cases and procedures were being used to ration services. The existence of different decision making arenas for child protection in Scotland was found to be cumbersome, with many professionals making referrals to the Children's Reporter in order to obtain services for children, rather than because they felt 'compulsory measures of care' were necessary (Scottish Executive, 2002).

Overall, despite nearly a decade of concern across the UK that child protection services needed to be 're-focused', the review underlined the extent to which preoccupation with investigation of and categorising situations as 'child protection' or 'child in need' continued to dominate the system and had become an end in itself (Stafford and Vincent, 2008; Daniel, 2004; Daniel, Vincent and Ogilvie-Whyte, 2007).

The Scottish Executive launched a three year Child Protection Reform Programme (CPRP) to build on the recommendations in the report. The aims were to provide better early support to children and families to prevent the need for protection at a later stage; to provide better direct help to children in need of protection; and to provide effective continuing support to children and families to prevent child protection concerns recurring. A number of initiatives were undertaken, including the development of a Children's Charter following consultation with children and young people, setting out what children wanted from these services:

- Get to know us.
- Speak with us.
- Listen to us.
- Take us seriously.
- Involve us.
- Respect our privacy.
- Be responsible to us.
- Think about our lives as a whole.
- Think carefully about how you use information about us.
- Put us in touch with the right people.
- Use your power to help.
- Make things happen when they should.
- Help us be safe.

Scottish Executive, 2004a

A Framework for Standards and a new structure for multidisciplinary inspection based upon the Charter was introduced (Scottish Executive, 2004b). New guidance was produced setting out new responsibilities for Child Protection Committees (Scottish Executive, 2005a). During the period of the CPRP there was an extensive programme of training and development, especially within education and health services.

There followed a round of multi-disciplinary inspections of services to protect children, led by HM Inspectorate of Education. Views are mixed about the effectiveness of such inspections in improving services for children, with anecdotal evidence suggesting that considerable police, social work, education and health resources have been diverted towards preparation for inspections. This of course is not unique to children's services, and in 2007 a Scottish review of all scrutiny processes concluded that mechanisms were unnecessarily complex and that 'providers believe that this has had a significant impact and is diverting resources from front-line delivery' (Crerer, 2007: 11) With the aim of simplifying the 'scrutiny landscape', in 2008 it was announced that a single body will look at care and social work in the future, including child protection services (Scottish Government, 2008b). Whilst the simplification is welcome, these developments have not challenged the assumption that inspection leads to improvements in outcomes.

In an evaluation of the impact of the CPRP, respondents considered that it had made a substantive contribution towards the improvement of child protection services in Scotland (Daniel et al., 2007). At the same time, significant concerns were raised about the implications of increased awareness of children's need for protection, subsequent increases in child protection referrals and increased resource implications for all services.

While the CPRP was underway, a review of the Children's Hearing System was undertaken. There were some concerns that the system, although highly regarded, could not deal effectively with entrenched offending by young people or with children requiring permanent substitute care (McGhee, 2003). There were concerns, too, that the system was not able to deal with the rise in referrals made on the ground of lack of care and that it could not remain true to its principles because it was under-resourced. At times it appeared that the Hearing system was being used by professionals as a route into an equally over-loaded child protection investigation system, thus compounding a view that the two systems were not sufficiently integrated. The initial review led to a wider review of arrangements for children's services, culminating in the *Getting it Right for Every Child* programme [GIRFEC] (discussed below) (Scottish Executive, 2005b).

During this period of reform there was a range of legislative policy developments in health and education services of relevance to child welfare and protection. Health visiting services in Scotland were, as in England, responding to *Health for all Children 4* with its call for a more 'public health' approach and for services to be targeted to those in most need (Scottish Executive, 2005c). More recent policy proposes a more generic approach to nursing in the community (Scottish Executive, 2006c). Contradictory elements of these different policy developments continue to preoccupy the service, which is also aiming to respond to GIRFEC requirements.

The *Education (Additional Support for Learning) Act 2004* introduced the requirement for schools to undertake assessments of children who may need additional supports for learning if affected by complex factors 'likely to have a significant adverse effect on the school education of the child or young person'. This definition potentially leads education staff into very wide territory. The broadening of expectations upon schools is also evident in the *Curriculum for Excellence*, formally launched in 2009, which aims to promote four 'capacities' of children so that they are:

- successful learners
- confident individuals

- responsible citizens
- effective contributors

Learning and Teaching Scotland, 2006

Education staff will also be attempting to integrate these developments with GIRFEC.

Scottish projects aimed at improvement

Changing Lives

The increased momentum towards integrated services led to questions about the role of social workers and whether the concept of generic social work was still sensible. While the CPRP was underway an independent review was commissioned to 'take a fundamental look at all aspects of social work in order to strengthen its contribution to the delivery of integrated services' (Scottish Executive, 2006a: 7). The resulting report *Changing Lives* (Scottish Executive, 2006a) asserted that 'it is and should remain a single generic profession, underpinned by a common body of knowledge, skills and values . . .' (p 27).

It also set out reserved functions of social workers, including:

Social workers should assess, plan, manage the delivery of care and safeguard the well-being of the most vulnerable adults and children, in particular, those who are in need of protection . . .

p 30

The report identified services and organisations as 'overwhelmed by bureaucracy' and advocated change to enable social workers to exercise professional autonomy. It also drew on two commissioned reviews (Kerr et al., 2005; McNeill et al., 2005) to suggest that, 'the quality of the therapeutic relationship between social worker and individual or family is critical to achieving successful outcomes' (p 27). The report also set out a role for social workers in building community capacity.

Social work education and training

Social work education has a distinct framework in Scotland and from 2004 onwards student social workers have had to achieve an honours degree in social work or an equivalent post-graduate award. Three projects aimed at improving social work knowledge and skills in relation to children

were established following the death of Caleb Ness, killed at the age of 11 weeks by his father, who was known to criminal justice social work services. The inquiry report noted the poor communication between adult and children's social work services and the lack of assessment of the risk posed to Caleb by his father (O'Brien, 2003). Crucially, the professionals working with his father saw themselves as working with an adult rather than an adult who was also a parent. The report highlighted that social work specialisation – in criminal justice, children's services and adult services – was associated with an erosion of a generic sense of responsibility for the well-being and protection of children. The first response was to introduce changes to the post-registration training and learning requirements for registered social workers such that five days had to:

Focus on working effectively with colleagues and other professionals to identify, assess and manage risk to vulnerable groups. This is in order to ensure that they are assisted to meet their primary responsibility of protecting children and adults from harm.

Scottish Social Services Council: 80

A second project to develop 'key capabilities in child care and protection' (KCs) started with an audit of social work course content in 2004 which suggested that it was possible, on some courses, for students to avoid engaging in depth with issues relating to the needs and safety of children. Following extensive consultation, a set of learning outcomes or 'key capabilities' was developed to ensure that all social workers at the point of qualifying:

- are aware of their roles and responsibilities in respect of children and young people.
- are able to demonstrate their knowledge, skills and understanding in relation to child care and protection.

Scottish Executive, 2006b

It was not intended that meeting the KCs would equip social workers to carry out child protection investigations, rather, it aimed to ensure that, in whatever setting they work, social workers are alert to children's needs, including their needs for protection from harm. Some Higher Education staff expressed concern about the imposition of another layer of requirements that had to be met by students; some objected to what could be viewed as top-down curricular constraint and others to the potential for fuelling a 'tick-box' approach to social work education. There was also concern that there might be a perverse incentive to increase children and families placements. In the event, practice teachers have developed a range of creative ways for students to consider issues of relevance to children within the context of adult services. An evaluation of early implementation was largely positive, with respondents, especially practice teachers, suggesting that KCs had improved students' awareness of issues relating to children (IRISS, 2008).

While this project was underway the 'Children at the Centre' project – a package of government funded training – brought together social workers in adult settings and children and families settings to explore the issues in relation to parenting, children, risk and needs. This training was delivered to over 1,600 social workers across Scotland and was positively evaluated by participants (Barlow and Daniel, 2007).

Some considered these projects to be simplistic 'knee-jerk' responses to an inquiry, into a child death and whether any of them have improved outcomes for children, or have affected childrens and parents' experience of services, has yet to be established. The extent to which training can significantly influence the culture of disconnected adult and child services is unclear. In conjunction with *Changing Lives*, however, the projects underline a generic role of social work for the protection of children. None of these projects has addressed the wider social work role set out in *Changing Lives*, of helping to build community capacity, although models for such approaches to the protection of children have been developed (Nelson and Baldwin, 2002; Jack, 2004). Whether social work education in Scotland adequately equips workers to engage effectively with communities would bear further exploration.

Scottish Child Care and Protection Network

The Scottish Child Care and Protection Network (SCCPN) is a Scotland-wide network of academics and representatives of key stakeholders in child care and protection. The SCCPN aims to provide a measured overview of available national and international evidence from research and practice, and promote the generation of new evidence so that practitioners

working with vulnerable children have access to evidence of best practice. The SCCPN was first proposed in 2006 and attracted seed-corn funding for initial work (Green Lister, 2009; Keys, 2007; Tarara, 2007; Tarara and Daniel, 2007). In 2008 the Scottish Government awarded three years funding for a dedicated co-ordinator, administrative support and dissemination activities. This was in response to a recommendation of an inquiry report that the Scottish Executive should establish a framework to assist staff involved in complex and challenging child protection work (SWIA, 2005). Ongoing SCCPN projects include a review of research evidence about effective intervention to support children affected by parental substance misuse and a multi-disciplinary survey of practitioners' views about perceived gaps in evidence for practice and about preferred methods of dissemination.

Multi-Agency Resource Service (MARS)

As a further response to the recommendation from the inquiry report the Scottish Government has recently established the national Multi-Agency Resource Service (MARS) to assist agencies with handling complex child protection cases by providing mechanisms for the exchange of expertise. If frontline practitioners, middle or senior managers and local policy makers identify a lack of expertise when addressing a particular issue, MARS will provide a structured opportunity to analyse the gap in expertise, to ensure a proportionate response and to draw, wherever possible, upon local expertise. Where needed, MARS will facilitate access to external skilled practitioners, consultants or trainers to reinforce or increase local levels of expertise. Similarly, if there has been a dramatic change in demography in an area, access to strategic planners from other areas may be of benefit. MARS would broker support in four tiers where there may be gaps in expertise in:

1. confidence and/or experience
2. specific knowledge about a topic or model for practice
3. skill in practice with a particular complex case
4. local changes as a result of demographic shifts

These initiatives are of a different order from the common response to an inquiry, to introduce further guidance; but it is too early to gauge whether these initiatives will lead to better outcomes for children.

Current context: 'Getting it right for every child'

As a result of the elections in 2007 there was a pause in momentum as the newly elected SNP negotiated a concordat with the Coalition of Scottish Local Authorities (COSLA) to underpin funding arrangements. An annual 'Single Outcome Agreement' is produced for every council, based on an agreed set of national outcomes (underpinned by agreed national indicators). Ring-fenced funding has been reduced and more autonomy has devolved to Local Authorities to meet local priorities. Whilst ring-fenced funding had been seen as restrictive, the danger of removal is that funding to some groups of children and adults in need of extra support will be vulnerable to cuts. The longer-term impact remains to be seen.

The SNP has continued the roll-out of GIRFEC and continued with a 'pathfinding' activity in the Highland Council area. Laying greater emphasis upon early intervention, the SNP has also developed the *Framework for Early Years and Early Intervention:*

> We will move away from a focus on 'picking up the pieces' once something has happened, towards prevention, becoming better at early identification of those individuals who are at risk and taking steps to address that risk. Early intervention must start in the early years, where it is most effective, but we must also look for opportunities to deliver early intervention through a broader range of policies.
> Scottish Government, 2008a: 1

The overall concept of GIRFEC is a common, co-ordinated approach across all agencies that supports the delivery of appropriate, proportionate and timely help to all children as they need it. Key aspects include a strengthened role for universal services to address concerns themselves where they can, without involvement of other agencies; a co-ordinated and unified approach to identifying concerns, actions and outcomes, based on the shared vision for children; and a lead professional to co-ordinate and monitor multi-agency activity where necessary.

There had been calls for Scotland to introduce a national, common multi-disciplinary assessment

framework, with substantial discussion and collaboration between government, local authorities, the voluntary sector and academics, culminating in a multi-disciplinary working group reporting to the Scottish Executive. The work of this group was incorporated into GIRFEC with the production of the 'My World' triangle which sets out developmental needs within three key areas, from the child's perspective:

1. how I grow and develop
2. what I need from people who look after me
3. my wider world

Although based on similar principles and a similar theoretical basis to the assessment framework for England (DoH, 2000) the Scottish version is distinct with its use of child-centred language and strong emphasis on the wider context of children's needs. This triangle has been joined with the Resilience Matrix (based upon Daniel et. al., 1999), the capacities identified in the curriculum for excellence, and the eight well-being indicators (included) safe, healthy, achieving, nurtured, active, respected, responsible, to produce a single model for children's services.

Issues of risk assessment and risk management are being addressed by Aldgate and Rose who propose a 'structured professional judgement approach' in which 'risk and need are two sides of the same coin' (Aldgate and Rose, 2008).

With its emphasis on refocusing services towards prevention, early intervention and family support, GIRFEC arguably moves Scotland further towards the child care systems of continental Europe (Stafford and Vincent, 2008). It is congruent with the research evidence that has led to a broad consensus about the importance of taking a holistic approach to the welfare of children. Because risks to children's development are frequently associated with unmet needs, there is recognition that a system focused tightly on 'risk' will provide impoverished responses. A paper in a recent high profile special edition of *The Lancet* on child maltreatment concludes:

> International comparisons emphasise the need for an approach that combines a focus on child safety with the broader benefits of a focus on child and family welfare.
> Gilbert et al., 2009: 177

One of the potential implications of GIRFEC is that if early intervention and family support becomes increasingly the preserve of the universal services, statutory social work could become even more of a residual service, reserved for situations where there is a need for investigation and compulsion. This could be dangerous and limiting for all, undermining the aim of integration. It is essential that all professions are alert to potential risks to children and equally important that the essential skills in assessment, relationship building and therapeutic work that social workers can bring to early intervention and family support are part of an integrated approach.

Conclusion

In a country the size of Scotland, it is relatively easy for debates to take place with government officials and ministers when new proposals are under discussion. Scotland has generally been able to avoid the kind of major re-organisation of children's services that swallow up additional resources in supporting new structures and divert resources from the front line. It is also attempting to avoid the introduction of a complex, bureaucratic and IT driven system to underpin the GIRFEC programme. However, despite substantial reform, there is a still a reluctance to unpick the fundamentally forensic, investigative core that lies at the heart of 'child protection' work. This means that social work in the local authority, the main agency charged with protecting the welfare of children, is still viewed with trepidation. It may be that GIRFEC will allow exploration of a model that provides children and parents some 'space for negotiation' over how allegations of abuse and neglect may be progressed, as proposed by Cooper et al. (2003). This would be compatible with the call for more professional autonomy set out in *Changing Lives* (Scottish Executive, 2006).

It is early days in the reform programmes and too soon to tell whether children's lives will improve as a result of the changes. If the aims are to be attained and the contradictions built in to policies – in Scotland as in all countries – addressed, practitioners must be genuinely released from current bureaucratic constraints, and fully supported to work creatively with, and on behalf of, children and families.

References

Action for Children (2009) *Factfile 2008–09*. Glasgow: Action for Children.

Aldgate, J. and Rose, W. (2008) *Assessing and Managing Risk in Getting It Right for Every Child*. Edinburgh: The Scottish Government.

Barlow, J. and Daniel, B. (2007) *Children at the Centre: A National Social Work Training Programme in Child Care and Protection: Final Report*. Glasgow: University of Glasgow and University of Dundee.

Clyde, J. (1992) *The Report of the Inquiry into the Removal of Children from Orkney in February 1991*. Edinburgh: HMSO.

Cooper, A., Hetherington, R. and Katz, I. (2003) *The Risk Factor: Making the Child Protection System Work for Children*. London: DEMOS.

Craig, G. and Manthorpe, J. (1999) *The Impact of Local Government Reorganisation on Social Services Work*. York: Joseph Rowntree Foundation.

Crerer, L. (2007) *The Report of the Independent Review of Regulation, Audit, Inspection and Complaints Handling of Public Services in Scotland*. Edinburgh: The Scottish Government.

Daniel, B. (2003) The Scottish Child Protection Review: Development of Methodology For a National Multi-disciplinary Audit of Child Protection Practice. *Qualitative Social Work: Research and Practice*, 2, 435–56.

Daniel, B. (2004) An Overview of The Scottish Multi-Disciplinary Child Protection Review. *Child and Family Social Work*, 9, 247–57.

Daniel, B., Vincent, S. and Ogilvie-Whyte, S. (2007) *A Process Review of the Child Protection Reform Programme*. Dundee: Dundee University and Barnardos, Scotland.

Daniel, B., Wassell, S. and Gilligan, R. (1999) *Child Development for Child Care and Protection Workers*. London: Jessica Kingsley.

Department of Health (2000) *Framework for the Assessment of Children in Need and their Families*. London: HMSO.

Dewar, D. (1998) *Children's Hearings: The 1997 Kilbrandon Child Care Lecture*. London: HMSO.

Fowles, R. (1988) Preventing Reception Into Care: Monitoring an Initiative Using Section 12 Funding. In Freeman, I. and Montgomery, S. (Eds.) *Child Care: Monitoring Practice*. London: Jessica Kingsley.

Fraser of Carmyllie (1995) Foreword. In The Scottish Office. *The Kilbrandon Report: Report of the Committee on Children and Young Persons*. Edinburgh: HMSO.

Gilbert, R. et al. (2009) Burden and Consequences of Child Maltreatment in High Income Countries. *Lancet.* Available: http://www.thelancet.com/journals/lancet/article/PIIS0140-6736%2808%2961706-7/fulltext.

Green Lister, P. (2009) An Analysis of Recommendations for the Police from Significant Case Reviews and Child Death Inquiries. Glasgow: Glasgow University.

Hammond, H. (2001) *Child Protection Inquiry into the Circumstances Surrounding the Death of Kennedy McFarlane, dob 17 April 1997.* Dumfries: Dumfries and Galloway Child Protection Committee.

Hill, M., Stafford, A. and Green Lister, P. (Eds.) (2002) *International Perspectives on Child Protection: Report of a Seminar Held on 20 March 2002.* Edinburgh: Scottish Executive.

IRISS (2006) *Key Capabilities in Child Protection.* Available: http://www.iriss.org.uk/keycapabilities.

IRISS (2008) *Student Focus on Child Care and Protection: Report on the Development and Embedding of Key Capabilities in Child Care and Protection into Social Work Programmes.* Dundee: IRISS

Jack, G. (2004) Child Protection at the Community Level. *Child Abuse Review.* 13, 368–83.

Kearney, B. (2001) Children's Rights and Children's Welfare in Scotland. In Baldwin, N. (Ed.) *Protecting Children: Promoting their Rights.* London: Whiting and Birch.

Kerr. B. et al. (2005) *Effective Social Work with Older People.* Edinburgh: Scottish Executive.

Keys, M. (2007) *The Role of Nurses and Midwives in Child Protection: A Report to the Scottish Executive Health Department.* Edinburgh: Napier University.

Learning and Teaching Scotland (2006) *Curriculum for Excellence: The Four Capacities.* Available *http://www.ltscotland.org.uk/curriculumforexcellence/* curriculumoverview/aims/fourcapacities.asp.

McGhee, J. (2003) The Social Work Role in the Children's Hearing System. In Baillie, D. et al. (Eds.) *Social Work and the Law in Scotland.* Houndsmills: Palgrave Macmillan.

McNeill, F. et al. (2005) *Reducing Re-offending: Key Practice Skills.* Glasgow. SWIA and Glasgow School of Social Work.

Nelson, S. and Baldwin, N. (2002) *The Craigmillar Project: Neighbourhood Mapping to Improve Children's Safety from Sexual Crime.* Dundee: University of Dundee.

O'Brien, S. (2003) *Report of the Enquiry into the Death of Caleb Ness.* Edinburgh: City of Edinburgh Council.

Parton, N., Thorpe, D. and Wattam, C. (1997) *Child Protection: Risk and the Moral Order.* Houndsmills: Palgrave.

Scottish Executive (2001) *For Scotland's Children: Better Integrated Children's Services.* Edinburgh: HMSO.

Scottish Executive (2002) *'It's Everyone's Job to Make Sure I'm Alright': Report of the Child Protection Audit and Review.* Edinburgh: Scottish Executive.

Scottish Executive (2004a) *Protecting Children and Young People: The Charter.* Edinburgh: Scottish Executive.

Scottish Executive (2004b) *Protecting Children and Young People: Framework for Standards.* Edinburgh: Scottish Executive.

Scottish Executive (2005a) *Health for All Children 4: Guidance in Implementation in Scotland.* Edinburgh: Scottish Executive.

Scottish Executive (2005b) *Getting it Right for Every Child: Proposals for Action.* Edinburgh: Scottish Executive.

Scottish Executive (2005c) *Protecting Children and Young People: Child Protection Committees.* Edinburgh: Scottish Executive.

Scottish Executive (2006a) *Changing Lives: Report of the 21st Century Social Work Review.* Edinburgh: Scottish Executive.

Scottish Executive (2006b) *Key Capabilities for Child Care and Protection.* Edinburgh: Scottish Executive.

Scottish Executive (2006c) *Visible, Accessible and Integrated Care: Report of the Review of Nursing in the Community in Scotland.* Edinburgh: Scottish Executive.

Scottish Government (2007) *Growing up in Scotland: A Study Following the Lives of Scotland's Children.* Scottish Government. Available: http://www.scotland.gov.uk/Publications/2007/01/17162004/0.

Scottish Government (2008a) *Early Years and Early Intervention: A Joint Scottish Government and COSLA Policy Statement.* Edinburgh: Scottish Government.

Scottish Government (2008b) *Improving Scrutiny.* Scottish Government. Available: http://www.scotland.gov.uk/News/Releases/2008/11/06103757.

Scottish Government and COSLA (2007) *Concordat.* Scottish Government. Available: http://www.scotland.gov.uk/Resource/Doc/923/0054147.pdf.

Scottish Office (1964) *The Kilbrandon Report: Report of the Committee on Children and Young Persons.* Edinburgh: The Scottish Office.

Scottish Social Services Council (2008) *Scottish Social Services (Registration) Rules.* Dundee: SSSC.

Stafford, A. and Vincent, S. (2008) *Safeguarding and Protecting Children and Young People.* Edinburgh: Dunedin.

SWIA (2005) *An Inspection into the Care and Protection of Children in Eilean Siar.* Edinburgh: SWIA.

Tarara, H. (2007) *Database of 10 Years of Scottish Child Care and Protection Research.* Scottish Child Care and Protection Network.

Tarara, H. and Daniel, B. (2007) *Audit of Scottish Child Care and Protection Research: Report to the Scottish Government, Directorate of Education and Lifelong Learning.* Scottish Child Care and Protection Network.

Tisdall, K. (1996) From the Social Work (Scotland) Act 1968 to the Children (Scotland) Act 1995. In Hill, M. and Aldgate, J. *Child Welfare Services: Developments in Law, Policy, Practice and Research.* London: Jessica Kingsley.

CHAPTER 4

The Understanding Systemic Caseworker: The (Changing) Nature and Meanings of Working with Children and Families

Harry Ferguson

My aim in this chapter is to consider the nature of children's services and child care practice and the direction they are taking in contemporary Britain. I want to explore what it means to work with children and families today and how such work can best be characterised and theorised. I will suggest that the nature of child care practice today can best be understood in terms of two main processes: firstly, the increasing importance of how practitioners are located within systems where their work is regulated by the government and integrated with other professionals. This is most evident in how, when children die in child protection cases, it invariably comes to light either that good systems to promote communication were not in place or that the systems that were in place were not used. Secondly, the importance of individual professionals being skilled, reflective and emotionally-intelligent (Howe, 2008) and acting creatively and on their own initiative has never been more apparent. It is clear that children have not been protected because certain key actions were not performed to establish the children's well being when professionals were face to face with them and their parents or carers. More positively, research shows that in situations where the outcomes for service users are good, this is in large part due to the skill and creativity of practitioners who are located in supportive organisational contexts.

We need a language that can capture how social work and child care practitioners today have to combine the ability to operate reflectively within the systems that increasingly govern their work, with the discretion and skill to act creatively and courageously in the best interests of children and their families. The identity and purpose of contemporary child care practice can be characterised in terms of what I will call 'systemic casework'. I will try to show how the understanding systemic caseworker has to meet the challenge of combining skills at the organisational or multi-professional level with

direct work with children and families. In doing so, they have to bridge the organisational and the personal; technology and emotion; multi-agency systems and casework. This requires us to develop theoretical approaches which integrate the sociology of bureaucracy and organisational life with understandings of psycho-dynamic processes, relationship based practice and the emotions and I will follow Kanter (2004) in conceptualising social workers as 'transitional participants' in children's and families lives.

Once upon a time: The restructuring of contemporary child care practice

There is in many accounts of social work with children and families today a pervasive sense of loss, or at least of an absence, a sense that something is missing and doesn't feel right. There is little doubt from the social work literature that what is thought to be lacking or lost is relationships, and having the time, capacity and capability to relate to children and families. Stephen Walker (2004: 162) describes this change as the 'subtle yet fundamental shift from the term caseworker to case-manager.' The implication is that while social workers once spent most of their time doing casework with families, they now spend most time in the office, writing up electronic case records and 'signposting' and managing the services that need to go into families, which are mostly delivered by other professionals and agencies. With more time being spent at computers and administration, less and less is available to work with service users. In any case, it is not necessarily the social worker's role to do the direct 'therapeutic' work any more but that of other agencies in a context where the increased emphasis on 'joined-up' multi-agency working has resulted in a loss of social work's traditional 'helping' role and function (Broadhurst et al., 2010).

This micro-management and intrusion into

previously autonomous areas of practice is in some measure a product of the new concern to manage risk of system failures that has arisen since the 1970s due to the deaths of children in child protection cases (Ferguson, 2004). Risk is being managed through increased accountability and integrated working. More structured information-sharing between agencies is thought to improve the likelihood that children at risk will not slip through the net. Many commentators worry that practitioners are being deskilled by having to follow the increasing volume of procedures and the audit and performance management that have come from closer monitoring of practice by management and, at a higher level, government. Stephen Webb exemplifies these concerns by arguing that, 'meaningful aspects of direct casework have given way to low-level functional tasks' (2006: 73). I am going to argue that this has accuracy in terms of some real changes that have taken place in child care social work, but ultimately it is too one-dimensional and it is necessary to do more justice to the nuanced nature of what practitioners do today. Not only does the direct work that does still go on with children and families contain significant emotional depth and meanings, but I will suggest that the case management and inter-professional dimensions of the role also have important emotional and therapeutic meanings for children and families.

The understanding caseworker and casework organisation

To develop this argument we need to examine in more detail what child care social work has been in the past and what it has become. It is certainly the case that in the 'old days' social workers largely constructed their own practice by deciding for themselves what was the best course of action to take in a case, and for the most part providing that intervention themselves. What went on between worker and client was seen as a largely private affair, with minimal interference by the state and limited requirement for social work to be accountable to the general public.

Social work drew on psychological theories such as psychoanalysis to understand their clients and to structure the work they did with them. The 'casework relationship' was at the heart of the enterprise, with the emphasis on emotional attunement as being the means to helping service users to deal with their problems. Practice was talked about through the language of relationships: warmth, holding, touch. In 1972 in *Social Work with Children* Juliet Berry wrote:

> Apart from the non-verbal communication of literally holding a distressed child, there are many ways of symbolising encircling warmth: one possibility is to keep a rug in the car. Children certainly understand such symbols.
>
> Berry, 1972: 55

Olive Stevenson, writing in 1963 in a paper called *The Understanding Caseworker*, gives a wonderful account of such 'encircling warmth' being practised with a 10 year old girl, Anne. Her foster placement, where she had lived for seven years, had broken down and the social worker was taking her to a residential care placement. Stevenson quotes at length from the social worker's case record, which begins from the start of the car journey:

> She (Anne) leaned out of the car waving to Miss N as we went off and then sat down, saying nothing. I was having difficulty in negotiating heavy traffic and could not get even a look at her for a while. When I was able to I could see that tears were pouring down her face though she was very quiet about it and turning her head away from me. I drew the car to the side of the road and said that I expect she was feeling a bit sad. She nodded and did not protest when I put my arm around her and cuddled her.
>
> Stevenson, 1963: 92–3

The child began to cry and wrapped herself in the social worker's travel rug which she referred to as her 'magic rug'. Safely wrapped in the rug and skilfully facilitated by the social worker to open up, Anne talked about her very mixed feelings towards her foster family, her grief, anger, fears about the move, and her fantasies about going to a lovely new family home with nice children and adults. At lunch, the social worker talked to Anne about what the children's home looked like, the names of the people there and the children who would be in her group. Commenting on the social worker's practice, Stevenson (1963: 95) observes that she 'comforts the child but recognises the need to keep the feeling open and flowing; her experience and knowledge will have shown her that if the feeling is damned up, the child's pain, anger, resentment may effectively block the later adjustment, in this case to the children's home and to the foster home to which she was to return for holidays'. This kind of relationship based casework went on with children and families in their homes, in clinics and social work offices and in practitioner's cars (for an extended analysis of the role of the car in the above case example and in child and family work in general, see Ferguson, 2010).

The theories that were drawn upon to understand and shape those helping relationships were drawn from approaches such as psychoanalysis and attachment theory, at the core of which was a concern with the potential for the worker to help the service user by addressing their emotional experience and the dynamics of the professional-client relationship in this. Olive Stevenson (2005) argues that the ways in which the influence of psychoanalysis on social work and child care has been written about in recent years is a caricature of what actually happened. The image has grown up – or been promoted – of a generation of practitioners whose main preoccupation was to delve into their client's unconscious and explore their fantasy lives while ignoring their social circumstances of poverty and discrimination. Just as in classical psychoanalysis Freud interviewed people on the couch and was preoccupied with their relationships with their mother and father and their sexual and other fantasies, the story goes that the social worker's focus was exclusively on their service user's internal lives to the exclusion of the external factors that influenced their experiences and life chances. The 'radical social work' movement which began in the mid-1970s was heavily based on this claim (see Bailey and Brake, 1975).

Stevenson (2005) points out that there were important differences between the impact of psychoanalysis on American and British social work and in actual fact the practitioners and academics who shaped British social work in the 1960s and 70s were wise enough to understand that effective social work was only concerned in very selective ways with the unconscious and the fantasy life of the client and that crucially this needed always to be in the context of their relationship to external reality (Kanter, 2004). It was experiences such as a move to a new placement, as in Anne's case, that brought the external reality of them having no family home into sharp focus for children, while also having a deep impact on their internal emotional life. The understanding caseworker was effective by engaging with both the internal and external aspects of children's experiences.

In fact even in the late-1950s and 60s social work came under attack for being too influenced by psychoanalysis and making what were regarded as grandiose claims for how it could change people. Barbara Wooton (1959) famously claimed that social workers were foolishly and ineptly attempting to be 'miniature psychoanalysts'. As Stevenson, responding to Wooton's criticisms, observes referring to the case-study of 10 year old Anne outlined above:

> *It is very clear in this record that the child care officer is not a 'miniature psychoanalyst' for her concern is not to explore deeply unconscious fantasy – which she is neither trained nor employed to do – but rather to recognise, as it were, the little pieces of the iceberg which show above the surface in order to help the child handle better the realities of the situation. On this long car journey, the child care officer is deliberately bridging the gap between the past and the future by the purposive references to both. The child care officer knows that in children who move from one place to another the images of people and places are often blurred and disturbed by the feelings – of anger, of fear, of sadness, which surround them, and that these are often intense. The task is therefore to try to keep the reality of the situation alive and relatively unclouded by fantasies. In order to do this, the child care officer must be alive to the significance of casual remarks or significant stories, such as Anne could tell when encouraged by the magic rug and the child care officer's interest.*
>
> Stevenson, 1963: 95

Stevenson's emphasis on 'keeping the feelings open and flowing' and the importance of helping the child to integrate her internal and external worlds reflects the influence of psychodynamic theories which held that a key task of child care social work was to enable children to process their experience and integrate thought and feeling by 'holding' or 'containing' them. Bion's (1962) notion of 'containment' was developed in this same period and influenced social work scholars like Stevenson. It refers to how the infant's dependence on its mother/parents for food and survival creates anxiety and feelings of love and hate, which they project onto their carer. The mother takes in the infant's anxious projections, processes them and gives them back in a concerned emotional form the child can tolerate, thus allowing the child to think more clearly about themselves and the external world. The mother/parent provides what Donald Winnicott (1953; 1957) called a 'facilitating environment' for the child to develop within. Winnicott developed the famous concept of the 'transitional object' (Winnicott, 1953) which describes how children become attached to objects like blankets and cling to them at times of transition, such as going to bed, or on journeys.

Joel Kanter (2004) who (like Winnicott and Bion) also draws on the psychoanalytic perspective of 'object relations' theory, opens up the possibility that social workers could be seen as transitional objects for children and indeed parents. But Kanter suggests that applying such terminology to social work is not sufficient because it is too inactive, implying the professional is a passive recipient of the child's feelings and projections. Social workers are active *participants* in the lives of those who use their services. Kanter (2004: 74) conceptualises social workers as 'transitional participants' in service user's lives. 'Through the reality of their contact with significant persons and experiences in the child's life, the social worker can help the child to maintain contact with positive life experiences that can enhance ongoing intrapsychic and interpersonal relationships' (Kanter, 2004: 74–5). The transitional participant gives children continuity throughout the changes to which they are subjected and a sense of someone able 'to gather together the separate threads of the child's life'.

Clare Winnicott (who was married to Donald) gives a wonderful example of this when writing in 1963 about her work with children in care:

> *(We would) go over the same ground again and again. It might begin with 'Do you remember the day you brought me here in your car?' And we would retrace our steps, going over the same events and explanations once more. This was no mere reminiscing, but a desperate effort to add life up, to overcome fears and anxieties, and to achieve personal integration. In my experience, feelings about home and other important places cluster round the caseworker, so that when the children see her they are not only reminded of home but can be in touch with the part of themselves which has roots in the past and the (outside) world.*
>
> Winnicott, C. 1963

Organisational change and transitional participation through case management

Moving now into examining practice in the present, as I have already suggested, many critiques of practice suggest that workers no longer have time to be understanding caseworkers because of the rise of case management and care planning which has pulled them away from forming direct meaningful relationships with service users (Webb, 2006; Parton, 2008). This analysis has value but it underplays the emotional meanings and relationships that remain within practice, reducing case management as well as the casework that does go on to technical and functional acts. I want to argue that this notion of the practitioner as transitional participant also has relevance to the increasingly significant role of the social worker as case manager and that within that a vitally important emotional and relational component is necessary and possible.

Ravi Kohli's research into social workers' responses to unaccompanied asylum seeking children provides compelling evidence for how, even in highly regulated bureaucratic systems like the UK, practitioners who are emotionally attuned to the needs of the child and prepared to act on their behalf with agencies, including and perhaps especially those who process their right to be in the country, can make a huge difference to their lives. He conceptualises the journey effective social workers take children on as being provided through creating safety, a sense of belonging and ultimately success (Kohli, 2007). Writing about the needs of children in care, Barry Luckock argues that the worker needs to take the young person in care on two kinds of journeys: one is 'to stable and permanent family and social life in childhood and beyond'; the other involves 'the journey to adulthood in its own right' (Luckock, 2008: 2). Echoing the influence of psycho-dynamic theorists like the Winnicotts, Olive Stevenson and Joel Kanter, he suggests that good practice in enabling successful journeys requires the worker to act as an emotional 'bridge' for children in and out of care, rather than just being a care manager, or 'tour operator'. The 'tour operator' role has become more prominent as the UK government has increasingly adopted the metaphor of 'travel' and viewed the role of social workers as being to help young service users to 'navigate' various services and help them through their care pathways. Both the emotional bridging and tour operator roles are important, Luckock argues, but they must not be at the expense of a third dimension, of a 'continuously engaged relationship' with the child. For this to occur, the social worker must commit to being 'the trusted ally' of young people in care (Luckock, 2008: 4). What Luckock, in a manner similar to Stevenson, refers to as the 'emotional bridging' role requires social workers to 'commit themselves as companions to be relied on, and allies to help in the struggle' (2008: 4). The social worker as transitional participant today has to involve a combination of being a tour operator, helping children and families to navigate their ways around different services and agencies, while supporting a continuously involved emotional engagement for the child and young person.

To fully appreciate how this can work, it is necessary to consider in more detail the nature of the organisational shift towards increased performance management and multi-agency working that has occurred in recent years. In the 1960s, 70s and 80s practice was performed by professionals who worked in bounded organisations that had an integrity and identity of their own. Social services teams were created in the early 1970s, taking over from the Child Care Officers described above (Packman, 1981). In the 1970s and 80s and prior to being disbanded in the mid-2000s, social services teams never fully took forward a therapeutic role in the psychodynamic sense described above. The expansion and professionalisation of social work at this time occurred in a context where social work education was influenced by the take up of radical ideas from Marxism and sociology in general (Bailey and Brake, 1975). Therapeutic work and the 'casework relationship' began to be seen as part of the problem, not the solution to people's ills. This was because it was held to focus on the individual causes of problems rather than the influence of social factors, especially power, inequality and the limited choices people had to live dignified lives free from struggle and problems. Empowerment of oppressed service users came to be seen as the key issue. Psycho-dynamic theories and practice became deeply unfashionable (Cooper and Lousada, 2005).

What is especially important to note in the context of the argument of this chapter is that in this context, social work teams and the 'personal social services' had integrity as bounded institutions with a clear identity. Social workers from social services departments would sometimes work with the NSPCC, probation, health visitors, other voluntary organisations and the police in child abuse cases, but social workers had distinct responsibilities in these cases. Social work was delivered through a distinct

organisation and by professional social workers who formed a primary relationship with the service user and largely provided that service themselves (Parsloe and Stevenson, 1978). While practitioners may not have provided 'therapy' in the psycho-dynamic sense, notions like the casework relationship could still exist and have explanatory power because, although group and community work went on, it was through one-to-one encounters that social work largely was done. For the most part the theoretical resources required for understanding and shaping those relationships also needed to be relational, individualistic and person-centred.

How this was changing became very apparent to me in the late 1990s through a research study which examined 286 child care referrals that were made to three social work teams over a three month period. The cases were tracked over the next twelve months to see what kinds of problems the children and families had and what services were offered. In 40 per cent of the cases where the children were considered to be either at risk or in need, social workers performed a case management role only, doing no direct casework themselves. Casework was undertaken by a range of other services, especially psychological and family support services. In 60 per cent, the social workers did some on-going work and this was usually alongside other agencies and support or 'care' staff (Ferguson and O'Reilly, 2001). The kind of configuration that typified this arrangement was for the social worker to act as case manager while various family support and/or other 'therapeutic' professionals did the intensive work (for an extended case study example, see Ferguson 2008a). This narrowing of social work to assessment and then 'signposting' of services rather than the direct delivery of a service now seems common. Since the mid-2000s, such multi-agency working has become more and more embedded in the system as part of the statutory duties embedded in integrated teams, reflecting the shift to a 'whole systems approach' which is at the heart of government policy such as Every Child Matters (Luckock, 2007).

The question arises of where have all the relationships and the emotional labour gone? Who, if anyone, is doing relational work? Does social work have any relationship to relationship-based therapeutic practice any more? Does the notion of the understanding caseworker have any relevance or meaning now? As I have pointed out, there are good reasons to be despondent here, as the impact of performance management, computerised case recording and information-sharing leave less time available for staff to do quality work with families. But my argument is that the notion of the understanding caseworker does still have relevance although not in the manner of a single professional delivering the care but in how this is done systemically through several workers. The scope that exists for emotionally significant, therapeutic practice today needs to be configured within a systems as well as an individual approach.

I want to ground the discussion by using a case example taken from my current study of children's social care. I recently shadowed a social worker on a visit to a single parent mother of two children, who had been referred by the school three months earlier due to concerns about her drug use and the children's welfare. 'Julie' (all names have been changed) had given up drugs soon after the social worker first visited and had now been off them for 12 weeks, having been using them for 24 years, since she was 12. Her children aged 13 and 5 were missing a lot of school and were often late when they did attend. During the visit the social worker gave Julie help with sorting out some housing and benefit issues and they discussed how she was coping. Julie presented the social worker with a drawing which her five year old daughter (who was at school) had done specially for the social worker, who was delighted by this. The social worker, Julie and I then travelled together to the school attended by her 13 year old son, James, for a meeting which also included a year teacher, year mentor, and a drugs worker who links to the school. James joined the meeting after about 30 minutes. It was an excellent discussion. Plans were agreed between mother, James and the school about homework and setting boundaries regarding his sometimes disruptive behaviour in class. The school will ring Julie weekly with a report, which can include positive feedback too. The social worker informed the meeting that she would be withdrawing from the case and agreed she would meet up with James on his own again (as she had done in the past) before doing so, which he was happy to agree to. The school seemed comfortable with the lead professional responsibility for the child's welfare going back to them. There had been huge improvement in James's attendance which was now 100 per cent for the seven weeks of the school year that had

passed, compared with 67 per cent attendance last year, over 50 per cent of which he was late for. James was suspected of having been a young carer for his mother and sister. The spirit of the meeting was very positive and highly respectful to the young person and his mother, who had never set foot in this school or spoken to a teacher there.

On the way back to the office the social worker commented in a self-critical tone: 'I haven't been able to do much in this case except be a case manager', by communicating with and co-ordinating other services – school, addiction and housing. This contrasted significantly with my own view in that the social worker clearly had a good relationship with Julie, who clearly liked and respected her, as did the children (note the five year old's gift of the drawing). She had developed and skilfully used the relationship with mother to 'hold' and contain her emotionally and build up her internal resources as she struggled to come off drugs. She was child focused, seeing the children on their own and doing similar kinds of containing work with them. She was clear about her role and the requirement to be authoritative and during the initial assessment had done the really hard emotional graft of child protection by insisting that she needed to see around the house, including the children's bedrooms. She also dealt skilfully with the relationship of Julie and the children to their external world by enabling Julie to relate to the school (for the first time ever) and other services. The multi-agency work I observed at the meeting in the school was superb, and the social worker, educational support person, teachers and an addiction worker did a very skilled piece of, well, 'understanding casework'. The improvement in the children's wellbeing clearly coincided with them becoming involved and working together in an integrated way.

I have learned from this kind of case example the importance of making sense of what individual professionals and their agencies contribute not only in terms of their own direct work with children and families but in the context of whole networks of inter-agency services. Child care work is no longer a bounded activity delivered by a single agency/ professional. It goes on through networks and flows of practices between organisations and service users, carers, the office and the home (Ferguson, 2008b). Within this, the role of the social worker as transitional participant is pivotal.

Kanter writes that as a transitional participant, the 'social worker actively positions him or herself in the child's life, making direct contact with an array of significant others and informing all parties of this array of contacts. With the knowledge of this participation, the child is then able to internalise the social worker as an embodiment of this life experience' (Kanter, 2004: 77). This speaks very clearly to what the social worker in the above case example did, both in the direct relationships she developed with the children and their mother and in how she worked so closely with other professionals. This has deep emotional resonances for children and their carers, because they know that the 'lead' professional is holding together different knowledge about them and activities which affect them. The social worker (or other lead professional) is relationally linked to the service user and coordinated services by holding the space within which care and control are delivered.

Conclusion

While commentators and critics rightly worry over social work's apparent loss of identity and purpose in an age of performance management and multi-agency working, the value and integrity of social work can no longer be seen just on its own terms but must be grounded in relation to the whole system of diverse professional, service user and community practices. Ultimately, it is service users' experiences of the total system and what it delivers that really matters, central to which is the regularity, flows, rhythms, skill and humanity with which interventions are carried out.

Social work interventions on their own – even short term ones – remain remarkably significant in terms of the skills and knowledge that are brought to bear on the lives of children and families. To realise this we only have to look at examples like the 'Baby Peter' case (Haringey, 2009) where children have not been protected because professionals did not walk across rooms to directly relate to, see, touch, or examine them (Ferguson, 2009). But these actions and how or if they are performed today also need to be understood in a systemic context. In social work, Karen Healy (2005) identifies 'three waves of systems theories'. The most recent of these waves draws attention to how social work is shaped within complex systems. As Eileen Munro puts it

when arguing that child protection needs to be understood as a 'systems problem':

> *Judgement and decision-making in child protection are best seen not as discrete acts performed by individuals in isolation but as part of a constant stream of activity, often spread across groups, and located within an organisational culture that limits their activities, sets up rewards and punishments, provides resources, and defines goals that are sometimes inconsistent.*
>
> Munro, 2005: 382

We need a new language to capture both individual casework practices and system complexity and their effects and I have drawn on Kanter's concept of the transitional participant and used the notion of the understanding systemic caseworker to try to contribute to advancing this. It is vital in this that the emotional dimensions and meanings of case management and face-to-face relating to children and families are fully acknowledged and their implications taken seriously in developing emotionally aware organisational cultures and good staff supervision. It is through skilled relational work, what Ruch (2007a, 2007b) calls 'thoughtful practice', that child care interventions can have real impact on children and their carers' lives. Both at individual casework and systemic multi-agency levels social work can be seen to be maintaining – or rediscovering – its connections to relationship based practice and the more the scope for this to happen is advanced the better it will be for vulnerable children and families.

References

Bailey, R. and Brake, M. (1975) *Radical Social Work*. London: Edward Arnold.

Berry, J. (1972) *Social Work with Children*. London: Routledge and Kegan Paul.

Bion, W. (1962) *Learning from Experience*. London: Heinemann.

Broadhurst, K. et al. (2010) Performing 'Initial Assessment': Identifying the Latent Conditions for Error at The Front-Door of Local Authority Children's Services. *British Journal of Social Work*, 40: 2, 352–70.

Cooper, A. and Lousada, J. (2005) *Borderline Welfare: Feeling and Fear of Feeling in Modern Welfare*. London: Karnac.

Ferguson, H. (2004) *Protecting Children in Time: Child Abuse, Child Protection and The Consequences of Modernity*. Basingstoke: Palgrave.

Ferguson, H. (2008a) Best Practice in Family Support and Child Protection: Promoting Child Safety and Democratic Families. In Jones, K., Cooper, B. and Ferguson, H. (Eds.) *Best Practice in Social Work: Critical Perspectives*. Basingstoke: Palgrave.

Ferguson, H. (2008b) Liquid Social Work: Welfare Interventions as Mobile Practices. *British Journal of Social Work*, 38, 561–79.

Ferguson, H. (2009) Performing Child Protection: Home Visiting, Movement and the Struggle to Reach the Abused Child. *Child & Family Social Work*, 14: 4, 471–80.

Ferguson, H. (2010) Therapeutic Journeys: The Car as a Vehicle for Working with Children and Families and Theorising Practice. *Journal of Social Work Practice*, In Press.

Ferguson, H and O'Reilly, M. (2001) *Keeping Children Safe: Child Abuse, Child Protection and the Promotion of Welfare*. Dublin: A&A Farmar.

Haringey (2009) *Serious Case Review, Baby Peter*. London: Haringey Local Safeguarding Children Board.

Healy, K. (2005) *Social Work Theories in Context*. Basingstoke: Palgrave.

Howe, D. (2008) *The Emotionally Intelligent Social Worker*. Basingstoke: Palgrave.

Kanter, J. (2004) *Face-to-Face with Children: The Life and Work of Clare Winnicot.*, London: Karnac.

Kohli, R. (2007) *Social Work with Unaccompanied Asylum Seeking Children*. Basingstoke: Palgrave.

Luckock, B. (2008) Living through the Experience: The Social Worker as the Trusted Ally and Champion of Young People in Care. In Luckock, B. and Lefevre, M. (Eds.) (2008) *Direct Work: Social Work with Children and Young People in Care*. London: BAAF.

Luckock, B. (2007) Safeguarding Children and Integrated Children's Services. In Wilson, K. and James, A. (Eds.) *The Child Protection Handbook*. London: Elsevier.

Munro, E. (2005) Improving Practice: Child Protection as a Systems Problem. *Children and Youth Services Review*, 27, 375–91.

Packman, J. (1981) *The Child's Generation*. London: Blackwell and Robinson.

Parsloe, P. and Stevenson, O. (1978) *Social Services Teams: A Practitioner's View*. London: HMSO.

Parton, N. (2008) Changes in the Form of Knowledge in Social Work: From the 'Social' to the 'Informational'. *British Journal of Social Work*, 38, 253–69.

Ruch, G. (2007a) Reflective Practice in Contemporary Child Care Social Work: The Role of Containment. *British Journal of Social Work*, 37: 4, 659–80.

Ruch, G. (2007b) Thoughtful Practice: Child Care Social Work and The Role of Case Discussion. *Child and Family Social Work*, 12: 4, 659–80.

Stevenson, O. (1963) The Understanding Caseworker. *New Society*, 1 August. Reprinted (1972) in Holgate, E. (Ed.) *Communicating with Children*. London: Longman.

Stevenson, O. (2005) Foreword. In Bower, M. (Ed.) *Psychoanalytic Theory for Social Work Practice*. London: Routledge.

Walker, S. (2004) Community Work and Psychosocial Practice: Chalk and Cheese or Birds of a Feather? *Journal of Social Work Practice*, 18: 2, 161–75.

Webb, S. (2006) *Social Work in a Risk Society*. Basingstoke: Palgrave.

Winnicott, C. (1963) *Child Care and Social Work*. Bristol: Bookstall Publications.

Winnicott, D.W. (1953) Transitional Objects and Transitional Phenomena, *International Journal of Psycho-analysis*, 34, 89–98.

Winnicott, D.W. (1957) *The Child and the Outside World*. London: Tavistock.

Wooton, B. (1959) *Social Science and Social Pathology*. London: George Allen and Unwin.

Part Two: Service Delivery Issues

CHAPTER 5

The De-professionalisation of Child Protection: Regaining our Bearings

Patrick Ayre and Martin C. Calder

Introduction

Within the tragicomedy represented by attempts to reform children's social care in England over the last three decades, child protection services have found themselves centre stage and under a glaring spotlight for much more of the time than those engaged in devising and delivering these services have found comfortable. However, despite the attention and resources which have been devoted to improving services during this period and despite or, we will argue, often because of, the many attempts to reform and recast provision which have taken place, public confidence in the ability of the English child protection system to keep children safe has remained stubbornly and alarmingly low (Ayre, 2001; Laming, 2009; Social Work Task Force, 2009). More alarmingly still, this lack of confidence has over recent years come to be shared by the ministers, managers and practitioners responsible for devising and delivering these services (Ayre, 2001; Clark, 2009; Parton, 2004). This chapter will argue that, unless we initiate substantial and fundamental change in both policy and practice, child protection services are in danger of entering a vicious spiral of decline from which it will be very difficult to recover. The malign forces which are driving this descent will be examined and a recovery plan will be outlined.

Work in the field of abuse and neglect in England has been affected greatly during the first decade of the 21st century by a government-mandated change of focus from child protection as narrowly defined to a more broadly defined concept of child safeguarding (Munro and Calder, 2005). This concept sees child protection not as a distinct activity but as located firmly within a wider range of issues affecting children's wellbeing. However, this chapter focuses not upon this definitional shift but upon the de-professionalisation of the workforce charged with meeting this challenge.

The evolving context of change

At first sight, it seems odd that child safeguarding services in early 21st century England should be so poorly regarded in comparison with other such services elsewhere in the world which are arguably less effective (Clark, 2009; Osbourne, 2009; Pritchard, 1992; 1996). In order fully to understand this, it is necessary to explore briefly the historical forces which have shaped their development. Throughout the 70s, 80s and 90s, indeed from the first inkling that child protection actually needed a system, work to protect children found itself thrust firmly into the grasp of England's legal system. Initially, a number of important and influential voluntary organisations were centrally engaged in this sphere of activity, but gradually they chose to withdraw to the calmer waters at the margins of safeguarding activity, and the dominant mode of service organisation and delivery became very strongly statutory. Day to day practice has been dominated by local authority social work agencies operating within a national framework incorporating strong elements of guidance, scrutiny and control by central government.

Until fairly recently at least, social policy in England and Wales has been founded primarily upon libertarian principles which have emphasised individual rights and have viewed the state as primarily controlling rather than enabling. In keeping with this tradition, it was felt to be important to constrain the exercise of power by the state in the field of child abuse by establishing a fairly rigid legal framework for intervention. Whilst this provided some defence against unwarranted state intrusion, the adversarial, rather than inquisitorial, character of the legal system in England and Wales has inevitable and unfortunate consequences when applied to child protection. In particular, it tends to place families and the authorities working with them in opposing camps rather than encouraging them to participate in mutual endeavour.

Typically, social workers have not been regarded by those who used their services as gathering evidence with them, or even about them, but rather against them, and the need to be able to prove a case in court, often against parental opposition, has made it inevitable that social workers have often been seduced into the same thinking. As a result the child protection process has been characterised much more by conflict and much less by co-operation than would be the case in countries such as France which have the benefit of legal systems founded on collectivism, citizenship and Roman law (Ayre, 2001; Calder, 1995; Cooper et al., 1995).

The development of the English child protection system has also been profoundly influenced by a series of notorious child abuse scandals and by a particular pattern of response to these which has become characteristic. Service development in other European countries has been affected by *causes célèbres* but the impact on child welfare in England and Wales has been greatly amplified by the large number of cases brought to public attention and by the intensity of the response in the print and broadcast media. Each of these scandals has been followed by an unholy trinity consisting of:

- the aggressive public pillorying in the mass media of those agencies deemed responsible
- the publication of ever more detailed recommendations to welfare agencies resulting from public enquiries convened to look into the tragedies
- the issuing by central government of ever more intricately wrought practice guidance intended to prevent recurrence.

Intense media scrutiny has the potential to contribute positively to the development of a more careful and accountable service. However, when it is associated with a swift, reactive and often condemnatory response from the national government (Butler, 2009) it seems entirely predictable that unhelpful biases and misplaced emphases will be introduced into the system. In considering these distortions, it may be helpful to explore the influence of this pattern of interaction between the media and the government on the emotional context within which child protection work has been undertaken and, in particular, to examine how they have contributed to the creation of a climate of fear, a climate of blame and a climate of mistrust (Ayre, 2001).

The emotional climate of child protection work

A climate of fear

Increased public awareness of abuse has been important in creating a more protective environment for our children and much of the coverage of this field in the creative media has been very helpful in this respect. The influence of the news media has been much less helpful.

News journalists are 'not in the business of faithfully recording the most common events, they are in the business of finding, constructing and selling 'news' (Kitzinger, 1996: 320). The qualities of immediacy and drama required of news stories inevitably slant the selection of stories towards the more sensational. As Gough (1996: 370) points out, the news media:

> *Tend to report rare hazards rather than commonplace events but in dramatising such extreme adversities as child murder, sex rings and social workers abducting children into care, encourage the development of moral panic, which over-sensitises people to the risks involved.*

It is important to recognise that the climate of fear which has been generated is not confined to the general public, but extends also to the professional groups most closely involved. The courage required to undertake work in the field of child protection has recently been recognised widely (Brody, 2009; Ferguson, 2008; Hughes, 2008; Laming, 2009; Social Work Task Force, 2009). Undertaking such work involves elements of fear for one's own physical and emotional wellbeing as well as for that of the children involved. Fear of the consequences of 'getting in wrong' is an ever-present consideration and all child protection workers from time to time lose sleep worrying about the potential impact of any error on their part. However, evidence suggests that whilst social workers and managers in France may lose sleep worrying about the impact of error on the children and families with whom they work, their English counterparts may find their anxiety focused, at least in part, on the consequences for themselves (Cooper et al., 1995).

Such underpinning fear does not provide a sound basis for service planning, and delivery and the development of services offering a balanced and confident professional response is not promoted by the fear of finding your name listed on the front page of a mass circulation daily under the heading 'Sack This Disgusting Lot' (*The Sun*, 2008). Lest we should doubt that involvement in a widely publicised child abuse tragedy is seriously damaging to one's professional health, it may be useful to note that the Director of Children's Services who convenes a press conference to discuss the findings of the public inquiry into the handling of a notorious case is seldom, if ever, the same Director who was in post when the scandal broke. Even the dogs in the street know the names of the workers most involved with Victoria Climbié and Baby Peter and the desire to avoid ever finding oneself in such a position may be felt likely to represent a significant driver in the fields of policy and practice.

A climate of blame

Over the past three decades, a climate of blame has come to be characteristic of child protection services in England. This may be seen, in part, as arising from the development of an influential discourse which centres on the responsibility of professionals for the abuse which they are attempting to prevent. The media have played an important part in creating and maintaining this discourse. As Hall, Srangi and Slembrouck (1997) perceptively point out, child abuse stories were once represented in the news media primarily as crime stories and accordingly reporting followed the standard formula for this genre: discovery of crime, arrest and charge, trial, conviction and sentence. This mode of presentation still seems to hold sway in much press reporting in continental Europe and North America. However, in recent years a further concluding element which concerns itself with the attribution of blame and 'how was this allowed to happen?' has begun to be added routinely to story lines in the British press.

When looking for explanations for how blame came to be displaced from the perpetrators to the (sometimes ineffective) protectors, it seems to have become conventional within the professions most associated with child abuse to place responsibility primarily on the news media and on the agendas and imperatives which drive them (Aldridge, 1994; Franklin and Parton, 1991a, Lombard, 2009a; Socialist Worker, 2008). However, a little reflection on the rôle played by the child protection system itself in the generation of this situation may be appropriate.

It is of course true that in the world of the media, 'good news is no news' and little or no attention tends to be paid to the routine daily successes of the system in detecting abuse and preventing death and serious injury (Clark, 2009; Osbourne, 2009; Pritchard, 1992). Unfortunately, it is in the nature of this work that it generates no spectacular successes to offset the impressions left by its occasional spectacular failures. Further, there can be little doubt that during the Thatcherite 1980s, the political climate was clearly right for the re-creation of the social worker as folk-demon (Ayre, 2001).

However, we must acknowledge that child safeguarding services too may have played a part, albeit unintentionally, in the process of transferring the blame for child abuse to their own agencies. By selecting the title 'child protection' for the service they offered, they were making a clear statement about the importance of its contribution to maintaining the social and moral fabric. However, we must recognise that 'when we choose for a service, a title which we cannot live up to, failure is inevitable' (Goddard, 1996: 304). Similarly, the widely publicised NSPCC 'Full Stop' campaign which was launched in March 1999 may be felt to have been unhelpful in giving the impression that we could, if we tried a little harder, potentially 'end child cruelty' (Devaney, 2002; Rothwell, 2009).

Unfortunately, the rather rash promise to keep children safe implicit in the name of the service was made even more rashly explicit during the 1970s, 80s and early 90s. During these decades, unremitting pressure on local government to reduce its expenditure seems to have induced senior managers to play on the climate of fear already described by deploying the argument that if the resources devoted to child protection services were reduced, children would die. The inevitable but unwelcome corollary of child protection managers' emotive argument for continuing generous funding was an expectation on the part of the public, the politicians and the press that if resources continued to be devoted to the service, children would not die. Yet of course they did, because no amount of expenditure can ever render human behaviour totally predictable nor totally eliminate error, incompetence or folly, whether corporate or individual. To this extent, it ill becomes those of us engaged in child protection to criticise the media for pointing out when we fail, sometimes in dramatic fashion, to deliver what we are perceived to have promised (Ayre, 2001).

A climate of mistrust

Whilst increased awareness of abuse undoubtedly has some impact on our general level of trust in our friends, neighbours, associates and fellow citizens, we wish to pay particular attention to trust between the general public and professionals working in child protection and, indeed, that between the professionals themselves. As we have seen, considerable tension is thrown into relationships by the primarily adversarial character of the child protection system. The climate of mistrust can only be increased when the values underpinning the selection of news stories inevitably emphasise drama and conflict.

Where people have little direct personal knowledge concerning an issue, the image portrayed by the media has been shown to come to shape their perceptions very powerfully (Hutson, Liddiard and Campling, 1994; Robinson, 1992). Newspaper quotations collected by Franklin and Parton (1991b) Kitzinger and Skidmore (1995) and Illsley (1989) demonstrate how the key news stories in the 1980s and 1990s contributed to the construction of the dominant popular image of English child protection services. Coverage often centred on criticism of the competence or motivations of child protection workers. On the one hand social workers were described as 'child stealers' (*Today*, 29 March 1991) who 'seize sleeping children in the middle of the night' (*Sunday Telegraph*, 10 July, 1988). In this guise they were 'abusers of authority, hysterical and malignant' (*Daily Mail*, 7 July, 1988) 'motivated by zealotry rather than facts' (*Daily Mail*, 6 July 1988) or 'like the SAS in cardigans and Hush Puppies' (*Sunday People*, 10 March, 1991). On the other hand, they were 'naïve, bungling, easily fobbed off' (*Daily Express*, 29 March, 1985) 'incompetent, indecisive and reluctant to intervene' (Kitzinger and Skidmore, 1995) and 'too trusting with too liberal a professional outlook' (*Guardian*, 19 December 1987). Such messages did little to generate public confidence in child protection services which came to be seen as sometimes too weak, sometimes too strong but never to be trusted.

Whilst the Baby Peter case yielded during 2009 a little media coverage offering a more rounded view (Brody, 2009; Hughes, 2008; Ferguson, 2008, Osbourne, 2009), it must generally be recognised that the handling by the popular press of the most notorious child protection cases during the current decade has served only to reinforce the stereotypes established in the 1970s, 80s and 90s. It must be a cause of considerable concern that the general public should have come to perceive professional practice in this field as generally unreliable and unsafe. However, it is of even more concern that this perception has come also to be shared by managers and policy makers at all levels of national and local government and that it may clearly be seen reflected in the approaches to regulation and management which have developed.

De-professionalisation and proceduralisation

This challenging emotional climate may be felt to have generated in the minds of all those engaged in child protection, from the highest to the lowest, the perception that this is essentially a very hazardous activity in which to be involved. Unfortunately the response to this challenge has not been wholly positive and has contributed in great measure to the de-professionalisation of child protection.

The de-professionalisation of child protection services may be seen to some degree as falling within a more general movement taking place within public services in Britain and elsewhere in the English speaking world in recent decades (Calder, 2008; Calder, forthcoming; Deem, 1989; Dressel et al., 1988). We have seen in most public agencies widespread shifts of culture and function associated with the advent of managerialism (Brewster, 1992), McDonaldisation (Ritzer, 1993) and the audit culture (Grayson and Rogers, 1997). The trend toward management by externally defined objectives, standardisation, routinisation and the attitude that 'if you can't count it, it doesn't count' is exemplified by the advent of comprehensive, nationally defined standards and performance targets in education, health care, policing and the Probation Service.

It may be felt these developments reflect a general view that the professions cannot be trusted to behave sensibly unless they are given very firm guidance about what to do. Such a view might be expected to be particularly prevalent in the sphere of child protection, where there has been so much emphasis on what has gone wrong. It is an entirely natural management response to seek to address problems which have arisen by writing new guidance and procedures. In doing so, we may hope to achieve two particularly desirable objectives. Not only are we helping our staff to act more appropriately next time, but also, and perhaps equally importantly, we are shifting the level of responsibility one level down the line. National government writes guidance for local authorities who then write guidance and procedures for their managers who in turn write detailed instructions for their staff. If anything then goes wrong, each can say 'I told you what to do and you failed to comply; the fault is yours'. In the blame oriented culture characteristic of child protection, this can be very comforting. Experience shows us that this argument can still be successfully deployed even when no new resources have been passed down the line to accompany the new demands (Ayre, 2001).

Dysfunctional organisational responses

This tendency to deal with serious systems failures by procedural proliferation is not confined to the fields of child protection or social welfare. Many useful parallels may be drawn with the analysis by Reason (1995) of the role of organisational error in large-scale disasters which have occurred in a wide range of hazardous, well-defended industrial technologies during the last half-century. He notes that the root causes of these accidents can in fact be traced to 'latent failures and organisational errors arising in the upper echelons of the system in question' (Reason, 1995: 1708).

The systemic weaknesses are 'transmitted along various organisational and departmental pathways to the workplace where they create the local conditions that promote the commission of errors and violations (such as high workload, deficient tools and equipment, time pressure, fatigue, low morale, conflicts between organisational and group norms and the like' (Reason, 1995: 1710). In this analysis, 'people at the sharp end are seen as the inheritors rather than the instigators of an accident sequence' (Reason, 1995: 1711). Yet, instead of dealing with the underpinning organisational weaknesses, 'sanctions, exhortations to be more careful, writing yet another procedure and 'blaming and training' operators are still the error management techniques of choice in most industries' (Reason, 1995: 1720). It may be felt that over the last four decades, this critique has applied as

uncomfortably accurately to the 'child protection industry' as it did to the railway, chemical or nuclear power industries which Reason had primarily in mind. Lord Laming's report into the tragic death of Victoria Climbié (Laming, 2003) may be felt to have broken new ground in the attention which it paid to systemic weakness and to failings 'in the upper echelons', but unfortunately, it has done little to undermine our misplaced faith in procedures and regulation as the answer to all our ills.

Under the dogma of proceduralisation, when a problem occurs new advice tends be added to what we already have, seldom replacing it. However, as Reason argues, ironically research suggests that 'one of the effects of continually tightening up procedures in order to improve system safety is to increase the likelihood of violations being committed' (Reason, 1995: 1715). During the last four decades, legislative change, statutory guidance, lengthy recommendations from public enquiries and research findings relevant to child protection have proliferated at such a rate that it has become virtually impossible for ordinary competent practitioners and managers to feel confident that they are aware of all the important guidance relevant to their work. The exponential growth of the government's advisory *Every Child Matters* website may be felt to illustrate this point particularly effectively. Launched in 2003, by June 2009 it hosted over 1300 items of content and over 400 publications relevant to child welfare.

However, it is not just the quantity of guidance available which causes concern; it is also its texture, in that it has become ever more closely woven. If an instance of error seems to have fallen through the net provided by existing guidance, we start to write on the spaces between the lines in the vain hope that we will eventually catch everything. The idea that we can control child protection and render it safe by writing increasingly detailed procedures describing right action is unfortunately fundamentally flawed. It rests heavily on the notion that if we could just get the system right, child abuse deaths could be eradicated. However, we are here straying uncomfortably into the territory of the 'myth of predictability'. Unpredictability is of the essence of human behaviour, both that of abusers and that of the professionals who work with them and no preordained set of rules can hope fully to address the infinite complexity of human interaction. Similarly, procedural proliferation has little to offer in situations in which workers know perfectly well what should be done in principle, but in the event do something else. Indeed, Reason (1995) suggests that over-regulation is likely to increase the likelihood of such infractions. Analysis of recent protection tragedies would suggest that the most damaging bad practice has been associated not so much with the absence of detailed and specific guidance, but rather with departures from the most basic principles which should have guided the work in question (Ferguson, 2007; Haringey Local Safeguarding Children Board, 2009; Laming, 2003; Newham Area Child Committee, 2002; Norfolk Area Child Committee, 2001).

Two basic models of control system are identified in the literature on human industrial and professional activity (Cantley, 1981; Kreitner, 1982). Feedforward control systems involve following pre-set procedures through from initiation of activity to termination. By contrast, in feedback systems, actions are not predetermined. Rather, they are based on judgements made following assessment of the situation at the time. Control systems theory suggests that feedforward control systems assume that 'interventions are programmable in advance as a known function of environmental disturbances' (Cantley, 1981). Systems leaning heavily on feedforward controls and prescriptive procedures are therefore best suited to areas of work where the relevant characteristics of the situation are easily captured and quantified, where seemingly similar circumstances may always be dealt with effectively by a similar response and where it is possible to define an unequivocally 'right' answer for each contingency. They may be used to guide workers engaged in relatively simple tasks like production line assembly in factories and also those undertaking relatively complex tasks like television or automobile repair. However, in either case, the work involved is primarily technical rather than professional. Professional activity more commonly involves drawing on an underpinning knowledge-base to make situation-specific judgements about the interaction of a multiplicity of diverse and relatively unpredictable elements, and is more typically regulated by feedback control systems.

It is understandable that concern about the dangerousness of child protection activity may lead to the desire to improve our control over it, but in doing so it is important that we understand the type of control which is most likely to prove effective. It may be felt that the child protection system in England has come to place rather too much emphasis on the feedforward aspects of the system at the expense of the feedback and is thus reconstructing itself as a technical rather than a professional activity. We may be felt to be expending too much effort in developing ever more detailed procedures and regulating compliance with respect to them, and too little in developing and encouraging sound professional judgement which is flexible enough to produce reliable results across a wide range of rapidly and erratically shifting circumstances. What we require, in effect, is research-informed professionals who thoroughly understand the underpinning general principles which should guide their action and are confident in using their judgment to apply these principles to whatever situation they may encounter.

Over-reliance on feedforward controls and the consequent proceduralisation and technicalisation of child protection over recent decades has had two important adverse effects on the workers involved. First, they have come increasingly to lack confidence in their own judgement and to be dependant on being told the right thing to do (Social Work Task Force, 2009). Excessive proceduralisation conveys to workers a clear message about the perceived limitations of their competence and they would seem to have ingested this message thoroughly.

Secondly, the system has become so wrapped up in process and procedure that it often loses sight of objectives and outcomes (Ayre, 2001; Social Work Task Force, 2009). When those involved are asked to explain why certain actions were taken, they are likely to respond in terms of compliance with procedures and regulatory requirements. They are much less likely to speak, or perhaps even to think, about what they were trying to achieve for the child with whom they are working. A question to a social worker about why a core assessment is being undertaken may be expected to elicit a response referring to the requirement in the relevant guidance that such an assessment be completed within 35 days (DoH, DfEE and Home Office, 2000). A response referring to the information and understanding which it is hoped to gain is much less probable. Similarly, ask why a review of a child protection plan is being planned and you will probably be told that it is because the last review was held five months ago and another is now due.

The desire to control risk through micro-management of professional performance which is evident in proceduralisation has also been reflected in the increasingly prescriptive approach to recording and reporting which has been evident during the last decade. The expression of this trend via computer-based information-management systems is explored by David Wastell and Sue White in Chapter 11. Whilst reports for court, assessment reports and the like have always tended to have a preferred outline format, this would traditionally have been fairly rudimentary, consisting of a small number of basic headings accompanied by some thought-starters about what it might be appropriate to consider under each heading. Such a format allowed workers to judge what needed to be included and what it was safe to omit in the context under review, and as a result a useable, coherent family assessment could be produced in somewhere between five and eight pages. However, under the procedures for the production of Core Assessments in 2009, a similar assessment might cover some thirty-six pages but produce a result which, in our experience, may be much less informative. Indeed, it may be argued that the relevant assessment templates provide an excellent example of the perils of confusing process and outcome. In seeking to perfect the process, controlling risk by imposing a rigid preordained structure, we may have ensured that reports are more consistent; unfortunately the outcome of our focus on process is that they are often no longer fit for purpose (Calder, 2007).

Because workers are no longer trusted to make judgments about what needs to be included, the proformas require that data be entered into each of a seemingly endless series of predetermined tick boxes and text boxes which seek to examine the child and family from every conceivable angle. The content is often highly repetitive as snippets of information may belong to several of the domains addressed. This makes the assessments tedious and irritating to read. Even worse, the data is disaggregated and scattered throughout the forms in a manner which can make it very difficult to get an overall impression of the family and its history. It is as though a photograph of the family had been cut up with scissors and the noses put in one place, the eyes in another and so forth. The reader is constrained to try to re-assemble all this data mentally, which can be quite a challenge when reports are so long.

Such an approach to assessment does not merely reflect the de-professionalisation and proceduralisation of child safeguarding which has taken place; in practice it further contributes to it. It reduces both the need for workers to exercise judgment, and their confidence in doing so, and subtly reshapes their conception of themselves and their role. Because those preparing an assessment are required to plod one by one through a predetermined and very lengthy list of 'fill-in-the gap'' text boxes, the assessment process almost inevitably becomes routinised and mechanistic. It is, in our view, an unusually able worker who can maintain a central focus on the child-centred objectives of assessment when the task being undertaken emphasises process so heavily (Calder, 2007).

In such circumstances it can be hard to maintain a grasp on the fundamental truth that the prime purpose, indeed in many ways the sole purpose, of assessment in a safeguarding context is to gain an understanding of what it is like to be this child, and what it will be like in the future if nothing is done. Assessment tools and proformas are only of benefit insofar as they contribute towards our achievement of this goal. When reporting to the courts and other key decision making forums, social workers are seeking to tell the child's story in a manner which is coherent, confident and compelling, but their ability to do so is being substantially undermined by the way in which their account is disassembled, disarticulated and reprocessed. The products of this process may be felt to have much in common with the vacuum-sealed packs of mechanically recovered, ham-like sandwich slices we find on our supermarket shelves. The slices are consistent in shape, identical in colour and uniformly lacking in any real flavour or substance.

'Getting the assessment done', in terms of filling all the boxes, must seem quite an achievement in itself and, indeed, the relevant performance target set by the government requires that an assessment be completed within 35 days, but makes no reference to the quality of that assessment, further emphasising the precedence of process over outcome (Social Work Task Force, 2009). In theory, the forms provide spaces in which the disaggregated data may be summarised and analysed, but we have seldom found these to be used effectively.

Regulating and guiding performance

It has been suggested that attempts to improve practice by means of proceduralisation and regulation may have unintended negative consequences on professional confidence and competence. Unfortunately, the potential for harm may be felt to have been exacerbated over the last two decades by the particular approaches to management which have been adopted. In particular, it will be argued that managerialism, the audit culture and over-reliance on quantitative targets and key performance indicators have interacted unhelpfully with the pervading climate of fear, blame and mistrust in such a way as to have a profound impact on the way in which child protection workers perceive themselves and the work in which they are engaged (Munro, 2008).

In this context, the heavy reliance which has been placed on Key Performance Indicators (KPIs) may be felt to have had a particularly harmful effect. The government has, very commendably, given considerable emphasis to securing better outcomes for children and young people. Unfortunately, within the field of safeguarding, the level of success in achieving such outcomes is extremely difficult to measure through the routine collection and collation of 'snapshot' monthly or quarterly statistics.

Having struggled with the complexity of measuring outcomes, it would seem that, in the absence of anything better, the government has settled for a set of KPIs which focus primarily on process instead (Laming, 2009; Social Work Task Force, 2009). These indicators have, in reality, often appeared to have a rather indirect, even speculative, connection with the quality of outcomes for the children and young people involved (Social Work Task Force, 2009). For example, local authorities have been judged on how many of those children whose names were removed from child protection registers (or, in the new language, children who had ceased to be the subject of a child protection plan) had been re-registered within two years. It is possible to conceive of circumstances in which re-registration might be indicative of a weakness in the safeguarding system, but it is equally possible to conjure up others in which re-registration might suggest something more positive, such as an increased robustness in decision-making and a realignment of thresholds to match those required by guidance. In either

case, the connection with outcomes for children may be felt to be so remote, and judgements based on it so dependant on assumptions which may or may not be justified, that re-registration may be regarded as virtually meaningless as a gauge of the quality of services.

It may be helpful to explore the impact of over-reliance on such indicators at all levels of the safeguarding system. At the level most remote from frontline practice, senior managers, elected members, Government departments, and for that matter reporters from the print and broadcast media, may have little detailed understanding of individual services and of how they function. In such circumstances, their perceptions of a service and of the quality of its outputs may come to be defined almost entirely by its KPI results. Quantitative indicator data is appealing to decision makers because it is readily obtainable and easily assimilated, particularly when presented as a cluster of stars or in the ever-popular 'traffic light' format with green for good, red for bad and amber for somewhere in between. For most official purposes, providing a certifiably good quality service has come to mean achieving good KPIs and to that extent, only aspects of a service which are measured are of any importance. Spending priorities and resource allocation will inevitably be affected, not to say distorted, by the desire to chase the stars. Were KPIs a reasonably accurate measure of service quality, these issues might be of limited concern. However, as we have seen, the government was obliged to select safeguarding KPIs more because they could be measured easily than because they were of real importance to the children and young people involved.

It has become clear in practice that over-reliance on KPI results may lead those with limited direct knowledge to misjudge the level of confidence which they should have in the services under consideration. The Department for Children, Schools and Families announced in February 2009 that it proposed radical adjustments to the inspection system pertaining to child safeguarding. It was suggested initially that the new inspection regime would demonstrate a welcome acknowledgement of the need for fundamental change, relying much less on performance indicators and much more on evidence of actual performance (Lombard, 2009b). However, it has been reported that in practice the predominant focus on process has been maintained, despite the apparent fallibility of such an approach (*Children & Young People Now*, 2009). Under the old KPI-driven regime, Children's Services in Haringey, the authority in whose area Baby Peter lived and died, had twice been rated as satisfactory, though later, more detailed inspection found them in reality to have been very seriously flawed (Haringey Local Safeguarding Children Board, 2009). Whilst routine quantitative measures are not without value, it may be regarded as essential that they are balanced by quality assurance activity which seeks to examine performance more directly. Indeed, in seeking to assure oneself of the quality of services for which one is responsible, it would seem unwise to permit routine statistical indicators to represent more than about a third of the mix, at most.

Focusing now on safeguarding workers closer to the frontline, for most the culture of the organisations in which they work will represent the strongest influence upon how they see themselves and their role. Though professionally qualified staff are socialised during their training to place considerable emphasis on values and standards of practice, when they enter employment it is their lived experience of the work they do which is likely to prove most significant in the long-run. Workers, qualified or unqualified, 'learn by doing' to identify what is truly important and valued about their work, and many will find themselves in a managerial climate which prioritises targets over outcomes and process over objectives. There is now a whole generation of workers and frontline managers whose practice experience has taken place entirely within such a climate, and whose conception of what really matters about what they do has been shaped accordingly. In this respect, apparent changes in the predominant focus of supervision may be felt to be highly indicative. Drawing on research terminology, we might suggest that there has been a shift of emphasis from qualitative supervision to quantitative supervision. Complying with targets, meeting deadlines and getting the right ticks in the right boxes at the right time have always been important in statutory child welfare practice, but the emphasis placed on them as an important component of what constitutes good practice has increased substantially (Social Work Task Force, 2009).

It may be felt that, within the prevailing managerialist climate, managers, senior or junior, who wish to remain in post have little choice but to prioritise the achievement of quantitative targets, however ill these seem to relate to outcomes. However, it must be recognised that in doing so they may be contributing to a substantial and unhelpful shift in the 'good practice' paradigm. Quantitative indicators are intended to be no more than that, indicators or clues as to the quality of the practice underlying them, but they have, in practice taken on a life of their own (Social Work Task Force, 2009). Pursuit of good KPI results has ceased to be a means to the end of improving outcomes, and has become instead an end in itself, indeed in many ways, the predominant end. There is a danger that, in a strange twist on Dorian Gray, the rather second rate portrait of good practice represented by the indicators has become the reality which walks abroad whilst the subject of the portrait, good practice in safeguarding itself, lies un-remarked and mouldering in the attic.

An example of the potential folly of this approach might be taken from nature. If you were concerned about a decline in the population of a garden favourite such as the robin, you might choose as an indicator of the health of the population the number of robins visiting your bird table between 11 and 12 in the morning. Reporting to the local naturalist group, you might be told that your figures were much too low and that something needed to be done. In response, you could start a campaign in the neighbourhood to improve the underlying environment for robins by encouraging people not to pave over their gardens, to leave some soil bare, to grow plants which attract insects to feed birds or what have you. This might result in a genuine growth in the robin population which would in turn improve your robin KPI, which you could report to the naturalists group to much commendation and acclaim. On the other hand, you could achieve the same improvement in your KPI, and receive the same plaudits, by collecting together some worms and tasty titbits and putting them out on your bird table every morning at 11am prompt. Improving KPI scores by chasing targets does not necessarily do anything to improve the underlying structures which the indicators are intended to measure. Indeed it may be felt sometimes to undermine effective performance by diverting resources and attention inappropriately.

Reversing the descent

It has been suggested, then, that child protection work in England has in recent decades been beset by issues of competence and confidence. The competence of the child protection system and its workers has been questioned widely, and there has been an associated loss of confidence on the part of the general public, successive secretaries of state, the managers of safeguarding services and, crucially, safeguarding workers themselves. It has also been argued that many of the well-intentioned steps which have been taken to address problems of competence have, in reality, diminished rather than enhanced the capabilities and the self-belief of those involved, and that, in consequence the child safeguarding system is in danger of entering a vicious spiral of decline. What then can be done to reverse the spiral? The key would seem to lie in pursuing simultaneously three closely interrelated strands of development. The first centres on enhancing the desirability of child safeguarding as a career, the second upon rebuilding the confidence and competence of the workforce and the third upon creating an operating environment which supports the first two strands.

The British government has made clear its intention that workers of the highest calibre should be engaged in child safeguarding, having accepted Lord Laming's recommendation that social workers employed in this field should be educated to postgraduate level (Laming, 2009). The Children's Workforce Development Council (CWDC) launched during 2009 a marketing campaign aimed at raising the profile of children's services social work as a destination for graduates and promoting a more positive public image for the profession. That such promotional activity can prove highly successful is suggested by achievement of the Training and Development Agency for Schools (TDA) in stimulating interest in teaching as a profession. In 1995, shortly after the agency was established, its communications centre received some 35,000 enquiries. After more than a decade of successful marketing, the enquiry rate has increased eightfold to about 300,000 per year (EWA, 2009). It may, however, be felt unlikely that, even after a sustained campaign such as that developed for the TDA, graduates with the level of ability required for Masters level study will in the longer run be attracted to children's services work in sufficient quantities unless there is also a substantial improvement in salaries and conditions. The proposed development by CWDC of an enhanced career framework for experienced social workers may assist in this regard, introducing the role of Advanced Social Work Professional to encourage the most experienced and able workers to remain in practice. Some scepticism may, however, be felt by those who recall how little lasting improvement flowed from similar initiatives relating to 'career grade' and 'Level 4' social work posts in past decades.

Attracting staff to join the child safeguarding workforce is, of course, only the first step. It is equally important that, having entered, they should be retained and that their ability to function effectively should be systematically supported and strengthened. In considering how to proceed with this, we must acknowledge the extent of the challenge we face. As a result of the unconducive climate within which child safeguarding work has been conducted and of the approach to performance management and regulation which has been employed, significant distortions have been introduced into how front-line workers and first line managers conceive of themselves and of what matters in their work. They have been progressively de-skilled and demoralised over an extended period and this situation will not be overcome by simple expedients such as improving the calibre of those entering this work and the quality of their training thereafter.

At the frontline, training and supervision present the most obvious mechanisms by which competence and confidence are developed. Much time and effort has been deployed in improving the quality of the training available to child safeguarding staff. For example, qualifying social workers are now trained to degree level and they have access to a framework of postqualifying training which has the potential to enhance their performance substantially. However, as experience suggests, the link between increased training and better outcomes has been, at best, a rather uncertain one. Whilst effective professional training should maximise the capabilities of students of all levels of ability, it has been recognised that optimal results can clearly only be realised if candidates of the highest calibre are attracted to enter the profession in the first place (Laming, 2009; Social Work Task Force, 2009). Further, what has been learned in principle may fail to yield fruit in practice if training fails to connect meaningfully with the lived reality of workplace activity, and there is some evidence that this may not always be the case.

Discussion with practice managers suggests a view that during qualifying training too much time is spent in exploring general underpinnings and too little in learning the specific procedures and processes required in practice. It has been noted that there is a lack of consensus between employers and educators about how to strike the right balance between 'on the one hand, educating students in terms of developing knowledge, critical and analytical thinking so they are better able to exercise judgement and apply knowledge to a range of situations; and, on the other hand, training students to carry out specific processes and prescribed tasks' (Social Work Task Force, 2009: 23).

In this context, it must be recognised that to shift the balance too strongly in favour of task-specific instruction inevitably risks further de-professionalising children's services work. It may be felt that in our focus on procedure we have come to forget that the likelihood of real change in the wellbeing of the children and families with whom we work is usually largely determined by the quality of our interaction with them, and seldom by our attainment of statistical targets. It is what we actually do when we are with them that holds the key to facilitating the transformation of their lives and it can be argued that it is this aspect of re-professionalisation which now most needs our attention. The implications of such an understanding for the future development of our services are explored in depth by Harry Ferguson in Chapter 4 and Donald Forrester in Chapter 12.

It is planned to reduce problems of fit between training and practice by developing employer-led routes to qualification to commence in 2011. Whilst training based largely in the workplace may yield substantial benefits, it is, of course, essential that one should be satisfied before one embarks on this that the workplaces in question will be able to deliver development which transcends the technical and encompasses the professional. In order to achieve this, mentors with the requisite skills and breadth of understanding will be essential, and such staff may be in short supply (Social Work Task Force, 2009).

In considering how training in children's services may be improved, analogies are sometimes drawn with the training of teachers, which is usually regarded as very successful. That teacher training should be regarded as an exemplar of successful practice is scarcely surprising when over 85 per cent of newly qualified teachers regarded their training as good or very good in 2008 (Training and Development Agency for Schools, 2008) whilst in the same year only one third of newly qualified social workers expressed similar levels of satisfaction with their level of preparation for practice (Children's Workforce Development Council Research Team, 2009). However, such analogies may not always be helpful. Whilst teaching is a highly skilled activity, the skill set required by teachers is, in practice, relatively narrow, compared with that required by social workers and it would be most unwise to conclude that what works for teaching would work for all other branches of children's services. In a week of formative training, a teacher may be able to practise the delivery of lessons for some thirteen or fourteen hours, and the delivery and preparation of lessons is very much the predominant focus of the work of most frontline teachers. The range of activity undertaken by a trainee childcare social worker during a similar period would be very much broader and work-based training does not, in such circumstances, allow a student to gain the same depth of hands-on experience in each key element of activity as that available to teachers because the range of such activities encompasses so much more variety. In such circumstances, training must, inevitably, concentrate more on principles and less on the details of practice, and newly qualified social work practitioners are likely to feel, with some justification, less well prepared for the tasks which they face than are newly qualified teachers.

With respect to the developmental contribution of supervision, much concern has been expressed recently by social workers and by independent commentators concerning the quality of the support being received by frontline staff (Laming, 2009; Social Work Task Force, 2009). A number of possible reasons for this have already been touched upon in this chapter. It has been reported that 'access to supervision is often threatened or put on hold due to staff shortages and mounting caseloads' (Social Work Task Force, 2009: 20). Retention problems mean that staff may sometimes be appointed to supervisory positions after comparatively little practice experience. Furthermore, less experienced managers who have only practised within a target-driven, process-oriented environment are likely to favour the administrative aspects of supervision over the educational and support functions (Kadushin and Harkness, 2002) and to have much less to offer in these latter aspects. It would generally be acknowledged that one of the most important aspects of professional supervision is to test, and where necessary challenge, the thinking underlying action (Laming, 2009) but this aspect of professional performance is not currently emphasised. Though investment in training and development for first-line supervisors may seem an appealing idea, this is unlikely to prove beneficial without more fundamental change.

As we seek to reverse the spiral, our greatest challenge will be to create a working environment in which the benefits of improved recruitment and enhanced training can fully be realised. Positive marketing and better learning opportunities will yield limited gains without fundamental change to the underpinning culture. We must first begin to tackle our addiction to blame, proceduralisation and targets. In doing so, we must begin actively to value quality as well as quantity, and outcomes as well as process. Whilst this change must be reflected at all levels, it must start at the top. It requires that the ministers and senior managers who set the context for children's services should take a step back and contemplate the cumulative harm which their current approach has done to levels of confidence and competence, and, straining credibility somewhat, that they should begin to favour effectiveness over expediency in their response to concerns over the quality of child safeguarding services.

Closer to the frontline, the lived reality of practice must change substantially if our workers and managers are to be able to re-connect with the fundamental objective of their work, which should lie primarily in promoting the wellbeing of vulnerable children and young people and only secondarily in meeting targets and deadlines. Their confidence and competence have been undermined by attempts to micromanage through procedures and proformas, and are unlikely to improve until we come to focus more on developing their understanding of the principles of practice and less on attempting to regulate their performance by means of prescriptive, predetermined processes. The system within which we work has, in recent decades, been so badly tossed on the stormy waters of controversy that it has lost its way, and

along with this, its grasp of its ultimate objectives. It has taken to steering by statistical beacons which are easily visible and close at hand. Though following such beacons is actively rewarded and failure to do so punished, there is little evidence that this system of navigation has brought us any closer to our intended destination. Indeed we have all too often continued to find ourselves on the rocks. Change is in the wind, but it is not clear that it has been fully appreciated that the rebuilding of confidence and competence requires, above all, a process of re-professionalisation. At this point, any new developments which are proposed should be judged primarily on their potential to contribute to this process.

References

Aldridge, M. (1994) *Making Social Work News.* London: Routledge.

Ayre, P. (2001) Child Protection and the Media: Lessons from the Last Three Decades. *British Journal of Social Work*, 31: 6, 887–901.

Brewster, R. (1992) The New Class? Managerialism and Social Work Education and Training. *Issues in Social Work Education*, 11: 2, 81–93.

Brody, S. (2009) Social Workers Deserve Better Treatment by the Press. *Journalism.Co.Uk*, 11 March. Available: http://www.journalism.co.uk/6/Articles/533768.Php.

Butler, P. (2009) Balls Under Attack for Scapegoating Social Workers after Baby P. *guardian.co.uk*. 2 June. Available: http://www.guardian.co.uk/Society/2009/Jun/02/Solace-Baby-P-Anti-Social-Worker.

Calder, M.C. (1995) Child Protection: Balancing paternalism and partnership. *British Journal of Social Work*, 25: 6, 749–66.

Calder, M.C. (2005) *Partnership and Child Protection: Origins, Theoretical Basis and Practice Application.* Careknowledge Briefing. London: OLM.

Calder, M.C. (2007) Child Protection in Changing Times: A Manager's Perspective. In Wilson, K. and James, A. (Eds.) *The Child Protection Handbook.* 3rd edn London: Bailliere Tindall.

Calder, M.C. (2008) Risk and Child Protection. in Calder, M.C. (Ed.) *Contemporary Risk Assessment in Safeguarding Children.* Lyme Regis: Russell House Publishing.

Calder, M.C. (forthcoming) Organisationally Dangerous Practice: Political Drivers, Practice Implications and Pathways to Resolution. In Kemshall, H. and Wilkinson, B. (Eds.) *Good Practice in Risk Assessment and Risk Management*. London: Jessica Kingsley.

Cantley, M. (1981) Strategic Control for a United Kingdom Regional Health Authority: A Conceptual Framework. *Behavioural Science*, 26, 1–28.

Children & Young People Now (2009) Social Care – Row over Inspection Rages On. *Children & Young People Now*. 23 July 2009. Available: http://wwwcypnow.co.uk/archive/921593/Social_Care_–_Row_inspections_rages/

Children's Workforce Development Council (2009) *Newly Qualified Social Workers: A Report on Consultations with Newly Qualified Social Workers, Employers and Those in Higher Education*. Leeds: CWDC.

Christopherson, J. (1993) The Children Act 1989 and Child Protection: European Comparisons. In Waterhouse, L. (Ed.) *Child Abuse and Child Abusers: Protection and Prevention*. London: Jessica Kingsley.

Clark, D. (2009) Talking Truth to Power. *Solace*. 28 May. Available: http://www.solace.org.uk/Blog.Asp?Blog_Id=MBafe30d7-Aaca-40d2-B460-415de4ad4c8c

Cooper, A., Hetherington, R., Baistow, K., Pitts, J. and Spriggs, A. (1995) *Positive Child Protection: A View from Abroad*. Lyme Regis: Russell House Publishing.

Deem, R. (1989) Educational Work and The State of Education. *Work, Employment and Society*, 3: 2, 249–60.

DoH (1995) *Child Protection: Messages from Research*. London: HMSO.

DoH, DfEE and Home Office. (2000) *Framework for the Assessment of Children in Need and Their Families*. London: HMSO.

Devaney, J. (2002) Moral Agendas for Children's Welfare. *Child Care in Practice*, 8: 4, 318–21.

Dressel, P. et al. (1988) Deprofessionalisation, Prolitarianisation and Social Welfare Work. *Journal of Sociology and Social Welfare*, 15: 2, 113–31.

EWA (2009) *TDA – Training and Development Agency for Schools*. EWA. Available: http://www.ewa.ltd.Uk/Case-Studies/Tda/. Accessed: 12/07/09

Ferguson, H. (2007) Human Errror. *The Guardian (Society)* 14 Februaury. p3.

Ferguson, H. (2008) To Protect Children We Must First Protect Social Workers. *The Guardian*. 13 November. p32.

Franklin, B. and Parton, N. (Eds.) (1991a) *Social Work, the Media and Public Relations*. London: Routledge.

Franklin, B. and Parton, N. (1991b) Victims of Abuse: Media and Social Work. *Childright*, 75, 13–6.

Goddard, C. (1996) Read All About It! The News about Child Abuse. *Child Abuse Review*, 5: 5, 301–9.

Gough, D. (1996) The Literature on Child Abuse and the Media. *Child Abuse Review*, 5: 5, 363–76.

Grayson, L. and Rogers, S. (Eds.) (1997) *Inlogov Informs on Performance Management 2*, Birmingham: University of Birmingham, Institute of Local Government Studies.

Hall, C., Srangi, S. and Slembrouck, S. (1997) Narrative Transformation in Child Abuse Reporting. *Child Abuse Review*, 6: 4, 272–82.

Haringey Local Safeguarding Children Board (2009) *Serious Case Review: Baby Peter (Executive Summary)* Haringey Local Safeguarding Children Board. Available: http://www.haringeylscb.org/Executive_Summary_Peter_Final.pdf.

Hughes, D. (2008) Baby P Case Shows that Social Workers Cannot Win. *Daily Telegraph*. 12 November. Available: http://blogs.telegraph.co.uk/News/Davidhughes/5705317/Baby_P_Case_Shows_That_Social_Workers_Cannot_Win/.

Hutson, S., Liddiard, M. and Campling, J. (1994) *Youth Homelessness: The Construction of a Social Issue*, Basingstoke: Macmillan.

Illsley, P. (1989) *The Drama of Cleveland: A Monitoring Report on Press Coverage between 23 June 1987 and 31 July 1987 of the Sexual Abuse of Children Controversy in Cleveland*. London: Campaign for Press and Broadcasting Freedom.

Kadushin, A. and Harkness, D. (2002) *Supervision in Social Work*. 4th edn. New York: Columbia University Press.

Kitzinger, J. (1996) Media Representations of Sexual Abuse Risks. *Child Abuse Review*, 5: 5, 319–33.

Kitzinger, J. and Skidmore, P. (1995) Playing Safe: Media Coverage of Child Sexual Abuse Protection Strategies. *Child Abuse Review*, 4: 1, 47–56.

Kreitner, R. (1982) The Feedforward and Feedback Control of Job Performance Through Organisational Behaviour Management (OBM). *Journal of Organisational Management*, 3: 3, 3–20.

Lord Laming. (2003) *The Victoria Climbié Inquiry: Report of an Inquiry by Lord Laming*, Cmnd 5730. London: HMSO.

Lord Laming. (2009) *The Protection of Children in England: A Progress Report*. London: HMSO.

Lombard, D. (2009a) Community Care Media Awards Expose Tabloid Hypocrisy. *Community Care*. 18 May. Available: http://www.communitycare.co.uk/Blogs/Social-Work-Media/2009/05/Community-Care-Media-Awards-Expose-Tabloid-Hypocrisy.html.

Lombard, D. (2009b) Ofsted Signals Shift in Inspection Priorities. *Community Care*. 5 May. Available: http://www.communitycare.co.uk/Articles/2009/05/05/111455/New-Ofsted-Inspections-To-Put-Onus-On-Outcomes-Not-Process.html.

Munro E. (2008) *Effective Child Protection*. 2nd edn. London: Sage.

Munro, E. and Calder, M.C. (2005) Where Has Child Protection Gone? *The Political Quarterly*, 76: 3, 439–45

Newham Area Child Protection Committee (2002) *Ainlee: Chapter 8 Review*. London: Newham Area Child Protection Committee.

Norfolk Area Child Protection Committee. (2001) *ACPC Overview Report Concerning Lauren Wright: Executive Summary*. Norwich: Norfolk Area Child Protection Committee.

Osbourne, P. (2009) The Child Murder Epidemic: Deaths as Shocking and Avoidable as Baby P's Happen Every Single Week. *Daily Mail*. 10 July. Available: http://www.dailymail.co.uk/News/Article-1198725/The-Child-Murder-Epidemic-Deaths-Shocking-Avoidable-Baby-Ps-Happen-Single-Week.htmlComments.

Parton, N. (2004) From Maria Colwell to Victoria Climbié: Reflections on Public Inquiries Into Child Abuse A Generation Apart. *Child Abuse Review*, 13: 2, 80–94.

Pritchard, C. (1992) Children's Homicide as an Indicator of Effective Child Protection: A Comparative Study of Western European Statistics. *British Journal of Social Work*, 22: 6, 663–84.

Pritchard, C. (1996) Search for an Indicator of Effective Child Protection in a Re-Analysis of Child Homicide in the Major Western Countries 1973–1992: A Response to Lindsey and Trocmé and Macdonald. *British Journal of Social Work*, 26: 4, 545–63.

Reason, J. (1995) A Systems Approach to Organisational Error. *Ergonomics*, 38: 8, 1708–21.

Ritzer, G. (1993) *The Mcdonaldisation of Society*. Newbury Park, CA: Pine Forge.

Robinson, J. (1992) Interpersonal Influence in Election Campaigns: Two Step Flow Hypotheses. *Public Opinion Quarterly*, 40, 304–19.

Rothwell, A. (2009) How the NSPCC's Failure Will Make The World a Better Place. *Intelligent Giving*. 23 April. Available: http://www.intelligentgiving.com/The_Buzz/The_Blog/How_The_Nspcc_S_Failure_Will_Make_The_World_A_Better_Place.

Social Work Task Force (2009) *Facing Up to the Task: The Interim Report of the Social Work Task Force*. London: Department for Children, Schools and Families.

Socialist Worker (2008) Media Witch-Hunt Over Baby P Puts More Children at Risk. *Socialist Worker*. 18 November. Available: http://www.socialistworker.co.uk/Art.Php?Id=16468.

The Sun (2008) Sack This Disgusting Lot. *The Sun*. 13 November. p 1

Training and Development Agency for Schools (2008) *Results of the Newly Qualified Teacher Survey 2008*. London: Training and Development Agency for Schools.

CHAPTER 6

New Labour and Youth Justice: What Works or What's Counted

John Pitts and Tim Bateman

New Labour: new youth justice

New Labour entered government in 1997 promising *'the most radical shake-up of youth justice in 30 years'*. Having spent the best part of the preceding two decades in a political cul-de-sac, Labour believed that if it was to revive its electoral fortunes it must bury its image as the natural party of penal reform and seize the mantle of law and order from the Conservatives. In the wake of the Bulger case, in 1993, the rebadged, 'New Labour' mounted a full-scale attack on the Tory record, orchestrated via their shadow Home Secretary, Tony Blair. New Labour, Blair maintained, would be *'tough on crime and tough on the causes of crime'* and, in the ensuing debate, the Labour Party deployed the entire lexicon of 'get tough' sound-bites in an attempt to wrest the political initiative from the Conservative's grasp. Their election pledge, to reduce by half the time from arrest to sentence for 'persistent young offenders', was an early indication of the weight the incoming administration placed upon time-based performance measures. Once elected, New Labour's legislative intentions, embodied in the portentously titled *No More Excuses* White Paper (Home Office, 1997) were translated into the *Crime and Disorder Act 1998* [CDA] in record time; attesting to the political centrality of youth crime and youth justice to the New Labour project.

In line with New Labour's eclectic politics, the Act embodied ideas from across the political spectrum. It specified that prevention of offending by children and young people should be the overriding aim of the youth justice system. The presumption that all youth justice sanctions would involve elements of reparation promised the victims of crime a stake in the outcome of criminal cases, while the new civil measures, such as anti-social behaviour orders, offered to 'empower middle England' by handing it the means to re-establish order and civility in its 'communities'. The ostensible rationale for these new statutory provisions was that criminal justice

policy would henceforth be evidence-led, and practice would be evidence-based. Moreover, this new 'joined-up' youth justice system would be administered, in accordance with the dictates of the very latest managerial techniques to ensure that it was 'SMART' (*specific, measurable, achievable, realistic*, and *timetabled*). However, from the outset, there were tensions between the administrative and scientific goals of the new youth justice and the political project it embodied.

An expanding system

Fortuitously for New labour, a blueprint for the new youth justice had been provided by the Audit Commission's (1996) *Misspent Youth*, published the year before the election. The report pointed to the fragmentation and inconsistency of the existing system and commended a model of joined-up 'service delivery' akin to that developed by the multi-agency diversion panels which emerged more or less spontaneously in some areas of England and Wales in the 1980s (Pitts, 1988).

At the national level, the CDA brought into being the Youth Justice Board for England and Wales [YJB] whose statutory function was *'to monitor the operation of the youth justice system and youth justice services'* (Great Britain, 1998: section 41(5)). It was soon charged too with reforming penal provision for children and young people; henceforth to be known as the 'secure estate' (Allen, 2005). At the local level, the legislation required that each local authority establish a multi-agency youth offending team [YOT] constituted from staff seconded from the police, social services, education, health, and probation (Tomlinson, 2005). These teams were responsible for the development and delivery of local youth justice services, but constrained in the way that they did so by the new powers at the centre. So while the expertise of the newly conjoined specialists was to be brought to bear on the diverse needs and problems of its young clientele, to fashion a 'joined-up response', each YOT was required to submit a youth justice plan to the YJB outlining its strategy for delivering centrally determined priorities at a local level.

However, the YOTs were modelled on the multi-agency diversion schemes that emerged in the 1980s, when diversion from prosecution and incarceration was still politically popular (Pitts, 2001). They had endeavoured, wherever possible, to deal with young people in trouble with the law outside the formal justice system. But by 1998, the politics of youth crime had changed.

The new youth justice

The CDA marked a repudiation of both 1960s 'welfarism' (Pitts, 1988) and 1980s 'progressive minimalism' (Currie, 1992). 'Welfarism' was composed of several strands. In its more radical moments, it emphasised the central role of social inequality in the aetiology of youth offending, while in its mainstream, 'technicist', moments it accorded primacy to individual pathology. Accordingly, the social legislation of the 1960s included both measures that allowed robust state intervention to ameliorate the personal and social circumstances of children who offended and those which prescribed the expert treatment of individual need (Curtis, 2005). 1970s 'progressive minimalism' marked a reaction to what many viewed as the 'over-reach' of welfarism, its tendency to stigmatise relatively innocuous behaviour and thereby accelerate young people's 'deviant careers'. Progressive minimalism strove to minimise professional intervention in the lives of young people in trouble and to divert them from potentially stigmatising formal involvement in the justice system (Rutherford, 1992).

The new youth justice supplanted these competing ideas with a strategy of early intervention informed by a focus on risk minimisation. The risk factor paradigm (Farrington, 2002) is predicated on the assumption that it is possible to:

Identify key risk factors that increase the probability of offending and lead to the conclusion that criminality can be prevented by implementing measures designed to counteract them.

Haines and Case, 2008: 5

In the process of transforming statistical correlates of populations into underlying causes

of individual delinquency, familial and personal factors inevitably come to occupy the foreground, hence the aetiological reductionism explicit in *No More Excuses* (Home Office, 1997) which highlights four key 'foreground' domains of risk: being male, poor parental discipline, criminal parents and poor school performance. In 1998, Jack Straw, Home Secretary, took this reasoning as far as it would go when he observed that:

. . . all the serious research shows that one of the biggest causes of serious juvenile delinquency is inconsistent parenting. We need to bring parenting out as a public issue so people feel able to talk about it.
cited in Pitts, 2003: 45

Thus, structural factors – poverty, restricted opportunity, institutional discrimination or neighbourhood socio-economic status – were relegated to the 'background' (Armstrong, 2006).

The social, economic and personal needs of young people became irrelevant to the development of services for children in trouble except to the extent that they could be shown to have contributed directly to their offending behaviour (Nacro, 2007). Having identified the relevant factors, intervention to ameliorate risk was required at the earliest opportunity; with young people who come to the formal attention of the youth justice system, and pre-emptively with those deemed to be 'crime prone' (Smith, 2008). The effect was to spread the reach of the youth justice system far wider:

. . . involving a clampdown on low level anti-social behaviour which was not in itself criminal and drawing in children, some below the age of criminal responsibility whose offending would not previously have warranted a criminal justice response.
Bateman and Pitts, 2005a: xviii

Far from endeavouring to avoid stigma, these interventions were rooted in the belief, the evidence for which was at best tentative, that early exposure to the youth justice system would have long-term deterrent and rehabilitative effects (Pitts, 2001). The YJB, for its part, worked to develop a raft of performance measures that would ensure that YOT practice was consistent with New Labour's account of the origins of youth crime and how it might best be tackled.

Welfarism and progressive minimalism were rejected on the grounds that they were ideologically inspired and pre-scientific. The new youth justice, by contrast, was presented as a child of progress. In this new era of post-ideological politics, policy was to be made in accordance with the dictates of scientific rationality rather than redundant ideological postures: what counted was 'what worked'. However, as many commentators have noted, government was in fact utilising criminological science rather more pragmatically than this, incorporating those elements which articulated most closely with its policy objectives, and so it is seldom clear whether theory was serving as a source of intellectual illumination or political legitimation (Muncie, 2000; Bateman and Pitts, 2005b).

The decline of diversion and the growth of incarceration

For all New Labour's scientific pretensions, the beliefs and assumptions underpinning the new youth justice were remarkably similar to those informing the policies of their Conservative predecessors (Curtis, 1999). For a time, the hectic pace of change served to obscure these important continuities between the policies of the two regimes; particularly with regard to the erosion of 'diversion', the increase in prosecutions and the consequent escalation of child imprisonment.

In the early 1990s, after a decade of minimalism, the Conservatives were goaded into action by a Labour party that had begun to play the Tories *'at their own law and order game'* (Downes and Morgan, 2007: 204). But it was the murder in 1993 of two-year-old James Bulger by two ten year olds which put youth crime unequivocally back on the 'front page'. In between the conviction and sentencing of the boys responsible, John Major had launched his *'crusade against crime'*, arguing famously that society should *'condemn a little more and understand a little less'* (Haydon and Scraton, 2002). Accordingly, in March 1993, only five months after the implementation of the *Criminal Justice Act 1991*, whose provisions would have effectively abolished custody for children below the age of 15, Home Secretary Kenneth Clarke promised to create 200 places for 12 to 14-year-old 'persistent offenders' in new secure training centres. This *volte face* signalled the advent of an era in which crime in general, and youth crime in particular, moved to the centre of the political stage. In October the same year, a new Home Secretary, Michael Howard, told the Tory Party Conference that:

Prison works, it ensures that we are protected from murderers, muggers and rapists – and it makes many who are tempted to commit crime think twice
Howard, 1993 cited in Rutherford, 1996: 128

However, it was New Labour that, in 1998, opened the first secure training centre. They also introduced a detention and training order, a generic custodial sentence that both increased the maximum length of detention available in the youth court and loosened the criteria for incarceration of the youngest children (Nacro, 2003).

Michael Howard's period in office marked a key transition in the English justice system from 'penal modernism' to 'penal populism'. Policies rooted in a commitment to the idea of rehabilitation and forged by 'experts' gave way to 'a new punitiveness (Pratt et al., 2005), policies and practices that resonated with 'popular' retributive sentiments. The victim, not the perpetrator, now emerged as the central object of penal policy and increasingly, being 'for' the victim implied being 'against' the offender. In this changed ideological climate, the primary focus of incarceration shifted from rehabilitation to incapacitation (Matthews, 1999) while community penalties were increasingly directed towards risk management. Inevitably, these latter penalties fed the former as further offending or minor acts of non-compliance produced 'evidence' that these risks could not be contained outside of the prison.

Between 1992 and 2002, the numbers of 10 to 17 year olds sentenced to custody rose by almost 90 per cent, while detected youth crime fell by more than a quarter (Nacro, 2004). Although the numbers sentenced to incarceration fell slightly from 2002, this was not reflected in reductions in the number of young people held in the juvenile secure estate, which rose from 2,868 in September 2000 to 2,934 in September 2008.

This escalation in youth imprisonment was not uniform however. Between 1992 and 2007, there was a five fold increase in custodial disposals for girls (Bateman, 2008a). For younger children aged 10 to 14 years, the equivalent rise since 1996 has been 550 per cent (Barnardo's, 2008). The overrepresentation of 'black and black British' young people has worsened in recent years (Audit Commission, 2004). During 2007/08, for instance, while 'black and black British young people made up three per cent of the 10–17 population nationally, they accounted for seven per cent of those coming to the attention of the youth justice system, 14 per cent of those receiving a custodial sentence and almost one in three of those sentenced to long term detention (Youth Justice Board, 2009a).

This growth in incarceration has been accompanied by a parallel development at the 'front end' of the system. Until the early 1990s, government had promoted the use of police cautions for a *'wide range of offences and offenders'* (Home Office, 1990: 3) as a mechanism for diverting young people from what was widely believed to be the stigmatising effect of a court appearance (Bateman, 2003). This optimistic viewpoint was swiftly sidelined with the development of the *'second order consensus on the fundamentals of law and order policy'* ushered in by what Reiner (2007: 122) describes as *'Blatcherism'*. Thus, a 1994 Home Office circular discouraged the extensive use of cautioning, arguing that it would bring the disposal into disrepute and, as a result, the rate of diversion fell from 73.6 per cent in 1992 to 61.4 per cent on the election of the Labour government in 1997 (Bateman, 2003).

The 'get tough' imperative and a commitment to nipping offending in the bud would have led to a greater resort to prosecution in any event, but the CDA limited pre-court disposals to one formal reprimand and a final warning (Pragnell, 2005). This 'three strikes' model guaranteed a continuation of the existing trend and, by 2002, the rate of diversion had dropped to 53.7 per cent (Nacro, 2004).

It seemed to have occurred to nobody in government that early induction into the system might, through a combination of stigmatisation, 'deviancy amplification' (Wilkins, 1964) and administrative drift accelerate young people's progress through it (Pitts, 2003), ultimately reinforcing the 'rush to custody' (Rutherford, 2002). In retrospect, the impact of that lack of foresight is clear:

> *The demise of diversion has . . . been a consequence of, but has also contributed to, the punitive environment in which decisions to deprive children of their liberty are taken.*
> Nacro, 2005: 29

The erosion of professionalism

The commitment to professionalism and the concern for the diverse needs of young people in trouble, expressed in the multi-disciplinary composition of the YOT, was to be short lived. The rapid increase in the numbers entering the system as a result of changes ushered in by the CDA meant that youth justice workers found it difficult to square the new governmental throughput targets with the needs of their young clientele. However, because the management model in operation was derived from the YJB's somewhat idiosyncratic understanding of how private sector markets were supposed to work, failure to meet targets threatened to place future funding, and hence jobs, in jeopardy. As a result, YOT professionals soon confronted the all too familiar public sector dilemma of whether to maintain the quality of the service or to tailor it to the achievement of prescribed targets (Pitts, 2001).

Typically, this resulted in an 'all hands to the pump' response, in which workers, irrespective of specialism, were engaged in supervising the burgeoning numbers of court orders flowing into the YOTs (Pitcher et al., 2004). By 2004, the Audit Commission (2004) reported that YOTs were spending no more time in face-to-face meetings with young people subject to statutory supervision than in 1996, when *Misspent Youth* (Audit Commission, 1996) had bemoaned the paucity of professional contact.

The erosion of professionalism was compounded by the micro-management of the professional task by the YJB and the prescription of a proceduralised knowledge-base (Habermas, 1976). Mandatory, actuarial risk assessments, conducted using *Asset*, a standardised tool developed by the YJB that requires practitioners to score children against 12 domains which had been highlighted as problematic by the risk factor paradigm, were placed at the heart of the relationship between young people and those who supervised them (Smith, 2007). Practice was to be developed within the constricting framework of a series of *Key Elements of Effective Practice*, developed by the YJB, each of which somehow managed to discern exactly 16 'indicators of quality' that supposedly ensured that interventions were evidence-based (Bateman and Pitts, 2005b). Moreover, YOTs were required to report to the YJB against a range of key performance measures relating to timeliness and administrative process (Pitts, 2001). If it ever had been the case that 'what counted was what worked', it was now clear that 'what counted was what was counted'.

Increasingly, court orders were underpinned by offence-focused programmes that aimed, quite explicitly, to eliminate the exercise of judgement or discretion on the part of the professionals administering them in order to avoid compromising 'programme integrity' (Pitts, 2007). Although the government made great play of the fact that the correctional techniques within the reformed youth justice system were 'evidence-based', the evidence for this was, at least, equivocal (Pitts, 2007). As to evaluation of practice, given the frequently ambiguous messages from research, it is not surprising that the YJB and the Home Office, as powerful 'claim-makers', have tended to cherry pick those which indicate that the practices they have championed 'work' (see for instance, Wilcox, 2003).

In consequence, the relationship between the youth justice professional and his/her knowledge base was changed from that of critical protagonist in a robust debate about policy means and policy ends, to one of uncritical operative in a milieu where the ideas were 'owned' by senior managers and their YJB overseers. But this process of intellectual de-skilling frustrates, and so squanders, the creativity of front-line professionals, compounding the pervasive sense of estrangement from the professional task which characterises 'audit culture' (Cooper and Lousada, 2005).

Latterly, the idea of the YOT as a group of multi-disciplinary specialists has been further subverted by considerations of cost. The massive expansion of youth justice has been achieved by drawing in ever larger numbers of unqualified or lesser qualified staff, who now outnumber the specialists whose expertise was, at the outset, perceived to be fundamental to successful multi-agency working. The 'professionals' of yesteryear have become 'case managers' whose primary role is to ensure that YOTs meet their prescribed targets and so face to face intervention with young people is increasingly undertaken by para-professionals, acting in accordance with models of intervention prescribed by the centre.

Every Child Matters?

Some observers had believed that the publication of the *Every Child Matters* Green Paper in 2003 (Boateng, 2003) would presage a renewed concern with the needs of children in trouble with the law. Those needs were however excluded from the agenda by the Home Office's

insistence that it should produce its own companion volume to *Every Child Matters. Youth Justice: the Next Steps* (Home Office, 2003), makes no reference to the five outcomes that would henceforth apply to all other children. Instead it extolled the virtues of the government's reform programme to date and confirmed that the youth justice system would continue to operate '*broadly on present lines*' (Home Office, 2003: 4). This caused some to observe wryly that it seemed that '*every child mattered unless they had broken the law*'.

The subsequent repositioning of the YJB, now jointly sponsored by the Ministry of Justice and the Department for Children, Schools and Families, has not resulted in any softening of New Labour's '*tough guise*' (Butler and Drakeford, 1997). The *Criminal Justice and Immigration Act 2008* introduced punishment as an explicit purpose of sentencing of children for the first time, and the 2008 *Youth Crime Action Plan*, adopted an unrelentingly punitive tone. The Action Plan endorsed a 'triple-track' approach to young people who offend, or display characteristics deemed to put them at risk of offending comprising: '*tough enforcement, non-negotiable challenge and support and prevention*' (HM Government, 2008: 8). The document has just one reference to child welfare and none to the best interests of the child. It dismisses the problematic escalation in custody as impacting on a '*small number of young people*' (HM Government, 2008: 49) and proposes, without any trace of irony, that YOTs should endeavour to conflate rehabilitation and restoration with punishment by developing interventions during young people's '*leisure time so that they feel the impact of their sentence*' (HM Government, 2008: 52). The *Standing Committee for Youth Justice* (2008: 2) observes that the government's strategy:

> ... with its emphasis on targeting large numbers of primarily disadvantaged children and young people as potential offenders, and the coercion of them and their families, is highly counterproductive and will serve to perpetuate social exclusion and will not achieve the [government's] aims.

The consistently punitive messages emanating from central government and the YJB have inevitably had an impact on professional practice. Recommendations for custody in court reports produced by YOT staff were, until recently, extremely rare; they are now commonplace (Bateman, 2005). Similarly, returning young people to court for a failure to comply with their order has evolved from an exceptional course of action to an everyday activity for many YOTs. Between 2003/04 and 2006/07, proceedings for breach of a statutory order in the youth courts rose by more than 93 per cent. In 2006/07 breach of an order accounted for more custodial sentences than any other offence type (Bateman, 2008b).

The persistence of need

The considerations that inspired the welfarist approaches of the 1960s have not evaporated. One in three young people within the secure estate have previously been in care; a staggering 86 per cent of boys have been excluded from school, and more than a third last attended education when they were below the age of 14. Ten per cent of the boys in custody are themselves fathers (Parke, 2009). While studies suggest that 16 per cent of children in the general population will experience maltreatment or abuse, the proportion of those in the secure estate who have experienced it ranges from one third to over 90 per cent, depending on the measures used (Day et al., 2008). Levels of sexual abuse are high, with one in three girls and one in twenty boys in custody reporting sexual victimisation (Social Exclusion Unit, 2002).

Problems of mental ill health are also significantly higher among young people in custody. An international review concluded that adolescents in correctional facilities are ten times more likely to suffer from psychosis than the general population (Fazel et al., 2008). These difficulties are frequently manifested in disquieting levels of self harm, which have risen rapidly within the past decade (Bateman, 2006). At its most extreme, the tendency to self harm manifests itself in a determination for children to take their own lives. Since 1990, 29 children have killed themselves while in custody (Goldson and Coles, 2005) and it has recently been calculated that the risk of suicide for incarcerated boys is 18 times higher than for young males in the community (Fazel et al., 2005).

Beyond the institutional walls, children who offend have scarcely less damaged and deprived backgrounds. A study of young people supervised by a London YOT undertaken in the late 1990s (Jones and Pitts, 2001) found that 46.5 per cent had previously been on the Child Protection Register, while a further 22 per cent had been subject to a social services or educational welfare service intervention. In the majority of cases, one parent at least had a diagnosable mental health problem and most of their children had been in and out of care as a result. The incidence of sexual abuse was also very high. A similar pattern of multiple, mutually reinforcing, problems was found amongst the 343 young people investigated by Berridge et al. (2001) in their study of the relationship between school exclusion and crime.

Bereavement and loss also loom large for young people known to youth justice agencies. Sixty eight of a randomly selected sample of 147 children and young people supervised by YOTs in Greater Manchester were found to suffer from anxieties generated by separation; 42 had experienced significant rejection by a parent or carer; 18 were not living in a permanent home and seven had recently experienced loss due to illness (Youth Justice Trust, 2003). One of these factors was present in 92 per cent of cases sampled, and at least two were present in 46 per cent of cases.

Significantly, although problems of loss and bereavement amongst those subject to statutory supervision were apparently both common and acute, the YOT response rarely endeavoured to address such needs. Instead, interventions accorded closely with those which, according to the YJB and the Home Office, 'worked'. The researchers note that:

In the history of the young people's official record of contact with the YOT, the case file, it appears that these events have almost been forgotten, or at least overlooked, whilst other pressing tasks have been undertaken – such as challenging offending behaviour.

Youth Justice Trust, 2003

Similarly, in her study of criminal justice interventions with children, Patricia Gray (2005: 952) found that while the young people were exposed to:

... acute levels of social exclusion ... intervention did little to provide participants with sufficient social support to establish stable family relations, resolve health issues and realise their aspirations in education, employment and training.

These children are precisely those who will eventually boost the ranks of the homeless and the addicted. It is they who will fill our prisons and psychiatric institutions. It is they who are most likely to be the suicides and the victims of non-domestic murder in the future (Pritchard and Butler, 2000). This was true in the 1960s, the heyday of welfarism. It is true today.

The conflation of need and risk

Karl Marx (1968: 93) once observed that history repeats itself, '*the first time as tragedy, the second as farce*'. Abel-Smith and Townsend's (1965) 'rediscovery' of poverty in the 1960s revealed that despite the unprecedented prosperity of the post-war years there were still people living in acute poverty and that it was their children who populated the youth justice system. This finding encouraged the development of a welfare-oriented policy for youth justice and other services for children and families, designed to ameliorate and compensate for the effects of privation and need.

Forty years on, the risk factor paradigm also addresses need but only to the extent that it can be shown to have precipitated a criminal act. Thus, the *Asset* assessment instrument, utilised by YOTs, measures 'criminogenic' rather than welfare need. However, as several commentators have noted, in the real world, it is virtually impossible to distinguish between those needs that are and are not 'criminogenic' in any given case and so the paradigm is prone to conceptual slippage (Bateman and Pitts, 2005b).The 'scaled approach', the YJB's most recent innovation, is indicative of the farcical, and egregious, consequences of this reconfiguration of 'need'.

Hitherto, the use of *Asset* has been confined to the identification of areas of risk that should be addressed to reduce further offending (Bandalli, 2005). As in the adult justice system, the extent and intrusiveness of the intervention has been constrained by a concern for 'natural justice', the idea that the penalty should be commensurate with the seriousness of the offence.

From November 2009, however, the YJB intends that the *level* of intervention should be directly related to the assessed risk of reoffending, established on the basis of a numerical score determined by *Asset* assessment (Youth Justice Board, 2009b). Thus, it is intended that the duration of the intervention and the intensity of compulsory contact should be determined primarily by *Asset* score and the risk of serious harm the child may pose to others.

Thus, a young person assessed as being in the highest band of risk will be required to keep six times as many appointments as a child who has committed a similar offence but has been allocated a lower risk score. The approach purports to build on evidence that:

> *interventions are more effective when their intensity is matched to an assessment of the likelihood of the person reoffending, and are focused on the risk factors most closely associated with their offending*
> Youth Justice Board, undated

This is a somewhat liberal reading of the evidence however. Indeed, Merrington and Stanley (2004) have considered the evidential base for two of the key assumptions underpinning the scaled approach:

- *The need principle* ('criminogenic' needs should constitute a major focus for intervention, while other welfare or structural considerations are less important)
- *The risk principle* (service levels should be matched to a young person's risk of reoffending, with higher risk individuals receiving more intensive services).

They contend that there is no home grown evidence that these principles, when operationalised, have any discernible effects on recidivism.

Reference has already been made to the recent escalation in the number of young people returned to court for failing to comply with the requirements of their order and the corresponding impact on custodial sentencing. Those generating higher *Asset* scores will, by and large, be children whose circumstances are such that they will find compliance more difficult than those assessed as requiring lower levels of intervention. The scaled approach will therefore demand a far higher level of compliance of the young people who are least equipped, socially and psychologically, to comply with the requirements of their order. Breach arrangements will, however, be uniform irrespective of the level of intervention. At present, YOTs are obliged to return a child to court on the third missed appointment. Accordingly, over a three month period, a low risk child could miss one third of his or her appointments and not incur breach action. A high risk co-defendant, by contrast, might keep more than 90 per cent of his or her appointments but, under the scaled approach, still be returned to court for non-compliance.

Because of this conflation of risk and need, the scaled approach discriminates against children drawn from the most deprived sections of the community. In most cases, a high *Asset* score will be indicative of social as well as *'criminogenic'* need. So young people from the most disadvantaged circumstances, with the least parental or adult support, who experience reduced educational and other opportunities, living in the most run down and crime prone neighbourhoods will, as a direct consequence of the scaled approach, be subjected to more intrusive levels of criminal justice intervention and a consequent increased probability of breach action resulting in custody.

Conclusion

The data generated via the YJB's PR machine notwithstanding, it is evident that, at present, the youth justice system routinely produces outcomes at stark variance with its stated intentions and that this is set to get much worse (Bateman and Pitts, 2005b). But what would it take to produce a youth justice system that did 'what it said on the tin'? Considerations of space preclude an extended articulation of the myriad changes that would be required (see for instance, Pitts, 2003) but it is possible to signpost several of the most fundamental.

Diversion not deterrence

In the 1970s, Edwin Lemert drew our attention to the inadvertent criminalising effects of welfare interventions with adjudicated offenders, thus presaging two decades of 'progressive minimalism'. New Labour's explicit rejection of such 'informalism' (Goldson, 2005) in favour of early intervention through criminal justice mechanisms is predicated upon the demonstrably erroneous assumption that young people can be dissuaded from offending by the introduction of deterrent penalties.

Nonetheless, from 2002, the government introduced a new target to increase the number of *'offences brought to justice'*. Between 2002 and 2007/8 the number of *'sanction detections'* recorded by the police rose from 1.025m. to 1.25m. This increase was, in large part, an artefact of shifts in police decision-making; dealing

formally with matters previously dealt with informally. But this process inevitably had a greater impact on those populations most susceptible to police intervention but also most likely to have benefited from police discretion: young people in general and girls and younger children below the age of 15 in particular (Bateman, 2008c). Thus, between 2002 and 2006, the overall number of young people drawn into the youth justice system rose by 16 per cent, while the increase in the proportion of 12 to 14 year olds was 26 per cent and the figure for girls was 31 per cent (Bateman, 2008c).

The government only recognised the problem belatedly, and having done so it promptly introduced a new 'target': to reduce the number of first time entrants to the youth justice system by 20 per cent by 2020 (HM Government, 2008). But this welcome *volte face* was a knee-jerk response to criminal justice services that had been overwhelmed by the sudden influx rather than a principled turn, and early intervention remained a government imperative.

Longitudinal research conducted by the *Edinburgh Study of Youth Transitions and Crime*, for instance, has demonstrated that system contact is itself profoundly criminogenic (McAra and McVie, 2007). South of the border, in the 1980s, the Northamptonshire Diversion Scheme dealt with the majority of young people in trouble outside the formal youth justice system, with diversionary measures supported by a range of voluntary schemes responding to the children's welfare needs as necessary. As late as 1997, 62 per cent of cases in Northamptonshire were being dealt with by an informal warning (Pitts, 1999). The authority was naturally concerned that the 'three strikes' philosophy of the CDA would undermine good practice and commissioned research to assess the impact of these legislative changes (Kemp et al, 2002).

The study revealed that one effect of the changes ushered in by the CDA had been to increase prosecutions by 22 per cent and formal pre-court disposals by 13 per cent. Overall, it appeared that the reforms had expanded formal throughput to the system by 35 per cent a year. At the same time, a logistic regression undertaken by the research team revealed that *'mode of case disposal'* was one of the two best predictors of re-offending over a two year period. Twenty seven per cent of those given an informal warning, 45 per cent of those referred to the Diversion Unit and 79 per cent of those prosecuted were reconvicted in that period, leading the researchers to observe that:

> *Prosecution at any stage has no beneficial effect in preventing re-offending. On the contrary, prosecution only seems to increase the likelihood of re-offending*
>
> Kemp et al., 2002: 4

The study concluded that in the interests of reduced recidivism and cost-saving it would, wherever possible, be beneficial to divert young people from court. The authors expressed concern that the introduction of the final warning scheme by the CDA would result in the escalation of children up the 'sentencing ladder' at a younger age and at an earlier stage in their offending careers. The potential consequences of reduced diversion, higher levels of compulsory intervention, and increased incarceration – particularly of younger children – have been discussed above.

So alarmed were the relevant agencies in Northamptonshire that, despite the provisions of the CDA, they maintained a system of *informal action* for children offending for the first time. The outcomes were compared with two YOT areas that had adopted the final warning scheme as intended by New Labour (Pitts, 2006).

In Northamptonshire, 76.5 per cent of new entrants were diverted out of the youth justice system altogether through informal action, a 'disposal' generating a reoffending rate of 23.51 per cent, significantly lower than that in the two YOT areas with which Northamptonshire was compared which had reoffending rates for new entrants of 50.56 per cent and 33.15 per cent respectively. Informality appears to reduce significantly the risk of system escalation, into the court and ultimately into the secure estate (Bateman, 2005). Diversion rather than deterrence would, accordingly, be the hallmark of a youth justice system that purports to be evidence-based or to provide justice to children.

De-politicisation and the rediscovery of the child

Since the early 1990s, England and Wales has been one of the few jurisdictions in Europe to separate its youth justice and child welfare systems. Optimists had hoped that this would obviate the *'spreading of the net of control'* (Cohen, 1979) and its corollary, the unnecessary incarceration of children and young people in

trouble. That optimism has proved misplaced. The evidence from Europe, where, pro-rata, youth crime and child and youth incarceration rates are substantially lower, suggests that a concern for justice and for the welfare of damaged and vulnerable young people who break the law can co-exist within one system, providing it is informed by a robust children's rights framework (Muncie and Goldson, 2006; Pitts and Kuula, 2006). At their best, such systems provide a space where two discourses, one concerning the establishment and reaffirmation of social expectations and the other concerning responses to a complex and chaotic social reality, can become a single dialogue: a place where the competing claims of rules and needs, guilt and suffering, justice and welfare can be squared. At present, such a dialogue appears to be too threatening for government to countenance.

Elliott Currie (1991) argues that desistence from crime will only be achieved by programmes which offer 'changed lives', rather than the inculcation of conformity. The YOT, though clearly located within a criminal justice framework rather than one that considers children holistically, was at least conceived as a multi-faceted service capable of responding to the complex and inter-related problems afflicting the hard core of young people who become involved in youth crime. But this new organisation was quickly over-burdened, both by a burgeoning, data-hungry bureaucracy and an influx of young people whose behaviour would not previously have brought them within the purview of the system. Professional discretion which, in an earlier era had enabled trained workers to respond intelligently to the personal deficits engendered by social disadvantage, offering young people compensatory experiences and equipping them to take advantage of legitimate opportunity, was now displaced by bureaucratic, pre-packaged, reactions to 'criminogenic' need. If we are to change lives and stop re-offending we can no longer continue to regard the 'young offender' simply as a repository of risks that we must neutralise via tough enforcement and off-the-shelf behavioural programmes. In the spirit of *Every Child Matters* we have to rediscover the child, and, in doing so, strive to achieve substantive justice where it is denied by attempting to vouchsafe their rights to education, healthcare, decent housing, freedom from want and freedom from fear. This is not some idealistic whim – it is an evidence-based strategy (Bateman & Pitts, 2005b).

References

Abel-Smith, B. and Townsend, P. (1965) *The Poor and The Poorest: A New Analysis of the Ministry of Labour's Family Expenditure Surveys 1953–54 and 1960.* London: Bell and Sons.

Allen, R. (2005) The Role of Central Government and the Youth Justice Board. In Bateman, T. and Pitts, J. (Eds.) *The RHP Companion to Youth Justice.* Lyme Regis: Russell House.

Armstrong, D. (2006) Becoming Criminal: The Cultural Politics of Risk. *International Journal of Inclusive Education,* 10: 2–3, 265–78.

Audit Commission (1996) *Misspent Youth: Young People and Crime.* London: Audit Commission.

Audit Commission (2004) *Youth Justice 2004: A Review of the Reformed Youth Justice System.* London: Audit Commission.

Bandalli, S (2005) The Legal Framework for Youth Justice and its Administration. In Bateman, T. and Pitts, J. (Eds.) *The RHP Companion to Youth Justice.* Lyme Regis: Russell House.

Barnardo's (2008) *Locking Up or Giving Up: is Custody for Children Always the Right Answer?* London: Barnardo's.

Bateman, T. and Pitts, J. (2005a) Introduction. In Bateman, T. and Pitts, J. (Eds.) *The RHP Companion to Youth Justice.* Lyme Regis: Russell House.

Bateman, T. and Pitts, J. (2005b) Conclusion: What the Evidence Tells Us. In Bateman, T. and Pitts, J. (Eds.) *The RHP Companion to Youth Justice.* Lyme Regis: Russell House.

Bateman, T. (2003) Living with Final Warnings: Making the Best of a Bad Job. *Youth Justice,* 2: 3, 131–40.

Bateman, T. (2005) Reducing Child Imprisonment: A Systemic Challenge. *Youth Justice* 5: 2, 91–105.

Bateman, T. (2006) Levels of Self Harm in Custody Rise. *Youth Justice,* 6: 3, 223–4.

Bateman, T. (2008a) *Review of Provision for Girls in Custody to Reduce Reoffending.* Reading: CfBT.

Bateman, T. (2008b) Breach a Major Contributor to Custody. *Youth Justice,* 8: 3, 267–8.

Bateman, T (2008c) '"Target Practice": Sanction Detection and the Criminalisation of Children', *Criminal Justice Matters* 73(1): 2–4

Berridge, D. et al. (2001) *The Independent Effects of Permanent Exclusion from School on the Offending Careers of Young People.* Occasional Paper 71. London: Home Office.

Boateng, P. (2003) *Every Child Matters.* Cm 5860. London: Stationery Office.

Butler, I. and Drakeford, M. (1997) Tough Guise? The Politics of Youth Justice. *Probation Journal,* 44: 4, 216–9.

Cohen, S. (1979) The Punitive City: Notes on the Dispersal of Social Control. *Contemporary Crisis,* 3: 4, 341–63.

Cooper, A. and Lousada, J. (2005) *Borderline Welfare: Feeling and Fear of Feeling in Modern Welfare.* London: Karnac.

Currie, E. (1991) *Dope and Trouble: Portraits of Delinquent Youth.* New York: Pantheon.

Currie, E. (1992) Retreatism, Minimalism, Realism: Three Styles of Reasoning on Crime and Drugs in the United States. In Lowman, J. and Maclean, J.D. (Eds.) *Realist Criminology: Crime Control and Policing in the 1990s.* Toronto: University of Toronto Press.

Curtis, S. (1999) *Children Who Break The Law, or Everybody Does It.* Winchester: Waterside Press.

Curtis, S. (2005) The Welfare Principle. In Bateman, T. and Pitts, J. (Eds.) *The RHP Companion to Youth Justice.* Lyme Regis: Russell House.

Day, C., Hibbert, P. and Cadman, S. (2008) *A Literature Review into Children Abused and/or Neglected Prior to Custody.* London: Youth Justice Board.

Downes, D. and Morgan, R. (2007) No Turning Back: The Politics of Law and Order into the Millennium. In Maguire, M., Morgan, R. and Reiner, R. (Eds.) *The Oxford Handbook of Criminology.* 4th edn. Oxford: Oxford University Press.

Farrington, D.P. (2002) Developmental Criminology and Risk Focused Prevention. In Maguire, M., Morgan, R. and Reiner, R. (Eds.) *The Oxford Handbook of Criminology.* 3rd edn. Oxford: Oxford University Press.

Fazel, S., Benning, R. and Danesh, J. (2005) Suicides in Male Prisoners in England and Wales 1978–2003. *The Lancet,* 366: 1301–2.

Fazel, S., Doll, H. and Langström, N. (2008) Mental Disorders Among Adolescents in Juvenile Detention and Correctional Facilities: A Systematic Review and Metaregression Analysis of 25 Surveys. *Journal of American Academy of Child and Adolescent Psychiatry,* 47: 9, 1010–9.

Goldson, B. (2005) Beyond Formalism: Towards 'Informal' Approaches to Youth Crime and Youth Justice. In Bateman, T. and Pitts, J. (Eds.) *The RHP Companion to Youth Justice.* Lyme Regis: Russell House.

Goldson, B. and Coles, D. (2005) *The Care of the State? Child Deaths in Penal Custody in England and Wales.* London: Inquest.

Gray, P. (2005) The Politics of Risk and Young Offenders' Experiences of Social Exclusion and Restorative Justice. *British Journal of Criminology,* 45: 6, 938–57.

Great Britain (1998) *Crime and Disorder Act.* Elizabeth II. Chapter 37. London: The Stationery Office.

Habermas, J. (1976) *Communication and the Evolution of Society.* Boston: Beacon Press.

Haines, K. and Case, S. (2008) The Rhetoric and Reality of the 'Risk Factor Prevention Paradigm' Approach to Preventing and Reducing Youth Offending. *Youth Justice,* 8: 1, 5–20.

Haydon, D. and Scraton, P. (2002) Condemn a Little More; Understand a Little Less: The Political Context and Rights Implications of the Domestic and European Rulings in the Venables/Thompson Case. *Journal of Law and Society,* 27: 3, 416–48.

Home Office (1990) *The Cautioning of Offenders.* Home Office Circular 59/90. London: Home Office.

Home Office (1997) *No More Excuses: A New Approach to Tackling Youth Crime in England and Wales.* London: Home Office.

Home Office (2003) *Youth Justice: The Next Steps: Companion Document to 'Every Child Matters'.* London: Home Office.

Home Office (2008) *Youth Crime Action Plan 2008.* London: Home Office.

Jones, K. and Pitts, J. (2001) *Early Childhood Child Protection Registration and Subsequent Involvement with a Youth Justice Team/Youth Offending Team in a London Borough.* Luton: Vauxhall Centre for The Study of Crime, University of Luton.

Kemp, V. et al. (2002) *Assessing Responses to Youth Offending in Northamptonshire,* Research Briefing 2. London: Nacro.

Marx, K. (1968) The Eighteenth Brumaire of Louis Bonaparte. In Marx, K. and Engles, F. (Eds.) *Selected Works.* London: Lawrence and Wisehart.

Matthews, R. (1999) *Doing Time: an Introduction to the Sociology of Imprisonment.* Basingstoke: Palgrave.

McAra, L. and McVie, S. (2007) Youth Justice? The Impact of System Contact on Patterns of Desistance from Offending. *European Journal of Criminology,* 4: 3 315–45.

Merrington, S. and Stanley, S. (2004) What Works: Revisiting the Evidence in England and Wales. *Probation Journal,* 51: 7–20.

Muncie, J. (2000) Pragmatic Realism? Searching for the Criminology in the New Youth Justice. In Goldson, B. (Ed.) *The New Youth Justice.* Lyme Regis: Russell House.

Muncie, J. and Goldson, B. (2006) (Eds.) *Comparative Youth Justice.* London: Sage.

Nacro (2003) *A Failure of Justice: Reducing Child Imprisonment.* London: Nacro

Nacro (2004) *Some Facts About Children and Young People Who Offend – 2002.* London: Nacro.

Nacro (2005) *A Better Alternative: Reducing Child Imprisonment.* London: Nacro.

Nacro (2007) *Effective Practice with Children and Young People Who Offend – Part 2.* London: Nacro.

Parke, S. (2009) *Children and Young People in Custody 2006–2008: An Analysis of 15–18 Year Olds in Prison.* London: HM Inspectorate of Prisons.

Pitcher, J. et al. (2004) *The Provision of Health, Education and Substance Misuse Workers in Youth Offending Teams and the Health/Education Needs of Young People Supervised by Youth Offending Teams.* London: Youth Justice Board.

Pitts, J. (1988) *The Politics of Juvenile Crime.* London: Sage.

Pitts, J. (1999) *Working With Young Offenders.* Birmingham: BASW.

Pitts, J. (2000) The New Youth Justice and the Politics of Electoral Anxiety. In Goldson, B. (Ed.) *The New Youth Justice.* Lyme Regis: Russell House.

Pitts, J. (2001) Korrectional Karaoke: New Labour and the Zombification of Youth Justice. *Youth Justice* 1: 2 3–16.

Pitts, J. (2003) Changing Youth Justice. *Youth Justice,* 3: 1, 3–18.

Pitts, J. (2006) Sometimes Less is More. *Community Safety Journal,* 5: 4 30–6.

Pitts, J. (2007) Who Cares What Works. *Youth and Policy,* 95: 5–24.

Pitts, J. and Kuula, T (2006) Incarcerating Young People: an Anglo-Finnish Comparison *Youth Justice* 5: 3 147–64.

Pragnell, S. (2005) Reprimands and Final Warnings. In Bateman, T. and Pitts, J. (Eds.) *The RHP Companion to Youth Justice.* Lyme Regis: Russell House.

Pratt, J. et al. (Eds.) (2005) *The New Punitiveness.* Cullompton: Willan.

Pritchard, C. and Butler, A. (2000) A Follow Up Study of Victims of Crime, Murder, and

Suicide Found in English Cohorts of 'Excluded from School' or 'In Care' (Looked After Children). *International Journal of Adolescent Medical Health*, 12: 4 275–94.

Reiner, R. (2007) *Law and Order: An Honest Citizen's Guide to Law and Order*. Cambridge: Polity Press.

Rutherford, A (1992) *Growing Out of Crime: The New Era*. 2nd Edition. Winchester: Waterside Press

Rutherford, A. (1996) *Transforming Criminal Policy*. Winchester: Waterside Press.

Rutherford, A. (2002) Youth Justice and Social Inclusion. *Youth Justice* 2(2): 100 – 107

Smith, R (2007) *Youth Justice: Ideas, Policy and Practice*. 2nd edn. Cullompton: Willan.

Smith, R. (2008) Early Intervention. In Goldson, B. (Ed.) *Dictionary of Youth Justice*. Cullompton: Willan.

Social Exclusion Unit (2002) *Reducing Reoffending by Ex Prisoners*. London: Cabinet Office.

Standing Committee for Youth Justice (2008) *Response to Youth Crime Action Plan 2008*. London: SCYJ.

Tomlinson, R. (2005) Youth Justice at the Local Level. In Bateman, T. and Pitts, J. (Eds.) *The RHP Companion to Youth Justice*. Lyme Regis: Russell House.

Wilcox, A. (2003) Evidence Based Youth Justice? Some Valuable Lessons from an Evaluation for the Youth Justice Board. *Youth Justice*, 3: 1 19–33.

Wilkins, L. (1964) *Social Deviance*. London: Tavistock.

Youth Justice Board (2009a) *Youth Justice Annual Workload Data 2008/09*. London: Youth Justice Board.

Youth Justice Board (2009b) *Youth Justice: The Scaled Approach. A Framework for Assessment and Interventions*. Post Consultation Version 2. London: Youth Justice Board.

Youth Justice Board (Undated) *Scaled Approach to Interventions* Available at www.yjb.gov.uk/En-Gb/Practitioners/ Youthjusticethescaledapproach/

Youth Justice Trust (2003) *'On The Case': an Investigative Study into Factors Affecting Young People in Four YOT Areas across Calderdale and Greater Manchester*. Manchester: Youth Justice Trust.

CHAPTER 7

Children in Need: The Challenge of Prevention for Social Work

Kate Morris

Introduction

This chapter seeks to explore the often fragile relationship between mainstream children's social work services and practices and the theory and application of prevention, focusing primarily on children in need of support, rather than protection. The discussion will explore the drivers that influence the extent to which preventative and supportive practices can be part of mainstream children's services activity and the argument will be made that progress has been limited in developing early helpful services within mainstream children's services provision. The core values and principles of social work are concerned with rights, with change and with well being (IFSW, 2000). Prevention and preventative practices speak uniquely to these values and principles and, it will be argued in the concluding section, the absence of serious concern in social work services and practices with the nature and role of prevention potentially diminishes the overall impact and worth of the services provided to children and their families.

The focus throughout will be on children's services in England, and to some extent Wales (although recent developments in Wales have resulted in some divergence in activity). The terms support and prevention are used in their changing legal and policy context – and reflect the shifting approaches to services to children in need. Consequently, preset definitions of the various terms are not offered; instead some underlying understandings are explored in the course of the discussions.

The legal and policy background

Much has already been written about the political change agenda that underscores New Labour's approach to services for children and families (see for example Fawcett et al., 2004 and Morris et al., 2009). What is of particular relevance to any discussion focused on prevention is the emergence of social exclusion as the primary driver for child welfare policies, and the consequential political support for large-scale preventative programmes. Prior to the arrival of the Labour government, policy and practice responses to vulnerable children and families were framed by an individualistic approach that sought to assess the need presented by a child and their family, using the principles set out by the *1989 Children Act*. The key concerns for providers and practitioners were those of eligibility and the intensity of the needs presented.

The *Children Act 1989* introduced a series of opportunities for local authorities to offer families helpful, supportive services and to do so in the first instance through a process of negotiation. As Frost and Parton (2009) rightly point out, the *1989 Children Act* (which predated the Labour government) was a legislative development largely at odds with the surrounding political context, in that it sought to promote working in partnership with vulnerable families at a time when punitive responses to welfare needs and difficulties were prevalent. The Act recognised the value of professional responses that sought to keep children within their kinship networks, and the guidance accompanying the Act prompted social workers to find ways of involving families in developing responses to the needs of their children. The Act introduced the concept of 'children in need' (a recognition of the value of responding to children's difficulties earlier through support services) and was heavily influenced by research that indicated that existing interventionist approaches at the point of crisis were often failing to help children in the longer term and did not always meet their more immediate needs for safety and protection (DoH, 1995).

The Act was implemented alongside a major policy and practice debate about the need to refocus children's services and to move the emphasis away from formal risk based interventions towards an early, supportive response that could prevent later crisis (Rose, 1994). The debate sought to identify ways in which local authorities could fully implement the expectations of the *1989 Children Act* and deliver services to children in need of support whilst maintaining a child protection service (ADSS and NCH Action for Children, 1996). This 'refocusing' debate, whilst at times intense, achieved little in terms of noticeable additional resourcing of prevention or a shift in professional culture – assessment of risk continued to dominate children's services' responses to children and families in need (Aldgate and Tunstill, 1995). Despite the intentions of the Act, the reality for many families remained uneven and poorly resourced support services. As studies of user experiences revealed, for many families there was real frustration that early requests for help had been rejected, but once needs escalated into a crisis there was a highly interventionist formal response (Lindley, 1994). Within this overall picture some groups and communities faced particular barriers to accessing support services, further reinforcing their marginalisation (Butt and Box, 1998; Clarke, 2006).

With the arrival of the Labour government came a series of cross cutting policy reviews – commissioned as part of a broader political change agenda. Of specific relevance to children in need was the Policy Action Team 12 [PAT 12] report (Social Exclusion Unit, 2000). This considered the services and arrangements for children and young people assessed to be at risk of exclusionary processes and poor long-term outcomes. The PAT 12 review argued that the implementation of the 1989 Act had significant shortcomings:

> PAT believes the philosophy which lay behind the Children Act 1989 has never been put into practice for a combination of reasons:
> * The fact that the costs of crisis intervention fall on different budgets from those that might fund earlier preventative activity – and services that might fund earlier preventative activity would not receive any payback from it.
> * The way the priorities for services for young people are set out in legislation and policy guidance, and the consequences this has for their deployment of resources.
> * Professional cultures.
> Social Exclusion Unit, 2000: 76

As a result of this review and other allied policy developments, the focus for children in need of

support began to shift. Central to this shift was Labour's concern with social exclusion and the impact of exclusionary processes on the longer term outcomes for children, young people and families. The concept of social exclusion is heavily contested and the subject of considerable theoretical and empirical enquiry (Morris et al., 2009) and is not the focus of this chapter. Nevertheless, the bringing together by Labour of economic strategies with social welfare projects (described as the 'social investment state') resulted in significant implications for children's services. Children were no longer simply the focus of individualised concern about their current conditions; instead the agenda addressed their longer-term roles as productive citizens. Fawcett et al. (2004) articulate the implications of this changing framework for service development:

* the development of strategies that are holistic, but also targeted
* understandings of children as investments for the future rather than simply a concentration on current well-being
* the forming of an alliance with parents (through mechanisms of support and control) to take forward the investment strategies
* a limited recognition of children as subjects in their own right, resulting in the emergence of ad hoc approaches to children's rights.
    Fawcett et al., 2004: 4

Essentially policy makers, in this new context of the analysis of the impact of social exclusion, considered it to be inadequate and ineffective to restrict the focus to individual children who presented particular needs. The *1989 Children Act* framework of 'children in need' was found wanting and was overtaken by a very different analysis. The argument was made for a broader set of policies that embraced all children '. . . with no child slipping through the net . . .' (Boateng, 2003). This change led to the emergence of the policy stream *Every Child Matters: Change for Children* (DfES, 2004) and the establishment of five outcomes which all child welfare services would be expected to seek to promote, for all children. These outcomes (staying safe, being healthy, enjoying and achieving, making a positive contribution and economic well being) illustrated well the focus of Labour's concerns – children and young people needed to be guided and supported to develop into socially and economically productive citizens, and parents and service providers should become partners in this endeavour. Services to children and young people in need who faced particular hardship or had specific requirements were now located within this broader framework of aims and purposes for children's services.

Other obvious policy and practice developments emerged from this change programme. Integrated service provision was piloted and supported, multi disciplinary teams were created to respond to children with additional needs, and social work became subsumed within a wider grouping of children's professionals. This was particularly evident in the inclusion of social workers in the footprint for The Children's Workforce Development Council (CWDC). They became 'one of many' rather than holding onto to their own distinct identity – unlike teachers who had successfully managed to retain their own professional identity during this time of considerable change). Frost and Parton (2009) point to the absence of any recognition of the role and value of social work in many of the children's services policy developments and statements issued by the Department for Children, Schools and Families (DCSF) during this period, and this absence was also noticeable in the plethora of preventative initiatives rolled out during the early stages of New Labour's term of office.

So, in summary, the past decade has seen the legal and policy context for services to children in need change from individualised responses to individual assessments of need to a set of concerns fuelled by a political analysis of the consequences of social exclusion. Children in need of additional support became absorbed into a more general preoccupation with children at risk of social exclusion, and prevention became the mechanism for responding to the potential consequences of exclusionary processes. In the following discussion, the theoretical frameworks for understanding prevention are discussed and the need for new understandings identified in the light of the changes described above.

Understandings for prevention

Social work and social care services have historically drawn on the work of Hardiker and colleagues to frame their approaches to prevention and intervention (Hardiker et al.,

1991). In the 2001 Children Act Now report summarising a collection of studies exploring the implementation of the 1989 Act, it was evident that a number of local authorities were using a diluted version of Hardiker's tiered model of prevention (DoH, 2001). Specifically children in need were being assessed against 'levels' of need – ranging from low levels (indicating universal or limited needs) through to high levels where risk and safety were the focus of concern. Hardiker's original work sought to make careful links between an analysis of the function of the welfare state and the preventative strategies that result. This complexity was lost in the translation of the model into policy and practice. The resulting framework was simply a tiered model – best illustrated by the version set out by the Children and Young People's Unit when providing guidance for developing the Children's Fund initiative:

> *Level One: Diversionary. Here the focus is before problems can be seen – thus prevention strategies are likely to focus on whole populations.*
>
> *Level Two: Early prevention implies that problems are already beginning to manifest themselves and action is needed to prevent them becoming serious or worse.*
>
> *Level Three: Heavy-end prevention would focus on where there are multiple, complex and long-standing difficulties that will require a customisation of services to meet the needs of the individual concerned.*
>
> *Level Four: Restorative prevention focuses on reducing the impact of an intrusive intervention. This is the level of prevention that would apply to, for example, children and young people in public care, those permanently excluded from school or in youth offender institutions or supervision and/or those receiving assistance within the child protection framework.*
>
> Children and Young People's Unit, 2001: 37

At the time of its inception the Children's Fund initiative was central in the policy drive to address the consequences of social exclusion for children and young people. The Fund was a £960m national initiative that sought to target children aged 5 to 11 years who were at risk of social exclusion. The programme was delivered by local multi-agency partnerships (including statutory, voluntary, faith and independent groups) and was guided by three principles: partnership, prevention and participation. The aim of the initiative was ambitious: to enable children and families to find pathways out of poverty and exclusion. In translating this broad aim into specific objectives, the Fund became focused on individual child attainment and change. The localised nature of the roll out of the Children's Fund programme allowed diversity in structures, services and practices to emerge. The National Evaluation of the Children's Fund [NECF] was able to capture this diversity and in doing so provide a better understanding of how prevention was being understood and taken forward by local managers and practitioners.

One outcome from the work of the evaluation was to reveal the complexity of need being experienced by children and families (Edwards et al., 2006). What was evident was that families did not contain their needs to a specific tier or category, and therefore there was limited value in policy makers and practitioners adopting such approaches when assessing needs or categorising services. For example, families who had experienced severe trauma requiring acute interventions also had lower level needs concerned with social support, access to services

and parenting advice. Families were presenting a range of cross cutting needs to which frontline services struggled to respond effectively. Whilst those using Children's Fund services experienced the services as helpful, positive and responsive, the evidence for sustained longer-term change was limited. In part as a result of the scale and complexity of need revealed by the development of the services, Children's Fund provision tended to focus on the excluded (changing the child) rather than the exclusionary systems and processes that contributed to the poor outcomes, and as a result significant long term change was difficult to achieve (Barnes and Morris, 2008).

Using the adapted Hardiker model therefore presented serious problems when set alongside this range of activity and intentions for prevention; significantly it failed to engage with what we now know about the complexities of children's needs and experiences and was not located within the new context of social exclusion. The preventative strategies adopted by the Children's Fund allowed a fresh analysis to be developed, and this is set out in the table below. The data gathered by NECF about practices and service aims revealed the

Table 1. (Morris and Barnes, 2008)

Category of activity	Intent – Primary driver	Description of provision	Assumptions about relationship between child, community and society
Integration (changing child focus)	integration into existing provision – which is perceived as functional and appropriate	focused on child's capabilities/capacities to engage with the existing provision	social exclusion can be addressed without structural/cultural change.
Adaptation (changing service focus)	increasing the responsivity of the mainstream services	focused on enhancing existing provision	increasing social cohesion requires greater diversity in service provision
Separated provision (child/their community focus)	certain groups need bespoke services to avoid problematic outcomes	highly focused and offered only to those meeting a specific criteria	specialist services to ensure marginalisation does not become destructive
Working with community models (mixed focus on child and services)	contextual knowledge building upon community understandings	developed by and reflecting existing community models of help and support	current social life is diverse and inclusion is achieved by building on networks
Promoting well being/achieving change (mixed focus on child and services)	mixed intent; promoting the child's potential and changing the services	aims to provide a broad service tackling a range of barriers	existing social organisation is not benign but children also need to change to engage with enhanced provision

understandings being utilised about exclusionary and inclusionary processes and allowed new understandings for prevention to emerge.

The analysis set out in the table is not exhaustive, nor are the categories mutually exclusive. Instead, the categorisation allows any analysis to focus on the purpose of the service and the assumptions that underpin that purpose. For example, within the Children's Fund there was evidence of a significant number of the preventative services seeking to build resilience and to enable children to access mainstream services. Such approaches focused on changing the child rather than changing the processes that excluded the child and revealed the assumptions being made by practitioners about the appropriateness and value of existing mainstream provision (Morris and Barnes, 2008).

This new framework for understanding approaches to prevention has considerable implications for the development of services for children in need and more generally for the analysis adopted by social work and social care when exploring roles and responsibilities in relation to children and families with support needs. The following discussion identifies these implications and considers the challenges posed for services to children in need.

The current context for prevention

With its sustained interest in preventing the longer term outcomes of social exclusion, Labour rolled out a series of preventative programmes including *Sure Start, the Children's Fund, On Track, New Deal for Communities* and, more recently, highly targeted programmes such as the *Family Nurse Partnership*. Behind these initiatives lay political interpretations of the substantial and growing body of work exploring risk and protective factors in long term outcomes for children and young people (France and Utting, 2005) and the potential for delivering targeted predictive early interventions (Hanson and Plewis, 2004; Hughes and Fielding, 2006). This research and political analysis is not the focus of this chapter but its influence on the direction and shaping of preventative strategies and services cannot be underestimated. Children who are particularly vulnerable to poor outcomes – because of where they live, their family environment, or their own capacities – have been the focus of specific, targeted national

programmes (the early development of *Sure Start*, for example, focused on geographical areas deemed to present particular risk factors and the Children's Fund was rolled out in waves with those areas presenting the higher risk indicators receiving the early funding). Some communities and their children are seen to present real challenges to the political aspirations for socially and economically viable citizens and as such additional interventions have been proposed as necessary to ensure that investment in childhood does deliver later benefits. For Labour the response to these 'at risk' children has repeatedly emphasised early interventions in family life through enhanced education and health provision (Morris et al., 2009).

The rapidly evolving legal and policy framework for children's services brought with it the expectations for integrated early intervention provision, working towards the generic Every Child Matters [ECM] outcomes. The ECM agenda meant that all children were argued to be the object of shared aspirations, with additional focused legislation developed to meet the needs of specific groups such as children in care, care leavers and young children at risk of crime. This included the *2004 Children Act* and various sets of guidance for practice and service planning (DfES, 2004; 2005). Mention needs to also be made of the development of the Common Assessment Framework [CAF] with the expectation by DCSF that this would support new directions for practice:

> *The CAF promotes more effective, earlier identification of additional needs, particularly in universal services. It aims to provide a simple process for a holistic assessment of children's needs and strengths; taking account of the roles of parents, carers and environmental factors on their development. Practitioners are then better placed to agree with children and families about appropriate modes of support. The CAF also aims to improve integrated working by promoting coordinated service provisions*
>
> DCSF, 2009

All local authorities were expected to be using CAF by 2008, but it is too early to establish the outcomes for children and families of this particular initiative.

Within what Warren described as this 'policy churn' (Warren et al., 2006) some patterns emerged. First, the speed of change was so fast that evaluations were seldom able to complete their work and thereby to inform subsequent policy and practice (Glass, 2005). As a result the potential learning about prevention offered by the national evaluations of Sure Start, the Children's Fund and On Track was diluted as the original services were changed and reformed before their impact could fully be assessed. Secondly, the ongoing difficulties for services in engaging and working with families experiencing enduring and multiple hardships became a recurring theme across the initiatives. The most vulnerable of families, who represented a significant percentage of the users of statutory children's services, were not accessing or using the preventative services rolled out in the drive to address the consequences of social exclusion (SEU Task Force, 2007). The evaluations of the major preventative programmes indicated the continued challenges of changing the experiences of the most marginalised families and in meeting the complex needs of families experiencing multiple difficulties. When evaluations revealed the limited reach of the preventative programmes, a new set of policy responses to these vulnerable families emerged. The early commitment to a partnership with families to address their needs was replaced by a more assertive tone that looked to identify families that failed to engage with mainstream support services, and adopted an increasingly interventionist approach (Cleland and Tisdall, 2005; Gillies, 2005).

The emphasis became targeted programmes that focused upon marginalised families with multiple and enduring difficulties (see for example the *Family Intervention Projects* (White et al., 2008) the *Think Family* policy stream (Morris et al., 2008; SEU Task Force, 2007) and the *Family Pathfinder* initiatives (DCSF, 2008). For those within children's services, this has become a complex and contradictory environment, not least because many of the families who are the subject of this new focus are also the families that historically have been the subject of statutory social care services, creating a policy and practice environment that can be difficult to navigate, both for families and for professionals.

The challenges for children's services

Provision: The tensions of core business

Recent preventative policy and practice developments, whilst often compromised by political interventions, have opened up

opportunities for new learning about the impact of preventative services, and new spaces for preventative practices to be either renewed or newly developed. Typically these opportunities were created by centrally driven initiatives (such as *Sure Start, New Deal for Communities* and the *Children's Fund*) and as a result mainstream local authority children's social care services could continue to perceive prevention as somebody else's responsibility. Initiatives such as the Children's Fund (which sought to extend and promote local approaches to prevention) often revealed the entrenched views of those delivering established services:

> There have been considerable difficulties in terms of defining prevention. Especially in reconciling notions of universal provision . . . and the focused targeting of groups with higher levels of need.
> Children's Fund Programme Manager.
> Morris and Spicer, 2004: 8

The limited resourcing for social care and social work services for children in need of support and the increasing administrative pressures on front line children's services have curtailed the extent to which services to children who have less acute needs can be delivered by local authority children's services. This is not a new phenomenon; Hargreaves and Hadlow noted in 1995 the significant reduction from 1970 in the number of 'preventative' cases held by front line social workers (Hargreaves and Hadlow, 1995). But recent pressures have exacerbated the constraints on preventative practice. In 2005 the Family Policy Alliance described the ongoing difficulties families faced in accessing support services, and they argued strongly for legislative change to ensure assessments and services for children in need were not curtailed:

> . . . the reality is that many children and families in need do not receive even minimal support and many have difficulties in accessing such services that are available.
> Family Policy Alliance, 2005: 2

Some developments, such as the Full Service Extended Schools (FSES) initiative have placed expectations on traditional services to develop and change – and the evaluation of these initiatives demonstrates the challenges presented by this process of change. For FSES the tensions between existing 'core business' (school standards and the attainment of pupils) and the new broader preventative agenda (the provision of child care, the engagement of families in learning and the development of the school as a community resource) are evident and largely unresolved. And, as with the other allied preventative policies, the most vulnerable of families have not accessed the extended school services (Cummings et al., 2007).

This tension in education services between perceived core business and expectations for the delivery of support services mirrors an enduring history for children's social care and within this for social work services for children in need. Child protection is frequently set out in recent policy developments as a primary responsibility for children's social care services, but as Corby notes, so too is family support for children in need:

> *The Green Paper emphasis on family support also provides opportunities for social workers to broaden their perspective in child and family social work, and thereby improve their image. It is important these opportunities are taken up.*
>
> Corby, 2006: 173

But, as the refocusing debate in the early 1990s illustrated, without difficult political decisions about resources, roles and purpose, the influence of child protection will dominate and social workers will remain understandably cautious in their willingness to work in other ways. Within this complex debate the new analysis for prevention also needs attention – services to children in need have a very different context from that in which the 1989 Act was implemented. Those planning and delivering children's services will need to reconsider the intended outcomes of their services and practices when set within the context of social exclusion and the evidence of the complexity of need.

Skills: Losing the capacity to support

The new approaches to understanding the role and purpose of preventative services and practices (set out earlier in this chapter) allow those engaged in delivering children's services to review the conceptual frameworks that underpin their practice with children in need. Important debates occur when consideration is given to, for example, the question whether the capacity to challenge and change an exclusionary service is compromised by adopting the integration approach to prevention. Such debates link into

core social work and social care discussions about the role and purpose of children's services. Spratt (2001), Parton (2006) and others point to the struggle of embedding family support and prevention in mainstream social work practice and despite the opportunities for new understandings and changing practices, there is an ongoing reluctance to promote the skills and knowledge necessary for effective preventative practice. In part this is perpetuated by the training frameworks for social workers, which make little if any mention of prevention, thus reinforcing the low status of the skills needed to deliver services to children in need of support

The policy decision to promote the profile of prevention via new national programmes rather than via internal changes to existing services for children in need has, it can be argued, been a costly one in terms of skills and knowledge. Whilst children and families have benefited in the short term from the funding for these new additional services, it has left the existing focus of practice within mainstream children's services largely unchanged, with little renewed attention being paid to effective preventative practices. The preventative programmes rolled out during the past decade have, at least initially, attempted to respond to many of the needs which services delivered under Part III of the 1989 Act were argued to have failed to address. The criticism of services to children in need was in part about their failure to engage with environmental factors such as unemployment, poor housing and poverty that stimulated many of the needs children and families presented.

By relocating the expectations and services associated with meeting these needs within new service configurations and arrangements outside established local authority provision, the opportunity to change the cultures and services within children's services that PAT 12 so starkly criticised was lost. The time limited funding arrangements for the high profile national prevention programmes resulted in limited enduring learning, because they were so consistently positioned outside the mainstream. Practitioners within children's services might therefore notice the absence of local family support services once funding ceased, but struggled to use the learning from these programmes unless effective 'knowledge bridges' were built between these different service streams.

Family needs and experiences

The experiences of the families that are the current focus of broader policy concerns remain in reality the same experiences that social work and social care services have long sought to change. Yet there is remarkably little evidence of any dialogue between existing providers and practitioners and the new targeted services. Indeed the most important message from any overview of the outcomes from a decade of prevention and family support evaluations might be the need to better use existing knowledge rather than repeatedly replicate learning.

Over the past two decades research has indicated that families who use social care services experience high levels of poverty, marginalisation and social and economic deprivation. Krumer-Nevo (2003) usefully describes 'defeated families' – those that are defeated by both their life experiences and by the services that seek to help them. (Whilst policy developments such as *Think Family* and the *Respect* agenda reflect an underlying, almost moralistic, analysis of transmitted deprivation, it is worth noting that it is not being suggested here that there are a core of failing families, instead a commonality of experience is being described, which may be more or less acute according to the specific circumstances of the family.) The growth in preventative initiatives over the past decade has failed to engage those experiencing the most difficulties. As a result, complex and difficult tensions have arisen for practitioners and for locality services. Historically, social work and children's services have sought to explore skills and practices that can enable change and can engage resistant service users. This set of knowledge and skills has yet to find a place in the new raft of targeted services, many of which draw on professionals outside social care and social work. Core social work values that are concerned with facilitation and respect rub against the assertive nature of the services being developed to catch and change resistant families. For frontline staff in children's services the reality may well be that they will now be expected to deliver a service in the context of this new assertive culture. Families who need help may be more rather than less resistant to intervention, having become the focus of a political process of 'othering', making the task facing children's services more rather than less difficult.

Services to childre morning after the

This has been a uniquel profile of prevention in have seen a flood of policy promoting preventative strate the majority of which sat outside care services and were delivered on the basis of fixed term funding. The outcomes of these initiatives are contested and in some cases still unclear (Buchanan et al., 2004) but there is little evidence of a reduced level of demand for services for children in need, and there is evidence of ongoing frustration at the paucity and inadequacies of those services that do exist. (This is not to deny the evidence that indicates that families do use and value the services that are available.) It is debatable whether those most needing support services have been able to use the services developed, and the reasons for this low take up by the most marginalised of communities and families are complex. It is apparent from the outcomes of a range of evaluations of preventative programmes (both national and international) that for some communities the capacity to access and utilise effectively the opportunities presented by the various funding streams are limited by a long history of under investment and alienation (Edwards et al., 2006).

Most recently, in the wake of the various analyses of a series of serious child protection cases, we have seen the emergence of a questioning of the efficacy and feasibility of sustained family support services and a call for early formal intervention to be more readily acknowledged as a preferred option:

> *Repairing families cannot be the primary, if rarely expressed criterion for success. But when the wake of Baby P has subsided we shall return to the status quo in which social workers who intervene to remove children from parents face vilification. The emphasis is – too much in my view – on fixing families.*
>
> Neary, 2009: 180

But, in the light of the preceding discussions in this chapter, this is a debate built on a false premise – it assumes that support services have been delivered and have failed. The decades of underfunding, the absence of robust support services to children in need and the limited transferred learning about effectiveness in means that few families have received planned and fully implemented early support. Inevitably, later failure for children and families is a consequence of this earlier non or partial intervention – rather than of support services failing *per se*. It is difficult to see how it can be judged that mainstream children's services to children in need have failed when all the evidence points to these services rarely being comprehensively delivered and the relevant knowledge and skills being significantly underdeveloped. Not all families can care safely for children and state responsibilities for ensuring protection must mean that some children need to live away from their parents/carers, but research shows that even families where there are serious concerns for the safety of children can and do respond protectively to children's needs (Burford et al., 2009). However, the absence of early support delivered on the basis of robust knowledge about prevention means that many families exhaust their reserves and reach a crisis point before services are forthcoming (Family Rights Group, 2008).

Whilst there is more yet to be learnt about how to plan, deliver and evaluate effective support services to children in need, there is a body of knowledge that demands serious consideration, and the potential for a sophisticated level of practice that currently few children's services are able to accommodate or support. This is the crux of the debate: to what extent are we prepared to fund and protect services to vulnerable and marginalised families that are based on practice frameworks for growth and change? There are complex questions about perceptions of entitlement and legitimacy woven into this debate. And, as Spratt identifies (2001), in this current climate there is certainty and relative safety in social work staying close to risk averse, interventionist models of practice and resisting the less well defined and proceduralised practices of support and prevention.

References

Aldgate, J. and Tunstill, J. (1995) *Section 17 – The First 18 Months*. London: HMSO.

Association of Directors of Social Services and NCH Action for Children (1996) *Children Still in Need: Refocusing Child Protection in the Context of Children in Need*. London: NCH Action for Children.

Barnes, M. and Morris, K. (2008) Strategies for the Prevention of Social Exclusion: An Analysis of The Children's Fund. *Journal of Social Policy*, 35: 2, 251–70.

Boateng, P. (2003) *Every Child Matters*. Cm 5860. London: Stationery Office.

Buchanan, A. et al. (2004) *The Impact of Government Policy on Social Exclusion Among Children Aged 0–13 and Their Families. A Review of the Literature for The Social Exclusion Unit*. London: SEU.

Burford, G. et al. (2009) *Family Group Decision Making: Annotated Bibliography on Engaging the Family Group in Child Welfare Decision Making*. American Humane Association. Available At: http://www.americanhumane.org/Protecting-Children/Programs/Family-Group-Decision-Making/Re_Annotated_Bibliography

Butt, J. and Box, L. (1998) *Family Centred: A Study of the Use of Family Centres by Black Families*. London: Race Equality Unit.

Children and Young People's Unit (2001) *The Children's Fund Guidance*. London: DfES.

Clarke, H. (2006) *Preventing Social Exclusion of Disabled Children and Their Families*, London: DfES.

Cleland, A. and Tisdall, K. (2005) The Challenge of Antisocial Behaviour: New Relationships Between the State, Children and Parents. *International Journal of Law, Policy, and The Family*, 19: 395–420.

Corby, B. (2006) The Role of Child Care Social Work in Supporting Families with Children in Need and Providing Protective Services-Past, Present and Future. *Child Abuse Review*, 15, 159–77.

Cummings, A. et al. (2007) *Evaluation of the Full Service Schools Initiative; Final Report*. London: DCSF.

Department of Health (1995) *Child Protection: Messages From Research*. London: HMSO.

Department of Health (2001) *Children Act Now: Messages From Research*. London: HMSO

Department for Children, Schools and Families (2008) *Family Pathfinders*. DCSF. Available: http://www.dcsf.gov.uk/Everychildmatters/Strategy/Parents/Pathfinders/Familypathfinders.

Department for Children, Schools and Families (2009) *Common Assessment Framework (CAF)* DCSF. http://www.dcsf.gov.uk/Everychildmatters/Strategy/Deliveringservices1/Caf/Caff ramework/

Department for Education and Schools (2004) *Every Child Matters: The Next Steps*. London: DfES.

Department for Education and Schools (2005) *Every Child Matters Outcomes Framework.* London: DfES.

Edwards, A. et al. (2006) *Working to Prevent the Social Exclusion of Children and Young People: Final Lessons from the National Evaluation of the Children's Fund.* London: DfES Research Report 734.

Family Policy Alliance (2005) *Supporting Children and Families.* Briefing Paper. London: FPA.

Family Rights Group (2008) *Submission to the Review of Arrangements for the Safeguarding of Children Conducted by Lord Laming.* London: Family Rights Group.

Fawcett, B., Featherstone, F. and Goddard, J. (2004) *Contemporary Child Care Policy and Practice.* Basingstoke: Palgrave Macmillan.

France, A. and Utting, D. (2005) The Paradigm of Risk and Protection-Focused Prevention and its Impact on Services for Children and Families. *Children and Society*, 19: 2, 77–90.

Frost, N. and Parton, N. (2009) Understanding Children's Social Care. London: Sage.

Gillies, V. (2005) Meeting Parents' Needs? Discourses of 'Support' and 'Inclusion'. *Critical Social Policy*, 25: 1, 70–90.

Glass, N. (2005) Surely Some Mistake? *The Guardian*, Wednesday 5 January.

Hansen, K. and Plewis, I. (2004) *Children at Risk: How Evidence from British Cohort Data Can Inform the Debate on Prevention.* NECF http:// www.ne-cf.org/Briefing.Asp?Section = 0001000 40009&Profile = 000100080003&Id = 639

Hardiker, P., Exton, K. and Barker, M. (1991) *Policies and Practices in Preventative Child Care.* Aldershot: Ashgate.

Hargreaves, R. and Hadlow, J. (1995) Preventive Intervention as a Working Concept in Child Care Practice. *British Journal of Social Work*, 25, 349–65.

Hughes, N. and Fielding, T. (2006) *Targeting Preventative Services for Children: Experiences from the Children's Fund.* London: DfES.

IFSW (2000) *Definition of Social Work.* IFSW: http://www.ifsw.org/P38000279.html

Krumer-Nevo, M. (2003) From a Collation of Despair to a Convent of Help in Social Work with Families in Distress. *European Journal of Social Work*, 6: 3, 273–82.

Lindley, B. (1994) *On the Receiving End.* London: Family Rights Group.

Morris, K. and Barnes, M. (2008) Prevention and Social Exclusion: New Understandings for Policy and Practice. *British Journal of Social Work*, 38: 6, 1194–211.

Morris, K. and Spicer, N. (2004) *The National Evaluation of the Children's Fund: Emerging Messages for Practice.* London: DfES.

Morris, K. et al. (2008) *Think Family: A Literature Review of Whole Family Approaches.* London: Cabinet Office.

Morris, K., Mason, P. and Barnes, M. (2009) *Children, Families and Social Exclusion: Developing New Understandings for Prevention.* Bristol: The Policy Press.

Neary, M. (2009) The Case for Care. *Public Policy Research*. 15: 4, 180–1.

Parton, N. (2006) *Safeguarding Childhood: Early Intervention and Surveillance in a Late Modern Society.* Basingstoke: Palgrave Macmillan.

Rose, W. (1994) *Address to the Sieff Conference*, 5 September.

Social Exclusion Unit (2000) *Young People at Risk: Policy Action Team Report 12.* London: SEU.

Social Exclusion Unit Task Force (2007) *Reaching Out: Think Family.* London: Cabinet Office.

Spratt, T. (2001) The Influence of Child Protection Orientation on Child Welfare Practice. *British Journal of Social Work*, 31, 993–54.

Warren, S. et al. (2006) Emergent Family Support Practices in a Context of Policy Churn: An Example from the Childrens Fund. *Child Care In Practice*, 12: 4, 331–46.

White, C. et al. (2008) *Family Intervention Projects: An Evaluation of Their Design, Set-Up and Early Outcomes.* London: DCSF.

CHAPTER 8

Inadmissible Evidence? New Labour and the Education of Children in Care

Isabelle Brodie

Introduction

Children in care have, over time, variously been viewed with pity, fear, anxiety and disdain. Their well-being and living-space, and their economic futures, have occupied the minds of prominent politicians and philanthropists for some two centuries (Frost and Stein, 1986). Over the past two decades, however, children in care have achieved a prominence in public policy that is remarkable in terms of the sheer volume of reporting, debate, legislation and guidance that has been generated. Analysis of this is far from easy, but reflection on the shape and direction of this policy is crucial, not least in view of the accumulation of evidence indicating the depressing nature of the care experience for many of the children and young people concerned. At the time of writing, the aftermath of the case of Baby Peter has led to yet more reflection on children in care and the need to improve practice. Two young boys have been charged with the serious assault of two other children while living in foster care (Walker, 2009). There is a heightened sense of a need or desire for the care system but at the same time the fact that the 'life chances of children in care are governed by luck to an unacceptable degree' (House of Commons Select Committee, 2009) means that a strong sense of ambivalence continues to permeate the commentary of press and politicians.

There are currently around 60,000 children in care at any one time in England. Most – 68 per cent – are of white British origin though there has been an increase in the number of children from Asian backgrounds and of African ethnic origin. Unaccompanied asylum seeking children represent a new and significant minority in the care population. The majority of these, some 41,000, live in foster care. A small number – around 6,500 – live in residential accommodation (DCSF, 2009a). A significant group of children and young people also experience short-break accommodation. In relation to all placement types, it is important to recognise that the care population is not static, and that children experience many different routes through the system. The main reasons for out of home placement are neglect, abuse, family dysfunction or an acute family crisis (DCSF, 2008). Such terms hide a constellation of parent and child difficulties, the depth and complexity of which should not be underestimated. Parental substance misuse and mental health needs are often present, while children frequently present emotional and behavioural difficulties and schooling problems (Stein, 2009).

This chapter begins by considering the legacy of the *1989 Children Act*, and the legislative, policy and research context in which Labour assumed power. An understanding of this context is crucial to understanding trends within the care system; some of these pre-date new Labour and seem to function in relation to broader social trends, including attitudes to risk (Rowlands and Statham, 2009). That said, the wide-ranging policy initiatives that have emerged under Labour are such that their impact on practice, even if not on service users, is important. This will be considered in relation to the educational experience of looked after children and young people.

Setting the scene

The Children Act 1989, implemented in 1991, had established a new set of principles in relation to care for vulnerable children and their families. It was evident, however, that significant problems remained, and New Labour's coming to power coincided with a Health Select Committee (1998) report on children in care which contained a number of potent criticisms. The influential Department of Health research summaries produced at about this time also proved significant. Research into adolescents, for example, pointed to an absence of inter-agency collaboration and communication, resulting in many teenagers 'falling through the net' (DoH, 1996). In 1998, a new series of studies into residential care (DoH, 1998a) highlighted the continuing problems of the sector: the 'exodus of the marginal' (Gooch, 1996) had resulted in residential children's homes becoming the repository of the most troubled young people, but the workforce continued to be largely unqualified and under-confident in meeting such serious and complex needs. Additionally 'new' problems had emerged, for example the over-representation of looked after children amongst those excluded from school.

Labour's approach to looked after children also needs to be considered in the context of wider anxieties about performance in social care, the extent to which children were being kept safe and their well-being enhanced within the system. Throughout the 1990s a series of scandals emerged relating to the abuse of children in residential care (see Berridge and Brodie, 1996 for a review of this issue). Although much of the abuse being uncovered had taken place in earlier decades, research was still producing evidence that children living in care continued to be at risk either from peers or in the community (Department of Health, 1998). Utting (1997) had also highlighted the paucity of research information relating to the safety of children living in foster care.

In addition to this existing body of information, children in care were ideally placed to fit within New Labour's thinking on social exclusion. As has been extensively documented, the term social exclusion was defined by politicians as 'a shorthand label for what can happen when individuals or areas suffer from a combination of linked problems such as unemployment, poor skills, low incomes, poor housing, high crime environments, bad health and family breakdown' (SEU, 1997: 1). Children in care – who are likely to come from precisely such environments – are cited as being at particular risk of social exclusion in a series of reports examining issues such as teenage pregnancy (SEU, 1999a), homelessness (SEU, 1998) difficulties in accessing training and unemployment (SEU, 1999b) and educational failure (SEU, 2003).

In undertaking this analysis, considerable emphasis was placed, by the Social Exclusion Unit and others, on the need for an 'evidence based' approach, that is, that sound research evidence, together with user views, should inform the development of policy and interventions with the care population. At face value this seems reasonable and indeed laudable. Within child care policy the relationship between

policy makers and researchers had traditionally been strong – witness the influence of Department of Health research programmes and summaries (Little, 1996; see also, for example, DoH, 1995). However, the extent to which the research base was fit for purpose was more questionable. For example, Berridge (1997) demonstrated serious gaps in knowledge relating to foster care, with only 13 major studies carried out in 20 years – even though the majority of the care population experienced, at some point, a foster care placement. Cross-disciplinary research – for instance in relation to medical and psychiatric research, social policy or educational research – was extremely limited, if not non-existent, in relation to children in care. More generally, the mainstream of child care research had been criticised as essentially 'pragmatic' and lacking methodological and theoretical transparency (Trinder, 1996). It seems, perhaps only with the benefit of hindsight, that the significance of this was not fully appreciated as Labour hit the policy trail.

Initiative led and target driven?

Crimmens and Pitts (2000) reflecting on the experience of the 1990s, note the flurry of activity that accompanied Labour's accession to power. They argue that, at that 'moment' what was needed 'was a set of policies which would underpin the development of good, safe practice, enabling the people who spent their lives working with children and young people in residential establishments to begin reconstructing the sector in accordance with the lessons of the 1990s' (pvii). The new initiatives which soon emerged did not, in their view, meet this need. Instead, the White Paper *Modernising Social Services* (DoH, 1998b) and the consultation paper *A New Approach to Social Services Performance* (DoH, 1998c) set out proposals for a new performance assessment system for social services within the Best Value regime for all government services. The vanguard of improvement in children's services was, however, the *Quality Protects* initiative (DoH, 1998d). This was launched in 1998 and aimed to 'transform children's services'. Crimmens and Pitts (2000) describe this as 'arguably the most significant development in the sector since the implementation of the *Children Act (1989)*' (pvii). The initiative offered:

- an extension of the local authority's duty of care in relation to young people leaving care
- new funding to provide a national 'voice' for children in care
- new initiatives to improve the educational attainment of 'looked after' children
- more effective regulation of all children's homes
- £375 million to be spent over three years.

Monitoring was to take place through eleven defined national objectives, with linked sub-objectives and performance indicators. Additionally, *Management Action Plans* and progress reports would be produced annually by local authorities. It also introduced the concept of 'corporate parenting', the idea that personnel and agencies in the local authority should recognise their responsibilities vis-à-vis children in care. Thus, for example, guidance was issued to local councillors outlining these responsibilities and arming them with a selection of relevant questions.

At this stage the investment of resource and attention to children in care at least seemed promising, though concerns about a managerialist and target driven culture were soon being expressed. However, the 'success' of these initiatives depended on the adequacy of the analysis, and the validity of the way in which problems were identified and defined. In order to consider this in more detail, the next section of the paper will focus on the education of looked after children. This provides a useful case study of Labour's approach, evidence concerning its impact and a means to consider the significance of the policy/research relationship.

New Labour and education in care: An evidence-based approach?

Looked after children have the odds stacked against them. Overall, they are five times less likely to get five good GCSEs than the rest of their peers; they are four times more likely to suffer from mental health problems; and young women in care are three times more likely to become pregnant as teenagers. This is true whether they are the subject of care orders made by the family courts, or provided with accommodation by local authorities with the agreement of their parents. Working with authorities and others, it is the Government's job to change those odds.

Speech by Children's Minister,
Kevin Brennan, 2007

One major thing to note is that whilst in care my education was allowed to suffer. I left care with no GCSEs whatsoever and this is absolutely unacceptable. I'm currently half way through my degree as an undergraduate at university, but the steps I had to take to get this far took me a lot longer than others due to lack of concern by my carers.

18-year-old male care leaver

Quality Protects contained the broad objective that children in need and children looked after should gain maximum life chance benefits from educational opportunities, health care and social care. The linked target stated that 50 per cent of all children in care should achieve an educational qualification by 2001, and 75 per cent by 2003. Statistical collections were introduced, initially focusing on GCSE qualifications.

The rationale for this target was at best unclear – as was privately acknowledged by government advisors of the time. This may be explained partially by the absence of existing data to inform such target setting. Surprising though it now seems, the education of looked after children was barely visible on the research horizon until 1987, when a seminal paper by Jackson (1987) brought the low achievement of children in care to the attention of both researchers and policy makers. During the 1990s, there was a gradual increase in research attention, but it is fair to say that in 1997 the quantity and quality of research available was, at best, limited (see Borland et al., 1998). The foundation for the targets was, therefore, weak – and yet, achievement of these was central to assessment of local authority performance. Managers and practitioners became first sceptical, then resentful of the gap between their efforts and the ways in which these were being measured.

Where there is little data available, the data that is collected assumes even greater importance. In the same way, the few research studies concerning the education of children in care exercised a crucial role in relation to new policy. An important plank in this body of work was the view that the low achievements of looked after children could be explained through deficits in the care system itself. Thus, Fletcher-Campbell (1998: 4) states unequivocally that the poor achievement of children looked after 'is a product of the system; the problem, though awesome, is solvable'. Therefore, if education is sufficiently prioritised through planning and the provision of appropriate support, and if those working with young people have a clear understanding of their responsibilities in this respect then 'there can be achievement in the normal range'. A similar line of thought is still apparent in government minister Kevin Brennan's statement (quoted above), and was reflected in the guidance issued in 2000 (DoH and DfEE, 2000). This aimed at improving planning through the use of personal education plans [PEPs] prioritising finding children school placements within specified time periods, and introducing designated teachers. Targets have remained in place.

As Young (2003) suggests in relation to New Labour's position on social exclusion more generally, the problem of the education of children in care was seen as 'a sort of hydraulic failure of the system'. Few would dispute the need for change in the care system: it is important to stress that the available evidence demonstrated that this did not support children's educational achievement and regularly jeopardised children's educational careers (Berridge et al., 1997; Berridge and Brodie, 1998; Brodie, 2001). Yet the weight given to the system seemed at odds with other evidence relating to the care population itself. Critically, neither policy makers – nor, indeed, the social care research community – were prepared to grapple with the complexity of the careers of children and young people entering the care system.

What this fails to recognise is that the experiences of children and young people in care are not confined to the care system itself. Attributing educational and other outcomes to the care system fails to take into account pre-care experiences and the highly variable routes taken through the system. As noted earlier, the majority of children and young people in care have come from situations not only of poverty and disadvantage but also abuse. Gallagher et al. (2004), describing a sample of 14 young people in one children's home, note that 10 had Statements of Special Educational Need for specific learning disabilities and/or behaviour, eight had been excluded from at least one school and in some instances several, and the majority had educational careers characterised by poor attendance, disruptive behaviour, lack of motivation and frequent changes of school. This is not unusual and is borne out by larger scale research (Berridge and Brodie, 1998; Francis, 2000; Brodie, 2001; Hicks et al., 2007). Other research has highlighted the high proportion of looked after children living in dual care/education registered facilities and not,

therefore, attending mainstream school (Berridge et al., 2008). This data has to be held in tension with other information demonstrating that significant elements of the care population, especially those living in foster care, will progress well at school and some will be high achievers (Jackson, Ajayi and Quigley, 2005).

National statistics relating to looked after children contain no 'value added' element that might take account of socio-economic inequalities, and the achievements of different groups of looked after children have not been compared with like populations (Berridge, 2008). In this respect, Labour's approach to the education of children in care is vulnerable to a more general criticism of the social exclusion model, namely the tendency to omit poverty and inequality as key factors in influencing individual life chances. This thinking has been reflected in the identification of outcome measures and the collection of data: for example, the fact that a cohort of looked after children in one year group will include children with serious learning disabilities or acute emotional and behavioural difficulties has been ignored in the collection of data. This is deeply frustrating to frontline professionals, who are conscious that their efforts are helping looked after children to progress educationally, but are unable to have this reflected in the data through which their local authorities are held accountable.

This may also help explain the failure of policy to impact on national data concerning the achievements of looked after children. Larger-scale evaluations have found evidence of much good practice, but this has not, it seems, translated into exam passes. Improvements at national level have been slow and small, leading to some frustration at policy level at the seemingly obdurate nature of the system (Brodie et al., 2009). This has largely taken the form of the issuing of further documentation and guidance, much of which either repeats or places further statutory force on existing provisions. It is difficult to be comprehensive, but since 2000 this has included:

- Guidance (DoH/DfEE, 2000)
- SEU report, containing over 100 recommendations (SEU, 2003)
- *Children Act 2004*, including amendment 52 imposing a new duty on local authorities to promote the educational welfare of looked after children

- Guidance (2005) (replacing 2000 guidance) on the education of children in care
- Guidance for governors (DfES, 2005)
- Working groups established to examine the issue of looked after children's education in more detail
- White Paper, *Care Matters*, 2006
- *Children and Young Persons Act 2008*
- *Improving the Educational Attainment of Children in Care (Looked After Children)* (DCSF, 2009b)

The irony is that this approach has prevented recognition of the positive contribution that the care system can make to the educational progress and achievements of looked after children and young people. Policy has made a contribution to this: there is greater awareness and understanding of the educational needs of looked after children, and a gradual building of expertise. The use of specialised posts in, for example, educational psychology and social work has been a positive innovation (Berridge et al., 2008; Harker et al., 2004). New strategic posts have helped co-ordinate work in this area and appear to have been effective, most recently in the form of Virtual School Heads (VSHs) (Berridge et al., 2009).

Recent consultation exercises have found that the majority of children find care to be more helpful than not in relation to education; care leavers interviewed by Jackson, Ajayi and Quigley (2005) believed that entry to care had been beneficial in terms of their educational achievement. That is not to say experience is uniform, or lacking in contradiction – as demonstrated by the quote from the young person cited earlier. However, where care is a trigger to improved educational experience and achievement, this is likely to be associated with a generally high quality of care, incorporating both practical attention to education and emotional support for the young person that endures through key transitions.

Part of the difficulty lies in the enormous amount of inspection effort that goes on the managerial aspects of the system, rather than its quality. An enormous number of different things are measured, and there is a great variety of measurement, but the failure to say that certain things really matter and that we will home in on them to try to get everybody up to a high standard across the board works against that inspection effort.

Professor Ian Sinclair to the House of Commons Select Committee, 2009, para 219

Research into all aspects of the care system has emphasised the fact that front-line carers and professionals play the most crucial role in supporting young people and providing the quality of care that helps improve outcomes in both the medium and longer terms. Significantly, this is also the factor most frequently identified by children and young people themselves as making them feel supported, cared for and able to achieve and make successful life transitions (see, for example, Morgan, 2009). This is not to downplay the role of other systemic factors – an adequate supply of care placements that make sensible planning possible will be important in ensuring that children are placed with appropriate carers, for example – but such evidence nevertheless highlights the importance of the skills and expertise of professional carers.

That said, the low level of qualified staff and carers working with children in the care system has long been a matter of concern in both foster and residential care: Utting (1997) described it as a 'chronic' problem (p11). The issues are well known: a shortage of foster carers, an absence of professionally qualified carers, a mismatch between the difficulties presented by children and young people in care and the skills of those caring with them, and a lack of structures through which carers can stay in the system while developing their careers. Initiatives such as the Residential Child Care Initiative (RCCI), which provided a 'residential care' stream within DipSW programmes, were valued but had a limited impact on the residential field as a whole (Hills and Childs, 1998). In this respect the UK has been compared negatively with continental Europe, where models such as social pedagogy are more likely to be in evidence (Pitts and Porteous, 2005; Cameron et al., 2007).

Some promising developments have taken place: in residential care, the Centre for Residential Care at the University of Strathclyde and the National Centre for Excellence in Residential Child Care (NCERCC) at the National Children's Bureau in England aim to serve as a focus for the development of excellent practice in residential care, through working collaboratively with key stakeholders. The last decade has also seen a growth in the knowledge available about the care workforce. This has generated some unexpectedly positive findings: Mainey and Crimmens (2006) surveyed 1, 243 workers in residential child care homes. Three-quarters of staff reported they were satisfied or very satisfied with their jobs, and almost three-quarters reported that morale was 'okay' or 'high' in their homes at the time of the survey. As with so much in child care, however, conditions were perceived to be fluid, and the maintenance of morale was seen to be dependent on how well teams worked together, the level of support available and knowing that good quality work was highly valued. This is not to say that long-standing problems do not remain within the care sector. These include the low status given to the work, lack of resources and low pay. Brannen et al. (2007) found certain differences in the approach taken by different groups of carers – thus foster cares emphasised the tensions between professional caring and warm parenting, while residential workers were frustrated by the nature of the system which they felt did not help children.

The 'somewhat tentative nature of both morale and job satisfaction' (Mainey and Crimmens, 2006: 84) is far from surprising. The research emphasises both the complexity of the task and the problems associated with facilitating long-term behavioural change. Wilson et al. (2004) describe the *a priori* conditions that, together with the characteristics of the child and the way in which the carer responds individually to the child, influence placement outcomes. These include the nature of care planning, the presence of a supportive social worker, the involvement of the birth family and the support of the carer's own family. The need for expertise in addressing emotional and behavioural difficulties, or meeting specific therapeutic needs, has long been recognised (DoH, 1998; Stein, 2009). The task of carers is crucial, but carers themselves continue to emphasise their need for support from other professionals, expert advice and the availability of respite. This should be available if the integrated model of care outlined by *Every Child Matters* is a daily reality – but the most recent research suggests that considerable progress is still to be made if professional expertise is to be delivered in a co-ordinated and effective way (Stein, 2009).

Care: a positive option?

The role of the care system remains uncertain. In some respects the reasons for this seem obvious, for example, when evidence comes to light concerning the dangers experienced by some children within care. Research findings can be alarming, revealing significant amounts of bullying, violence and victimisation. Barter et al. (2004), in their study of peer violence in residential care, found in their interviews with 71 children and young people that verbal and physical attack was considered commonplace. Almost half had been the victim of physical attack, and a similar proportion had experienced attacks on personal property and invasion of personal space.

Part of this uncertainty lies in the question of how children should best be protected and given the best life chances available when there is evidence that families are not able, for whatever reason, to provide acceptable standards of care. The kind of services that should be delivered, and the threshold at which children should enter the care system, continues to be a matter for contention.

In fact, the word 'contention' is perhaps misplaced, because the processes that underpin a child's entry to care, or a family's receipt of support services, are subject to a complex series of informal and formal decision-making that is by its nature hidden from the view of policy makers and researchers. What statistical evidence demonstrates consistently is the variation that results, most obviously in the number and proportions of children entering care in different local authorities, even where areas are similar in levels of socio-economic disadvantage. Research suggests a wide variation in the decision-making process through which children and young people enter the care system (Oliver et al., 2001; Dickens et al., 2007). Research on statistics for 2000–2001 in 24 English local authorities suggests that while differential levels of need explain differences in the numbers of those in the care system, they do not help to predict the numbers who will enter care. Overall, examination of data from authorities with both the highest and lowest start rates said little about the appropriateness of those entering the system: rather 'they were all children who, on the face of it, needed to be looked after, even if only for a short time' (Dickens et al., 2005: 606). Indeed, Dickens et al. make the point that the authorities with low start rates may not be admitting to care some children who *should* be admitted.

Interpretations of such trends must also take account of the economy of the care sector. A limited number of foster carers, an expensive (and increasingly privatised) residential sector, and the cost of specialised treatment services are also key drivers of managerial decision making (Stein 2009). Understanding of the workings of this market continues to be limited, with a serious lack of related research. These issues also, of course, predate New Labour. Beckett (2001: 94), reporting on trends in the use of accommodation in the years 1991–1998, noted that the 'single most striking feature of these statistics is the steady increase in the number of care order applications and of care orders actually made'. He attributed this 'explosion' to the context of social work decision-making, identifying a series of possible explanations including: the perceived ineffectiveness of preventative work resulting in a move back into the use of care proceedings; a general move towards defensive social work practice to avoid scandal; and inadequate resourcing.

At the same time policy over the past decade has emphasised the provision of family support services and the delivery of an integrated style of working. While the case for family support appears self-evident, the evidence for the capacity of this style of working to prevent entry to care is considerably weaker (Forrester, 2007). Again, the difficulties associated with identifying thresholds for intervention, and the point at which care may be the best way of ensuring a child's welfare, remain problematic. Evaluative studies suggest that while family support services are welcomed and may have short-term benefits, they are less effective in addressing complex and chronic family difficulties. Evidence on children returning home from care also indicates that even where this is planned, there is too often a lack of work undertaken with the family while the child is in care. A significant proportion of the cases examined by Farmer, Sturgess and O'Neill (2008) oscillated between home and care, with chronic and serious problems unaddressed. A high proportion of the children and young people concerned said they would have preferred to remain in care.

Conclusions

Policy over the past decade has seen some interesting and useful developments. The evaluation of the Quality Protects initiative concluded that the initiative had succeeded in developing a coherent policy framework and had generated a new understanding of 'quality' in children's services (Stein, 2009).

There are a number of areas in which improvements can be observed, and some children within the care system have benefited from improved resources and the presence of a broader range of professionals within the system. Worryingly, however, these benefits have not been equally distributed and there is a serious gap in the knowledge base about the experiences of some groups. Too often 'care' is the defining characteristic of both policy and research, and the interaction between care, gender, ethnicity and learning or other disabilities is unknown (Brodie et al., 2009; Bostock et al., 2009; Fish et al., 2009). There is still a serious deficit in the provision of services for children who have been abused or have serious mental health needs – and a lack of evidence through which to understand this.

Throughout the past ten years, the body of research knowledge has grown and some neglected areas of the care system have been addressed, most notably in relation to foster care. The gaps which remain are, however, all too visible, and the search for an evidence-based approach to policy has highlighted profound areas of disagreement both within the research community and between researchers and policy makers. The positive consequence is that some important questions are being raised and the complexities associated with applying research messages are ever more apparent. In time this may be considered a positive aspect of New Labour's legacy.

Unexpectedly, as well, there is much evidence to demonstrate the value that is placed on care by the children and young people who are looked after within the care system. Paradoxically, the effects of government policy have often been to obscure the positive and to emphasise the failure of 'the system' to meet externally imposed targets. If high quality care is to be delivered by the individuals who undertake this difficult task, then more building on these positive achievements needs to be undertaken.

References

Barter. C. et al. (2004) *Peer Violence in Children's Residential Care*. Basingstoke: Palgrave Macmillan.

Beckett, C. (2001) Critical Commentary: The Great Care Proceedings Explosion. *British Journal of Social Work*. 31, 493–501.

Berridge, D. (2008) Theory and Explanation in Child Welfare: Education and Looked-After

Children. *Child and Family Social Work*. 12: 1, 1–10.

Berridge, D. et al. (2009) *Looked After and Learning: Evaluation of the Virtual School Head Pilot*. Research Report DCSF-RR144. London: DCSF.

Berridge, D. (2007) *Foster Care: A Research Review*. London: The Stationery Office.

Berridge, D. and Brodie, I. (1996) Residential Child Care in England and Wales: The Enquiries and After. In Hill. M. and Aldgate. J. (Eds.) *Child Welfare Services: Developments in Law, Policy, Practice and Research*. London: Jessica Kingsley.

Berridge, D. and Brodie, I. (1998) *Children's Homes Revisited*. London: Jessica Kingsley.

Berridge, D. et al. (1997) *Hello: Is Anybody Listening? The Education of Young People in Residential Care*. Warwick: University of Warwick.

Berridge, D. et al. (2008) *Educating Difficult Adolescents*. London: Jessica Kingsley.

Borland, M. et al. (1998) *Education and Care Away from Home*. Edinburgh: Scottish Council for Research in Education.

Bostock, L. et el. (2009) *Increasing the Number of Care Leavers in 'Settled, Safe Accommodation'*. C4EO vulnerable children scoping review 3, London: Centre for Excellence and Outcomes in Children and Young People's Services.

Brannen, J. et al. (2007) *Coming to Care: The Work and Family Lives of Workers Caring for Vulnerable Children*. Bristol: Policy Press.

Brennan, K. (2007) *Children in Care White Paper*. Speech 11 July 2007 at Ministry of Justice Children's Act 1989 Consultation Event. Available at http://www.dcsf.gov.uk/speeches/search_detail.cfm?ID=665.

Brodie, I. et al. (2009) *Scoping Review: Improving Educational Outcomes for Looked After Children and Young People*. London: C4EO http://www.c4eo.org.uk

Brodie, I. (2001) *Children's Homes and School Exclusion: Redefining the Problem*. London: Jessica Kingsley.

Cameron, C., McQuail, S. and Petrie, P. (2007) *Implementing the Social Pedagogic Approach for Workforce Training and Education in England: A Preliminary Study*. London: University of London, Thomas Coram Research Institute.

Crimmens, D. and Pitts, J. (2000) *Positive Residential Practice: Learning the Lessons of the 1990s*. Lyme Regis: Russell House Publishing.

Department for Children, Schools and Families (2008) *Children Looked After in England (Including Adoption and Care Leavers) Year Ending 31 March 2008*. London: DCSF.

Department for Children, Schools and Families (2009a) *Outcome Indicators for Children Looked After: Twelve Months to 30 September 2008. England*. London: DCSF.

Department for Children, Schools and Families (2009b) *Improving the Educational Attainment of Children in Care (Looked After Children)*. London: DCSF.

Department for Education and Skills (2005) *The Education of Children in Public Care: Guidance for Governors*. London: DfES.

Department for Education and Skills (2006) *Care Matters: Transforming the Lives of Children and Young People in Care*. London: The Stationery Office.

Department of Health (1995) *Child Protection: Messages from Research*. London: HMSO.

Department of Health (1996) *Focus on Teenagers*. London: HMSO.

Department of Health (1998a) *Children Living Away from Home: Messages from Research*. Chichester: Wiley.

Department of Health (1998b) *Modernising Social Services: Promoting Independence, Improving Protection, Raising Standards*. London: The Stationery Office.

Department of Health (1998c) *A New Approach to Social Services Performance*. London: DoH.

Department of Health (1998d) *The Quality Protects Programme: Transforming Children's Services*. London: DoH.

Department of Health and Department for Education and Employment (2000) *Guidance on the Education of Children and Young People in Public Care*. London: HMSO.

Dickens, J. et al. (2007) Children Starting to be Looked After by Local Authorities in England: An Analysis of Inter-authority Variation and Case Centred Decision Making. *British Journal of Social Work*. 37. 597–617.

Farmer, E., Sturgess, W. and O'Neill, T. (2008) *The Reunification of Looked After Children with their Parents: Patterns, Interventions and Outcomes. Report to the Department for Children, Schools and Families*. Bristol: University of Bristol.

Fish, S. et al. (2009) *Scoping Review: Improving Emotional Health for Looked After Children and Young People*. C4EO vulnerable children scoping review 2, London: Centre for Excellence and Outcomes in Children and Young People's Services.

Fletcher-Campbell, F. (1998) *The Education of Children who are Looked After*. Slough: National Foundation for Educational Research.

Forrester, D. (2007) *Evaluation of Option 2: Report to the Welsh Assembly*. Welsh Assembly Government.

Francis, J. (2000) Investing in Children's Futures: Enhancing the Educational Arrangements of 'Looked After' Children and Young People. *Child and Family Social Work*. 5: 1. 23–33.

Frost, N. and Stein, M. (1986) *The Politics of Child Welfare*. Oxford: Blackwell.

Gallagher. B. et al. (2004) Good Practice in the Education of Children in Residential Care. *British Journal of Social Work*. 34. 1133–60.

Gooch, D. (1996) Home and Away: The Residential Care, Education and Control of Children in Historical and Political Context. *Child and Family Social Work*. 1. 19–32.

Harker, R. et al. (2004) *Taking Care of Education: An Evaluation of the Education of Looked After Children*. London: National Children's Bureau.

Hicks, L. et al. (2007) *Managing Children's Homes: Developing Effective Leadership in Small Organisations*. London: Jessica Kingsley.

Hills, D. and Child, C. (1998) *Leadership in Residential Care: Evaluating Qualification Training*. Chichester: Wiley.

House of Commons Health Committee (1998) *Children Looked After by Local Authorities. Volume 1: Report and Proceedings of the Committee*. London: The Stationery Office.

House of Commons Select Committee (2009) *Looked After Children. Third Report of the Committee*. London: The Stationery Office.

Jackson, S. (1987) *The Education of Children in Care*. Bristol: University of Bristol School for Applied Social Studies.

Jackson, S., Ajayi, S. and Quigley, M. (2005) *Going to University from Care*. London: Institute for Education, Thomas Coram Research Unit.

Little, M. (1996) Whispers in the Library: a Response to Liz Trinder's Article on the State of Social Work Research. *Child and Family Social Work*. 3. 49–56.

Mainey, A. and Crimmens, D. (Eds.) (2006) *Fit for the Future? Residential Childcare in the United Kingdom*. London: National Children's Bureau.

Mainey, A. (2004) *Better Than You Think: Staff Morale, Qualifications and Retention in Residential Child Care*. London: Social Education Trust and the National Children's Bureau.

Morgan, R. (2009) *Life in Children's Homes*. London: Ofsted.

Oliver, C. et al. (2001) *Figures and Facts: Local Authority Variance on Indicators Concerning Child Protection and Children Looked After*. London: Institute of Education.

Pitts, J. and Porteous, D. (2005) Nobody Should Feel Alone: Re-introducing Socially Excluded, Cultural and Ethnic Minority Children and Young People to Educational and Vocational Opportunity. *European Journal of Social Work*. 8. 435–50.

Rowlands, J. and Statham, J. (2009) Numbers of Children Looked After in England: A Historical Analysis. *Child and Family Social Work*. 14. 79–89.

Social Exclusion Unit (1997) *Social Exclusion Unit: Purpose, Work Priorities and Working Methods*. London: HMSO.

Social Exclusion Unit (1998) *Rough Sleeping*. London: SEU.

Social Exclusion Unit (1999a) *Teenage Pregnancy*. London: SEU.

Social Exclusion Unit (1999b) *Bridging the Gap: New Opportunities for 16–18 year-olds not in Education, Employment or Training*. London: SEU.

Social Exclusion Unit (2003) *A Better Education for Children in Care*. London: SEU.

Stein, M. (2009) *Quality Matters in Children's Services: Messages from Research*. London: Jessica Kingsley.

Trinder, L. (1996) Social Work Research: The State of the Art (or Science). *Child and Family Social Work*. 1. 233–42.

Utting, W. (1997) *People Like Us: The Report of the Review of the Safeguards for Children Living away from Home*. London: The Stationery Office.

Walker, P. (2009) Doncaster Child Services Criticised over Brothers who Attached Boys in Quarry. *The Guardian*. 19 January, p 4.

Wilson. K. et al. (2004) *Knowledge Review: Fostering Success: An Exploration of the Research Literature in Foster Care*. London: Social Care Institute for Excellence.

Young, J. (2003) *Social Exclusion*. Available at http://www.malcolmread.co.uk/JockYoung

Part Three: Research Evidence on Services

Looking After Social Work Practice in its Organisational Context: Neglected and Disconcerting Questions

Michael Preston-Shoot

Introduction

The Chairman of the House of Commons Select Committee (2009) Barry Sheerman MP, has expressed considerable wariness of professors who have an answer for everything, even when they cannot draw upon research for evidence. The evidence in this chapter comes from more than twenty years' experience of researching and teaching about the interface between law and social work practice. This followed fourteen years' experience as a social work practitioner and manager, during which the quality and frequency of supervision was highly variable, employer supported continuing professional development erratic, and caseloads often unreasonably high. This author's experience is that, in social work as elsewhere, a study of history often uncovers a litany of lessons unlearned.

In the aftermath of the death of Baby Peter, the focus has fallen most powerfully on the degree to which social workers have been adequately prepared by their qualifying training, and subsequently supported in their practice, for the roles and tasks expected of them by employers. Detailed scrutiny has been given to how intra- and inter-agency arrangements for safeguarding children have been implemented.

The argument in this paper is that, in the feverish policy activity following the death of Baby Peter, crucial aspects of the lived experience of social workers have been overlooked. The chapter begins with evidence of unlawful and/or unethical practice, drawn from case law, inquiry reports and research projects. Awkward questions that emerge from this evidence are then named, particularly those concerned with social work's organisational location, followed by a critique of relevant parts of Laming's progress report (2009a) and evidence to the select committee (2009b). The analysis is further extended with scrutiny of government and regulator responses, and of some research findings about the organisational context for social work practice. The chapter concludes that, without addressing deeply ingrained and underlying fault-lines, lessons will not be learned from the deaths of children known to health and welfare services.

Case law evidence

The detailed scrutiny of social work practice, following the deaths of Victoria Climbié and Baby Peter, could leave an impression of widespread incompetence. However, children and their families should also know that most social workers are conscientious (Re F [2008]) and many departments perform valuable work that demonstrates dedication, skill and care in meeting people's complex needs (Re X (Emergency Protection Orders) [2006]; Re B [2007]; Re D [2008]).

Nonetheless, social workers are also overworked and lacking the resources to practise as they would like (Re F [2008]). A review of child care case law judgements finds some disconcerting evidence of:

- flawed assessment and service provision, as in Pierce v Doncaster MBC [2007] where a looked after young person had been returned to abusive parents with inadequate safeguards in place, and in R (LH and MH) v Lambeth LBC [2006] where a care plan for a disabled child and family was unlawful because needs had not been properly assessed
- failure to follow statutory guidance, as in R (AB and SB) v Nottingham CC [2001] when assessment of children's needs did not accord with framework guidance (DoH, 2000), and in R (G) v Nottingham CC [2008] when a child was removed from parents without lawful authority
- seeking to avoid legal duties, as in Councils with Social Services Responsibilities attempting to limit the support given to asylum seeking young people (R (Behre and Others) v

Hillingdon LBC [2003]) and to those leaving young offender institutions (R (S) v Sutton LBC [2007]), contrary to the *Children Act 1989* children in need provisions and the duties contained in the *Children (Leaving Care) Act 2000*

- expressed attitudes and values, as in Re F [2008] where the Court of Appeal heavily criticised a local authority for failing to respond to a birth father's late application to contest a placement order for adoption and to be considered as his child's carer, and in R (L and Others) v Manchester CC [2002] where a policy of paying kinship carers less than other foster parents was ruled unlawful because it did not meet a child's welfare requirements and was arbitrary and discriminatory
- resource driven decisions, as in R (M) v Hammersmith and Fulham LBC [2008] where responsibility that was passed to housing officials for a young person leaving care showed no evidence of a commitment to ensure that their needs were properly identified and the most appropriate services made available
- poor practice standards, as in R (CD and VD) v Isle of Anglesey CC [2004] where a review of a respite care package failed to meet the requirements of the *Children Act 1989* in ascertaining and giving due consideration to the expressed wishes and needs of a disabled child and her mother.

Similar themes may be identified from investigations of maladministration by the Local Government Ombudsman (LGO, 2002; 2007). Thus, Ombudsman reports expose:

- flawed assessment and service provision, as when local authorities fail to assess the needs of parents as carers, omit to review and update care plans, or neglect to assess disabled children's needs and to make proper arrangements
- failure to follow statutory guidance, resulting in significant neglect and ill-treatment of children whose welfare should have been safeguarded
- negative attitudes and values, for example in failing to respond adequately to complaints
- resource driven decisions, for instance in failing to provide support workers for disabled children on grounds of insufficient resources
- poor practice standards, for example failing to identify alternative forms of respite care

despite recognising that the service being provided was inadequate.

Other child care cases, together with parallel instances in adult services, have been analysed elsewhere (Braye and Preston-Shoot, 2009; Preston-Shoot, 2010). This evidence asks awkward questions of social workers and their employers.

Awkward questions

Owing to the nature of judicial review and Ombudsman proceedings, often little information can be gleaned from their judgements and reports about the stance taken by individual social workers. However, in one case of care proceedings (Bath and North East Somerset Council v A Mother and Others [2008]) where a local authority failed to complete core assessments of the children, evidence did emerge of newly qualified social workers having reported that they felt out of their depth. They were required to take on too much work and to accept excessive responsibility at an early stage, post qualification. They also gave evidence of feeling unsupported within and pressurised by a management culture and style which placed them in vulnerable positions because of staff shortages and neglected to provide them with adequate supervision. In another judicial review, a social worker's needs assessment and proposed care package for a disabled young man was overturned unlawfully by managers (R v Avon DC, ex parte Hazell [1995]). Managers also subsequently overturned the recommendations of a complaints procedure investigation and appear either to have been unaware of, or to have chosen to ignore, policy guidance on choice of residential care.

Further disconcerting evidence about the organisational context in which social workers have to practise comes from rulings on registration from Care Standards Tribunals. In several cases, applications by the General Social Care Council [GSCC] or the Care Council for Wales to have social workers removed from the professional register have been overturned. Whilst the social workers' practice might have amounted to misconduct, or at the very least been inadequate, mitigating factors were found in inadequate supervision, chaotic departments, absence of support, lack of resources to cope with the volume of demands, and lack of effective management action (LA v GSCC [2007]; Forbes v GSCC [2008]; Cordingley v Care Council for Wales [2009]). In the Welsh case, the Care Council was criticised by the Tribunal for a disproportionate response to the social worker's actions following a child protection referral. It had also failed to give reasons for removing the social worker's name from the register and had been unduly influenced by the high profile death of a child.

Qualified and student social workers have also provided this author with accounts of unethical organisational behaviour. One example is of reports for care proceedings, written by social workers, being altered by managers without them being informed and submitted over their signatures. Another is of managers attempting to scapegoat those who highlight local authority failings in safeguarding children. The evidence from practice teachers and social work students (Braye et al., 2007) also highlights how practice is powerfully shaped by organisational procedures rather than by either legal rules or ethical standards. Service users and carers have also given accounts of being excluded from decision-making, misinformed about the legal rules, and feeling that local authority targets and resources are elevated in importance above their needs (Braye and Preston-Shoot, 2006; Preston-Shoot, 2010).

Regrettably it is not just within child care social services where practice does not fulfil the obligations in professional codes of conduct, namely that it should enhance people's well-being, protect their rights and emphasise their human dignity and worth (GSCC, 2002), whilst also demonstrating effective inter-professional relationships and team working (QAA, 2004; GTC et al., 2007). Investigations into services for people with learning disabilities have found significant and distressing service failures, and unremedied injustice, causing suffering and sometimes death (LGO and PHSO, 2009). Complaints have not been handled satisfactorily, standards of care have been unacceptable, and legal rules on disability equality, mental capacity and human rights have been breached. People's needs have not been assessed, managers and inspectors have failed to monitor performance adequately, learning disabled people have been stereotyped and ignored, and communication between the NHS and social services has been poor (LGO, 2008; LGO and PHSO, 2009; Michael, 2008).

Since the practice of health and welfare professionals should be underpinned by core values of care, safeguarding, and counteracting discrimination, how can these shortcomings be explained and prevented? Why has it become necessary, in nursing as well as social care, to rediscover and foreground dignity and respect?

Significantly, neither is the research evidence about unlawful and unethical practice restricted to the United Kingdom. Research from Australia (Lonne et al., 2004; McAuliffe and Sudbery, 2005), the United States (Strom-Gottfried, 2000; 2003) and Europe (Musil et al., 2004; Papadaki and Papadaki, 2008) reports disturbing evidence about the moral probity of service providers, and the erosion of ethical and effective practice. With a familiar ring for UK practitioners and researchers, it too highlights concerns over heavy workloads, lack of continuing professional development, absence of management support and supervision, and the impact of procedural monitoring and resource constraints.

In the Isle of Anglesey case quoted earlier, the judge suggested that a virus had entered and corrupted the council's decision-making system. Just what are the viruses that have entered health and welfare services, and especially child care services? To what degree are these viruses acknowledged by policy-makers?

Neglected practice questions

In his progress report, Laming (2009a) refers to the vital importance of professionals understanding the legal framework and suggests that the law on information sharing and inter-agency collaboration for child protection is not well understood. He demands the robust and consistent implementation of policies, procedures and legislation designed to safeguard children. Subsequently (Laming, 2009b), he has also stated that front line practitioners are not well equipped in relation to the legislative base. A similar critique is offered by Ofsted (2009) in its analysis of lessons to be derived from serious case reviews. It highlights lack of compliance with statutory requirements and guidance, such as care planning, as one contributory factor behind some child deaths and serious incidents. Serious case reviews also found that disabled children did not always receive an assessment of needs, to which they were entitled, and that legislation and regulations had not been followed when assessing or placing children with foster carers.

Recommendations to foreground the legal framework as social work's mandate have a long history in child protection inquiries (Blom-Cooper, 1985). Law teaching and assessment on social work education programmes has been a prescribed component of the curriculum for approaching twenty years. Student satisfaction with law teaching on social work programmes appears to be increasing (Braye and Preston-Shoot, 2009). However, the inclusion of legal literacy and skilled implementation of legal knowledge remains under-developed in the practice curriculum. On occasion this aspect of assessment of social work students is also problematic because practice assessors prioritise agency procedures which may not be an accurate interpretation and/or implementation of the legal rules. Indeed, the conflation of legal rules with agency procedures permeates official pronouncements also. The Ofsted analysis of serious case reviews (2009) argues that the absence or adequacy of procedures is seldom the issue but rather staff ignorance of, or failure to follow them. It is unclear whether what is meant by procedures are the requirements in statute and statutory guidance or local agency interpretations of them. This process of interpretation or translation remains unacknowledged and unexplored.

Thus, Laming (2009a) urges social workers to be confident and decisive in using the full range of legal options and to have a thorough knowledge and understanding of the legal framework. There is, however, no detailed analysis of, or response to the case law and Ombudsman evidence reported in this chapter, or to research findings about how managers give priority to their own organisational procedures at the expense of legal rules (Braye et al., 2007). How power is constructed and exercised in hierarchical and bureaucratic organisations is similarly neglected, with no analysis of how social workers might experience the processes or outcomes of challenging the legality, ethics and evidence-based content of their managers' decision-making.

Moreover, nowhere does Laming refer to whistle blowing and specifically to what has happened to social workers when they have highlighted serious concerns about agency practice on safeguarding. There is no detailed exploration of how the *Public Interest Disclosure*

Act 1998 has failed to provide adequate protection for professionals who act in accordance with their code of conduct (GSCC, 2002) and bring attention to resource and operational difficulties. Similarly, although Laming appears to recognise the importance of creating environments where practitioners may share feelings and anxieties without being labelled as inadequate, his focus here is on the work itself and not the organisation's attitude towards the legal rules, ethics and the profession's knowledge-base. There is no analysis of what may deter social workers from highlighting when employers are jeopardising their ability to comply with the code's requirements.

There is equally no analysis of the law-in-between (Preston-Shoot, 2011) the process by which the law-in-theory, that legislated by Parliament and amplified in central government guidance, is translated into local authority procedures. Neither is there any analysis of the speed with which the legal framework changes and the failure accordingly to highlight legal literacy in the continuing professional development available to social work practitioners and managers. Finally, the competence of the regulators, now the Care Quality Commission and Ofsted, in respect of their knowledge of the legal rules and their audit oversight of this process of translation, has escaped question.

Laming (2009a) does recognise that social workers face demanding tasks, which must be accommodated in training, caseloads and supervision. He criticises the low quality of training and support, and notes the impact of high workloads on effective practice. He appears to recognise the danger to reflective social work practice presented by over-emphasis on targets, and to appreciate the need for a supportive learning environment that validates continuous development of professional judgement and skills. The Ofsted report on learning lessons (2009) also recognises the impact of a lack of staff training and of insufficient staff resources with appropriate expertise, for instance on services for looked after children. It also comments that findings recur through time across serious case reviews but does not venture any analysis as to why this might be so.

However, the prevailing assumption is that social workers practise in benign organisational environments that are ethically and legally literate. The evidence presented in this chapter casts some doubt on the wisdom of neglecting this organisational context. Nor does Laming appear to stand back and ask the penetrating, searching question; namely, given that systematic analyses of serious case reviews over two decades point to the same failings (DHSS, 1982; Reder et al., 1993; Sinclair and Bullock, 2002; Ofsted, 2009), why is national and local policy yet to provide consistently manageable case loads; reflective and challenging supervision; and learning and containing environments where the effect of families on practitioners and managers can be explored? The analysis offered by Laming and by Ofsted is curiously ahistorical. Laming calls for renewed energy to implement the structures ushered in by his earlier report (Laming, 2003) and the *Children Act 2004*, without a thorough scrutiny of long-standing barriers to recognised good practice, which now should include the additional challenges to inter-departmental and inter-agency co-operation occasioned by the separation of social work and social care services for children and for adults.

Laming (2009a; b) advises that managers of locality services must recognise the importance of early intervention, of supporting children as soon as they are recognised as being in need. He comments that financially it is in everyone's interests to intervene early and to take preventative work seriously. He criticises the use of thresholds, especially when inconsistent and/or high, to limit access to services, noting that it undermines the intention of section 17 (*Children Act 1989*). However, nowhere is there any analysis of how resource constraints distort recognition of need and limit options when the needs of children in need must be balanced against those of children requiring protection. Nowhere is there any analysis of why the difficulties with use of section 17 persist, despite findings from research evidence across the decades (Colton et al., 1995; Reder and Duncan, 2004; Morris, 2005).

Finally, Laming (2009a) comments approvingly on giving the employers' section of the code of practice (GSCC, 2002) statutory force. Whilst this may be a welcome development, nowhere does he reflect on the employment status of social workers and the impact this may have on how they perceive their obligations towards the code vis-à-vis their employers. Nor does he explore the effectiveness of practice and ethical codes in ensuring ethical, lawful and evidence-informed or knowledge-driven practice, despite research-based reservations in this respect (Preston-Shoot, 2010).

Parliamentary scrutiny and missing answers

The report of the House of Commons Children, Schools and Families Committee (2009) similarly fails to appreciate the historical and repetitive cycle of analyses of lessons from child protection failures. The report explores the quality of social work education, recruitment and retention questions, and the organisational context in which social workers practise. It proposes reforms to social work education, improvements to practitioners' working conditions, and changes to workforce modelling and planning. The Committee reports evidence received to the effect that requiring more practice placements from local authorities may be impractical when councils are struggling to meet their statutory commitments (para. 99). However, it does not in its analysis or recommendations address the evidence of unlawful decision-making presented in this chapter, nor does it pause reflectively before recommending that all social work students should have a placement in a statutory social work agency (paragraph 110). The committee rightly questions whether all placements are of good quality (para. 112). It also reports evidence from witnesses that lack of knowledge results in unlawful practice. However, it does not question the organisational location of statutory social work or what kind of learning student social workers may experience when placed in statutory organisations that are failing to implement the legal rules appropriately.

The committee stresses the importance of employers being confident in their role as learning communities and enabling social workers to maintain a 'state of the art' understanding. It disapproves of newly qualified social workers being given too much responsibility too soon (para. 123) and of inconsistent and poor quality supervision (para. 125). It warns that local authorities already under resource pressures may struggle to accommodate newly qualified social worker requirements within overall caseloads and time available for supervision (para. 127). It reports evidence that social workers may find it hard to implement what they know to be good practice because of the employer-employee relationship and the tendency of managers and practice assessors to emphasise agency procedures. However, the committee stops short of questioning these deep-seated organisational arrangements and practices. There is no examination of whether social work's location in local authorities is helpful any longer. The analysis is also ahistorical in that the committee conveys no sense of analysing familiar themes or repeating routine recommendations. Yet, reviews of child protection inquiries (for instance, Reder et al., 1993) and research on the impact of professional education (Karban and Frost, 1998) highlight the challenges that newly qualified practitioners have faced in introducing their knowledge and learning into individual and agency procedures.

The committee does recognise that resource strapped local authorities will find it difficult to protect social work and that a workforce stretched beyond its capacity will need investment. It does not, in the context of the current economic climate, challenge government in relation to past and future investment in social work practice.

To date central government has shown little taste for exploring and answering these neglected but disconcerting questions. The *Apprenticeships, Skills, Children and Learning Act (2009)* places Children's Trusts on a statutory footing, extends the multi-agency duty to cooperate on safeguarding to schools, requires the publication and monitoring of a children and young people's plan, and clarifies every Trust's relationship with its Local Safeguarding Children Board. It allows the setting of new statutory targets for safeguarding the well-being of young people. As yet, however, there are no legislative proposals to address the processes uncovered by judicial reviews and Ombudsman reports. Employers will still not be held accountable in law for their failure to adhere to the code of practice (GSCC, 2002).

The initial government response (DCSF, 2009) to Laming's progress report (2009a) indicates the intention to require more rigorous inspection of services, to improve support for newly qualified social workers, to tackle perceived shortcomings in social work education, and to expect Children's Trusts to improve staffing and supervision and to lead a culture change in front line services to protect children. The response does not address questions of resource investment, how councils understand and construct their response to legal mandates, and

how the messages from whistle blowers are heard. The response appears not to appreciate that Laming made recommendations relating to social worker caseloads, and managers being clear with practitioners about what action was required in allocated cases, in his earlier inquiry into the death of Victoria Climbié (2003). The recommendations have been repeated without analysing the reasons for non-implementation hitherto. Interestingly, there is a parallel to this missing reflexivity in Ofsted's comment (2009) that more evidence is needed of whether recommendations from serious case reviews, when implemented, have actually improved the quality of child protection services.

The Social Work Taskforce (2009a; b) recognises that the forced timing of performance indicators leads to perverse incentives to make hasty and risky decisions, and can mean poor quality assessments. It goes further by arguing that the system for managing social work performance is not addressing quality and by stressing the crucial importance of high quality supervision. It has also expressed concern about the volume of cases being carried by practitioners and about how the demands of information collation, recording and sharing reduce the amount of time that social workers spend with children and their families. Laming (2009a) also recognises the danger to reflective social work practice created by the impact of excessive workloads and over-emphasis on targets. The taskforce (2009a) criticises employers for holding unrealistic expectations, especially of newly qualified social workers, and recommends without apparent amazement that they should engage with practitioners about the reality of front line practice. However, these features of social work practice are long-standing. Moreover, the taskforce has yet to recognise, let alone address, the disconcerting evidence that emerges through judicial reviews and Ombudsman and Ofsted reports. Its reports too are ahistorical. There is no analysis of why it should be necessary to recommend (again) that practitioners should have the resources and conditions needed to practise effectively.

Discovering viruses

Given the evidence presented in this chapter, one question in need of an answer is why the General Social Care Council (2008) has had so few notifications of breaches of section 1 of its code, namely that registrants should promote service user rights and protect their interests, or of section 4, which relates to risk assessment. Reports of misconduct have largely revolved around inappropriate relationships and poor practice concerned with record keeping, breaches of confidentiality and failure to follow procedures.

The Council (GSCC, 2009) has provided a partial response in noting that social worker whistle blowing goes unheard and that employers fail to act when concerns about, or barriers to, ethical and lawful practice are reported. In its own survey, half of all respondents had no confidence in employers being prepared to act in response to concerns raised. Although the code (GSCC, 2002) requires social workers to challenge and report dangerous, abusive and discriminatory practice, respondents feared victimisation and a negative impact on their careers if they did so. They have good reason to. Preston-Shoot and Kline (2009) in written evidence to the House of Commons Select Committee, note the fate of key social work whistle blowers, including in the London Borough of Haringey prior to the death of Baby Peter. Nowhere yet have the barriers to speaking out, a professional and codified obligation on social workers, been addressed. There are currently no proposals to make the code an express term of a social worker's contract of employment (Preston-Shoot and Kline, 2009). It remains unclear why the taskforce recommendation (2009a) that employers should guarantee standards for support and supervision, to make good practice possible, has not been prioritised previously by organisations charged with inspecting services, and how it will enable front line staff to insist on the resources necessary to meet their professional obligations.

As yet, official reviews of, and responses to, 'deep-dive' inquiries into social work practice have not addressed the limitations within the code of practice (GSCC, 2002) which registered social workers must uphold. These include an embedded assumption that registered practitioners are autonomous agents, able to act independently of their organisational context (Lonne et al., 2004). In hierarchical organisations, personal judgement may prove little match against institutional routines and decision-making (Preston-Shoot and Kline, 2009), where social workers follow institutional patterns of conduct to avoid practice dilemmas (Musil et

al., 2004), even if registered practitioners appreciate that their ultimate accountability is to the code rather than their employer (Kline, 2009).

The code does not contain clear statements about the type of unlawful practice reported in this chapter. Moreover, its clauses are open to interpretation (Preston-Shoot, 2010), with the result that practice standards are unclear. Finally, management support may be variable, especially when managers are part of problematic organisational contexts. Research evidence suggests that organisations play down ethical breaches, are not always responsive to concerns about practice standards, and are ineffective in tackling issues concerned with resource allocation (Lonne et al., 2004; McAuliffe and Sudbery, 2005). It further pinpoints bullying (Collins, 2001; Gillen, 2008), for example in relation to changing recommendations arising from assessments or compromising assessment quality in order to meet target-driven timescales.

Significantly, the erosion of lawful and ethical practice extends beyond social work. Investigations in health care have also uncovered bullying, harassment and abuse of staff by managers. They have found that practitioners have few avenues to raise concerns about standards of care, that cultures do not openly welcome such expressions of unease, and that inaction may be the outcome (Healthcare Commission, 2009a; b). Research into medical practice has also found a reluctance to report unethical and/or unlawful behaviour. In one study, for example, 40 per cent of respondents had engaged in unethical or unlawful behaviour, when instructed to do so by their superiors, whilst nearly two-thirds had witnessed such behaviour but felt too uncomfortable to challenge or report it (Feudtner et al., 1994). As for social workers, an overdue reform may be to provide a contractual right for practitioners to raise concerns safely with a regulator, such as the Care Quality Commission or Ofsted.

How might these phenomena be understood? The focus on the content of social work education, and on the support at long last proposed for newly qualified social workers, by the select committee (House of Commons, 2009) and Laming (2009a) overlooks one crucial point, namely that half of qualifying programmes are delivered in practice settings and that these locations where students and newly qualified practitioners develop their competence for practice have been criticised in judicial reviews and Ombudsman reports. Health care and medical education have similar structures. It is here that students are socialised into their profession and often assume an identity similar to that of their mentors (Hudson, 2002). If the authority exercised by the workplace is incompatible with codified professional and legal requirements, students and qualified practitioners may feel too insecure in their knowledge and employment position to resist bureaucratic demands. Indeed, research has found that mentors, in the shape of practice assessors, supervisors and managers, do foreground agency requirements and encourage students and newly qualified practitioners implicitly or explicitly to depart from the formal curriculum that they have learned. In so doing they are essentially distorting professional formation (Braye et al., 2007; Green, 2009).

Horwath (2000) describes this as collusion between managers and practitioners to accept organisational misuse of power. This can be underpinned by threats of disciplinary measures and exclusion, adding to the pressure to comply with the managerial line and undermining social workers' human agency and moral responsibility (Green, 2009). Institutional patterns of conduct and organisational compliance, rather than professional norms, come to dominate responses to cases and to distance practitioners from people's needs (Musil et al., 2004, McAuliffe and Sudbery, 2005; Papadaki and Papadaki, 2008). Put another way, what is brought to the fore is a hidden curriculum of organisational policies, resource allocation procedures and evaluative activities which undermine social work's knowledge base and formal curriculum. The phenomenon is widely recognised in medical education (for example, Roff and Preece, 2004; Goldie et al., 2004) but largely unrecognised in social work. In this context, recommendations that there should be a prescribed curriculum and at least one placement in a statutory social work setting (House of Commons, 2009; Social Work Task Force, 2009a) entirely miss the point. Just what are students and newly qualified practitioners learning in settings where practitioners are overworked, stressed and required to take on situations beyond their level of competence, where the work has to fit into performance indicators and time limits, and where legal rules and ethical considerations are sidelined in order that demands on available resources can be managed?

If one concern about organisational location is the impact on professional formation, another is the impact on how case scenarios are perceived. Horwath (2007) describes this as the missing child and family assessment domain, suggesting that the organisational situation is overlooked even though inquiries routinely highlight the impact of anxiety, workplace culture and resources on perceptions of role and cases. Organisational structures and rules, both overt and covert, influence behaviour, adjust vision, and frame beliefs about cases (Reder et al., 1993). Richards (2000) offers an adult services example, demonstrating what can happen to assessment of older people's needs when that process is dominated by agency agendas. Similarly, Noble and Irwin (2009) caution that supervision is not immune to the retreat to residual welfare and managerialism. In other words, it is a fertile ground for an uncritical adoption of agency procedures where a worker's performance is evaluated in organisational terms and a focus on organisational functioning is seen as guaranteeing a place in the workplace. The overall concern here is that narrowing definitions of need become institutionalised in organisational arrangements which become difficult to dislodge. Professional standards are compromised, whilst management expectations circumscribe professional autonomy, erode the capacity to retain an ethical orientation and express contrary opinions, and exert a strong pressure to maintain silence (Marsh and Triseliotis, 1996; Hunt, 1998; Banks and Williams, 2005; Beckett et al., 2007; Preston-Shoot, 2010). Thus far, insufficient attention has been paid to practitioners' emotional and practical lived experience of social work in framing future policy regarding safeguarding children. In some settings, legal literacy, ethical codes and professional knowledge appear to have held and to hold little validity. Practice is bureaucracy led.

Conclusion

New Labour's modernisation agenda (DoH, 1998) for health and social care was founded in part on a critique that services had been reflective of institutional rather than individual needs. That critique remains pertinent across child and family social services. The argument in this chapter can finally be summarised quite succinctly. It is welcome once again to hear acknowledgement that high caseloads, aspects of performance and information management systems, and poor supervision will inevitably mean that practitioners cannot practise effectively. That conclusion is nothing new. However, for as long as serious case failures are seen as temporary departures from standards, as the responsibility of individuals and singleton agencies or groups of agencies locally, whole system change will remain elusive. The focus on selection for and the content of social work education, and on support for newly qualified practitioners, whilst important, will not significantly challenge features that recur in the findings of judicial reviews, Ombudsman reports and serious case reviews. Equally, it is unclear how increased or improved inspection alone will significantly impact upon service quality and on the ability of managers and practitioners to identify cases of serious concern.

This chapter suggests that social work's organisational location should be rethought. A more critical gaze should be cast over the technical and managerial culture in which social work has become embedded and the nature of the compromises asked of professional social workers. It should ask how safe the environment is for the highest standard of social work and child protection practice. This gaze will alight upon legal and ethical literacy, and on the interactions between organisations and their practitioners. It is a gaze that will question the coherence of public policy, for instance the balance between supporting families and intervening to protect children, and the commitment of sufficient resources to counter the subversion of professional judgement about need and thus ensure that every child really matters.

Case Law References

Bath and North East Somerset Council v A Mother and Others [2008] EWHC B10 (Fam)

Cordingley v Care Council for Wales [2009] UKFTT 213 (HESC)

Forbes v GSCC [2008] CST 1267. SW

LA v GSCC [2007] CST 985. SW

Pierce v Doncaster MBC [2007] The Times, 27 December

R (AB and SB) v Nottingham CC [2001] 4 CCLR 295

R (Behre and Others) v Hillingdon LBC [2003] The Times, 22 September

R (CD and VD) v Isle of Anglesey CC [2004] 7 CCLR 589

R (G) v Nottingham CC [2008] 11 CCLR 273

R (L and Others) v Manchester CC [2002] 1 FLR 43

R (LH and MH) v Lambeth LBC [2006] 9 CCLR 622

R (M) v Hammersmith and Fulham LBC [2008] UKHL 14

R (S) v Sutton LBC [2007] EWCA Civ 790

Re F [2008] EWCA Civ 439

Re X (Emergency Protection Orders) [2006] 2 FLR 701

Re B [2007] 1 FLR 482

Re D [2008] EWHC 1306 (Fam)

R v Avon DC, ex parte Hazell [1995] Family Law 66

References

Banks, S. and Williams, R. (2005) Accounting for Ethical Difficulties in Social Welfare Work: Issues, Problems and Dilemmas. *British Journal of Social Work*, 35: 7, 1005–22.

Beckett, C., McKeigue, B. and Taylor, H. (2007) Coming to Conclusions: Social Workers' Perceptions of the Decision-Making Process in Care Proceedings. *Child and Family Social Work*, 12, 54–63.

Blom-Cooper, L. (1985) *A Child in Trust: The Report of The Panel of Inquiry Into the Circumstances Surrounding the Death of Jasmine Beckford*. London Borough of Brent.

Braye, S. and Preston-Shoot, M. (2006) *Teaching, Learning and Assessment of Law in Social Work Education: Resource Guide*. London: Social Care Institute for Excellence.

Braye, S. and Preston-Shoot, M. (2009) *Practising Social Work Law*. 3rd edn. Basingstoke: Palgrave Macmillan.

Braye, S., Preston-Shoot, M. and Thorpe, A. (2007) Beyond The Classroom: Learning Social Work Law in Practice. *Journal of Social Work*, 7: 3, 322–40.

Collins, S. (2001) Bullying in Social Work Organisations. *Practice*, 13: 3, 29–44.

Colton, M., Drury, C. and Williams, M. (1995) Children in Need: Definition, Identification and Support. *British Journal of Social Work*, 25: 6, 711–28.

DCSF (2009) *The Protection of Children in England: Action Plan. The Government's Response to Lord Laming*. London: The Stationery Office.

DoH (1998) *Modernising Social Services*. London: The Stationery Office.

DoH (2000) *Framework for the Assessment of Children in Need and Their Families*. London: HMSO.

DHSS (1982) *Child Abuse: A Study of Inquiry Reports, 1973–1981*. London: HMSO.

Feudtner, C., Christakis, D. and Christakis, N. (1994) Do Clinical Clerks Suffer Ethical Erosion? Students' Perceptions of Their Ethical Environment and Personal Development. *Academic Medicine*, 69, 670–9.

Gillen, S (2008) Who's Making the Decisions? *Community Care*, 20 November, 20–21.

Goldie, J. et al. (2004) The Impact of a Modern Medical Curriculum on Students' Proposed Behaviour on Meeting Ethical Dilemmas. *Medical Education*, 38: 9, 942–9.

Green, J. (2009) The Deformation of Professional Formation: Managerial Targets and the Undermining of Professional Judgement. *Ethics and Social Welfare*, 3: 2, 115–30.

GSCC (2002) *Codes of Practice for Social Care Workers and Employers*. London: GSCC.

GSCC (2008) *Raising Standards: Social Work Conduct in England 2003–08*. London: GSCC.

GSCC (2009) *Social Worker Whistle Blowing Goes Unheard*. Media Release, 9 September.

GTC, GSCC and NMC (2007) *Values for Integrated Working with Children and Young People*. London: GTC.

Healthcare Commission (2009a) *National NHS Staff Survey 2008*. London: Healthcare Commission.

Healthcare Commission (2009b) *Investigation into Mid Staffordshire NHS Foundation Trust*. London: Commission for Healthcare Audit and Inspection, Healthcare Commission.

Horwath, J. (2000) Child Care with Gloves on: Protecting Children and Young People in Residential Care. *British Journal of Social Work*, 30: 2, 179–91.

Horwath, J. (2007) The Missing Assessment Domain: Personal, Professional and Organisational Factors Influencing Professional Judgements when Identifying and Referring Child Neglect. *British Journal of Social Work*, 37: 8, 1285–303.

House of Commons Children, Schools and Families Committee (2009) *Training of Children and Families Social Workers. Seventh Report of Session 2008–09*. London: The Stationery Office.

Hudson, B. (2002) Interprofessionality in Health and Social Care: The Achilles' Heel of Partnership? *Journal of Interprofessional Care*, 16: 1, 7–17.

Hunt, G. (Ed.) (1998) *Whistleblowing in the Social Services. Public Accountability and Professional Practice*. London: Arnold.

Karban, K. and Frost, N. (1998) Training for Residential Care: Assessing the Impact of the Residential Child Care Initiative. *Social Work Education*, 17: 3, 287–300.

Kline, R. (2009) *What If? Social Care Professionals and the Duty of Care. A Practical Guide to Staff Duties and Rights*. Wakefield: Association of Professionals in Education and Children's Trusts.

Laming, H. (2003) *The Victoria Climbié Inquiry: Report of an Inquiry by Lord Laming*. London: HMSO.

Laming, H. (2009a) *The Protection of Children in England: A Progress Report*. London: HMSO.

Laming, H. (2009b) *The Protection of Children in England: Lord Laming's Progress Report*. Evidence to The Children, Schools and Families Committee, House of Commons. London: The United Kingdom Parliament.

LGO (2002) *Report Summaries: Social Services*. London: Local Government Ombudsman.

LGO (2007) *Report Summaries: Social Services*. London: Local Government Ombudsman.

LGO (2008) *Injustice in Residential Care: A Joint Report by the Local Government Ombudsman and the Health Service Ombudsman for England. Investigations into Complaints Against Buckinghamshire County Council and Oxfordshire and Buckinghamshire Mental Health Partnership*. London: HMSO.

LGO and PHSO (2009) *Six Lives: The Provision of Public Services to People with Learning Disability*. London: The Stationery Office.

Lonne, B., Mcdonald, C. and Fox, T. (2004) Ethical Practice in the Contemporary Human Services. *Journal of Social Work*, 4: 3, 345–67.

Marsh, P. and Triseliotis, J. (1996) *Ready to Practise? Social Workers and Probation Officers: Their Training and First Year in Work*. Aldershot: Avebury.

McAuliffe, D. and Sudbery, J. (2005) Who Do I Tell? Support and Consultation in Cases of Ethical Conflict. *Journal of Social Work*, 5: 1, 21–43.

Michael, J. (2008) *Healthcare for All. Report of the Independent Inquiry into Access to Healthcare for People with Learning Disabilities*. London: The Stationery Office.

Morris, K. (2005) From 'Children in Need' to 'Children at Risk': The Changing Policy

Context for Prevention and Participation. *Practice*, 17: 2, 67–77.

Musil, L. et al. (2004) Do Social Workers Avoid the Dilemmas of Work with Clients? *European Journal of Social Work*, 7: 3, 305–19.

Noble, C. and Irwin, J. (2009) Social Work Supervision: an Exploration of the Current Challenges in a Rapidly Changing Social, Economic and Political Environment. *Journal of Social Work*, 9: 3, 345–58.

Ofsted (2009) *Learning Lessons from Serious Case Reviews: Year 2*. Manchester: Ofsted.

Papadaki, E. and Papadaki, V. (2008) Ethically Difficult Situations Related to Organisational Conditions: Social Workers' Experiences in Crete, Greece. *Journal of Social Work*, 8: 2, 163–80.

Preston-Shoot, M. (2010) On the Evidence for Viruses in Social Work Systems: Law, Ethics and Practice. *European Journal of Social Work*, (In Press).

Preston-Shoot, M. (2011) On Administrative Evil-Doing within Social Work Policy and Services: Law, Ethics and Practice. *European Journal of Social Work*, (In Press).

Preston-Shoot, M. and Kline, R. (2009) *Memorandum of Written Evidence in House of Commons Children, Schools and Families Committee Training of Children and Families Social Workers. Seventh Report of Session 2008–09.* Volume II. London: The Stationery Office.

QAA (2004) *A Statement of Common Purpose for Subject Benchmarks for the Health and Social Care Professions*. Gloucester: The Quality Assurance Agency for Higher Education.

Reder, P. and Duncan, S. (2004) Making the Most of the Victoria Climbié Inquiry Report. *Child Abuse Review*, 13, 95–114.

Reder, P., Duncan, S. and Gray, M. (1993) *Beyond Blame. Child Abuse Tragedies Revisited*. London: Routledge.

Richards, S. (2000) Bridging the Divide: Elders and the Assessment Process. *British Journal of Social Work*, 30: 1, 37–49.

Roff, S. and Preece, P. (2004) Helping Medical Students to Find Their Moral Compasses: Ethics Teaching for Second and Third Year Undergraduates. *Journal of Medical Ethics*, 30, 487–9.

Sheerman, B. (2009) Question 37. in *The Protection of Children in England: Lord Laming's Progress Report*. Evidence to the Children, Schools and Families Committee, House of Commons. London: The United Kingdom Parliament.

Sinclair, R. and Bullock, R. (2002) *Learning from Past Experience: A Review of Serious Case Reviews*. London: DoH.

Social Work Taskforce (2009a) *Building a Safe, Confident Future. The Final Report of the Social Work Task Force*. London: DCSF.

Social Work Taskforce (2009b) *First Report of the Social Work Taskforce*. London: DCSF.

Strom-Gottfried, K. (2000) Ensuring Ethical Practice: an Examination of NASW Code Violations, 1986–1997. *Social Work*, 45: 3, 251–61.

Strom-Gottfried, K. (2003) Understanding Adjudication: Origins, Targets and Outcomes of Ethical Complaints. *Social Work*, 48: 1, 85–94.

CHAPTER 10

Managerialism – At the Tipping Point?

Alex Chard and Patrick Ayre

Managerialism has now become so rampant, so invasive in its practices, so convinced of its pre-eminence, so all-consuming in its lust for attention, that it fills the days and nights of practitioners and managers alike in organisa-tions around the world with its unending requirements for measurement, assessment, evaluation, report-writing and presentation. Yet its invasion has been so drawn-out, and its approach so stealthy, that we have scarcely noticed how profoundly it has altered the organisational landscape.

Theodore Taptikilis, 2008

Introduction

This chapter argues that managerialism has failed as a guiding principle for the management of children's services, and outlines and explores alternative strategies. As we do so, we feel it important to distinguish between management, which can take many forms, and managerialism, which represents a specific, ideologically driven approach within the general field of management. As Dillow (2007: 12) suggests 'management is a technique, the skill of organising resources effectively, which may be done well or badly. Managerialism is an ideology, the belief that government should behave like company managers and has the skill to do so.'

Understanding managerialism

Dixon et al. (1998) described managerialism as 'the private sector "solution" to the public sector "problem"', concerning itself particularly with efficiency and the application of management methods such as strategic planning, quality assurance, performance management and risk management. Dillow (2007: 11) argues that managerialism has been a defining feature of New Labour, describing it as 'an ideology which tries to eliminate political debate about the rival merits of competing ideals. In its stead, managerialism relies on a central elite which believes that it, and it alone, has the skill and know-how to devise policies to cope with the inexorable forces of economic change'.

The terms managerialism and *New Public*

Management (NPM) are closely associated and often used interchangeably. Hood (1991) has suggested that NPM arose from the fusion of two strands of change within the management of public services. The first of these was an increased interest in *New Institutional Economics*, which emphasises such factors as user choice, market contestability and management incentives. The second was the adoption of private sector business methods. Key features of NPM include attention to outputs and performance rather than inputs; the representation of organisations as chains of low-trust relationships; the separation of the roles of purchaser and provider, and client and contractor; the breaking down of large scale organisations; and the decentralisation of budgetary and personal authority (Clarke, Gerwitz and McLaughlin, 2000).

Pollitt (1993) traces the roots of managerialism to a single paper, *The Principles of Scientific Management* by Frederick Taylor (1911: 14–15) which is now nearly a century old. He outlines the key elements of 'Taylorism', noting that:

First there is the assertion that management can be a 'true science' (with all the connotations of discovering precise, impersonal laws). Second, a parallel claim is made for universality of application – all human activities are subject to the laws thus discovered. Both these claims, but perhaps especially the second one can still be heard today – anything can, and should, be managed.

He regards the managerialist approaches to public services introduced by Margaret Thatcher in the UK and by Ronald Reagan in the US as having their origins in Taylor's principles and describes them as 'neo-Taylorism'.

Dixon et al. (1998: 164) have suggested that a managerialist view now pervades public administration in Australia, New-Zealand, the UK, Canada and the USA, though, as Langan (2000: 158–9) notes, the ideological impetus for New Public Management was primarily American, arising from the work of Osborne and Gaebler. The cover of their influential 1993 volume *Reinventing Government* proclaims: 'To cut taxes and improve services at the same time may seem too good to be true. Yet now we have in our hands a way to make it come true' (Osborne and Gaebler, 1993). All that was required was that politicians of all parties and persuasions should read the book and follow its prescriptions.

In the UK, the Thatcher administration (May 1979–November 1990) laid the foundations for the managerialist approach to the management of public services which has been adopted by all subsequent governments. The Thatcher years saw the creation of the Audit Commission which scrutinises local government and the re-definition of the role of the National Audit Office which focuses on government departments. Both held mandates 'stressing the "three Es" of economy, efficiency and effectiveness' (Pollitt et al., 1999: 52). Pollitt notes that during this period 'the public services were frequently chastised for inefficiency and self-interest while a series of business people and consultants were brought into central government in an attempt to transfer their allegedly superior management skills, techniques, and insights to the civil service'. Charting the shaping of what he calls the 'social work business', Harris (2003) notes that the "community care reforms instituted in the late 1980s and early 1990s, served as the proving ground for many of the developments that spread subsequently to other areas.' Harris identifies the *Children Act 1989* and the *NHS and Community Care Act 1990* as formative legislation introduced by the Conservatives which remain at the root of managerialism within social work.

In the 1980s and 1990s, managerialist principles began to pervade all aspects of public services and by September 1999, an editorial in the Observer was able to state confidently that 'in economic and social policy, the Government accepts wholeheartedly the so-called "Washington consensus" that deregulation, privatisation, hire-and-fire labour markets, balanced budgets and low taxes are not only the key to policy success but unopposable' (Sim, 2000: 168).

Managerialism and the public sector

Managerialism suggests that public sector services should be run as quasi-businesses but this ignores fundamental differences between public and private sector undertakings. It is of the essence of private sector businesses that they sell goods or services in order to make a profit but public services are not, for the most part, driven in the same way by the profit motive, being funded mainly through taxation. The social accountability of public services, and the structural and political context within which they operate, can be contrasted with the independent, entrepreneurial environment typical of private business, which answer primarily to the shareholders who own them (Kolthof et al., 2007).

Within business, selling more goods or services increases the income of the organisation but in the majority of public services, increased service supply simply increases costs. As a result, managers within public services will typically seek to limit demand, whereas businesses will seek to increase it. Within a fixed budget, the only way in which public services can be expanded is through greater efficiency. Characterising the recipients of public services as consumers fails to take account of the fact that they may also be citizens with inherent rights to many of the services under consideration. Furthermore, across a range of public services, there is in reality limited or no choice. In some services including for example mental health, child protection and youth justice, not only there is no element of consumer choice, but services may be compulsorily delivered (Pollitt, 1993).

A central tenet of managerialism is that workers are primarily self-seeking. In the absence of the profit motive, this suggests that artificial incentives must be created to drive up attainment. Performance measures and associated league tables with the potential for shaming for poor performance are the primary managerial motivators employed within public services. However, such an approach conflicts with the ideology of most public services where the primary motivation of staff is to help others.

Managerialism fails to recognise that public services operate within an administrative and political environment which is risk-averse, and which thus tends to resist the entrepreneurial and behaviour reforms which managerialism seeks to achieve (Dixon et al., 1998). Such considerations are particularly relevant to children's social care services, where there is the clear need to be highly risk-averse or at least highly risk-aware, when delivering services designed to protect individuals or the public from harm. Within the context of child protection, Munro (2004: 25) argues that 'concern with risk to members of the public has been augmented with concerns with risk to the agency.' This leads agencies to introduce 'more and more formal procedures to guide practice so that they create a "correct" way to deal with a case'. When a tragedy occurs, this allows agencies to focus on whether procedure has been followed rather than whether assessments or professional judgement were correct (Munro, 2004).

A central aspect of managerialism is the pursuit of 'general ideals, of decontextualised models or theories as to what would constitute a desired outcome in the situation in question' Shotter (2009a: 1). He suggests that this idealisation of the 'perfections of a tomorrow' prevents us from seeking the 'alleviations of a felt wrongness in the present moment'. Writing in a similar vein, Sen (2009: 26) comments that: 'The principal theories of justice in contemporary political philosophy draw in one way or another on the social contract approach, and concentrate on the search for ideal social institutions.' He goes on to argue that: 'What moves us is not the realisation that the world falls short of being completely just, which few of us expect, but that there are clearly remediable injustices around us which we want to eliminate'. Arguably, the focus of managerialism on idealised outcomes distracts agencies and workers from addressing the intrinsic social injustice faced by many service users.

Is managerialism working?

In recent years, quality assurance and improvement activity across a range of English public undertakings, including children's services, has come to be governed principally through the application of performance indicators and externally defined targets. However, as Ayre and Calder have argued at length in Chapter 5, it is far from clear that such an approach has yielded, or could ever yield, wholly satisfactory outcomes. It is difficult to develop quantitative indicators which assess the effectiveness of performance meaningfully when the 'raw materials' with which the work is undertaken (those who use services) are infinitely varied, when the context for the work is ever shifting and complexly interactive, and when outcomes can thus only sensibly be measured in relative, 'added-value' terms, rather than against absolute standards. By their nature, performance indicators measure process, and it is much harder

to evaluate practice, which inevitably requires that qualitative judgments be made.

This highlights one of the intrinsic problems that is inherent within a managerialist approach to managing services that are based upon human interactions. A Taylorist approach is based upon 'task management', which in turn allows measurement of task completion and the development of performance indicators. However as Shotter (2009b: 11) observes:

> There is hardly any more efficient way of evading the complexities of our ordinary everyday activities and practices, than to divorce them from the actual people performing them and the actual situations in which they occur, to find an order in the 'data' so collected, and to then go on to invent mythical ideals in terms of which that order can be supposedly explained.

The managerialist approach of breaking human processes down into a range of prescribed task or processes also denies the inherent complexity of human interaction. In relation to the management and delivery of practice, managerialism has the effect of constraining choice and limiting negotiability. Such a procedural approach serves to stifle a dialogical collaborative approach which is essential when seeking joint solutions to complex problems of human relations.

Speaking of the impact of a target driven approach to children's services, Seddon (2008) comments that 'the fear engendered by the regime means that everyone dealing with children worries about ensuring they have the right "ticks in boxes" when their inspectors come knocking. The safest route is to focus on "activities" to meet the stipulated outcomes' (Seddon, 2008: 190). However, as Ayre and Calder have argued, the quest to improve performance indicator scores and to chase targets not only distorts patterns of service development; it also distorts fundamentally the way in which workers and managers think about themselves and about what is important in their work. It may be argued that less experienced children's services workers who have spent their whole careers working within a target-driven environment are likely to conceive of themselves and their roles in ways which are substantially different and, it may be argued, less professional, than those socialised into regimes more focused on quality than quantity.

Quantitative performance indicators do, of course, allow comparisons to be made between authorities, but the usefulness of such comparisons may be questioned. One of the statistics currently scrutinised is the proportion of the total child population within a local authority area who have a child protection plan, as compared with the proportion found in demographically similar areas (statistical neighbours). These data may have some intrinsic interest but it is not evident that they would assist a judgement about how good or bad services may be. Leaving aside the problems of establishing demographic comparability, a local authority may have a lower rate of child protection plans because it has very good preventive services that intervene effectively at an early stage; another local authority may have a low rate because it has very high service thresholds for acting to protect children. In the first scenario, children may be being protected promptly and effectively whilst in the other they may be being exposed to risk, but this performance indicator cannot distinguish between the two.

Management by indicators may also create difficulties when the targets set for different agencies, or for different services within the same agency, seem to conflict. In 2002, the police were set demanding targets for the prosecution of offenders under the 'offences brought to justice' initiative (HM Treasury, 2002). One of the consequences was a significant rise in the number of children and young people being prosecuted for trivial offences. Subsequently, Youth Offending Teams were required under a Youth Justice Board initiative to reduce 'first time entrants' to the criminal justice system (Youth Justice Board, 2005). The inevitable conflict occasioned by this absence of joined-up thinking was not, however, resolved at the national level, where the problem originated. Instead, this led to HM Inspectorate of Probation expecting the management boards of YOTs to try to resolve the position locally (HM Inspectorate of Probation, 2007).

It may be argued that the tragic death of Baby Peter in 2009 provides a very poignant reminder of the limitations of the managerialist approach to managing and monitoring children's services which has been adopted by the current UK government. Prior to his death, Children's Services in Haringey, where he had lived, had been favourably reviewed in a Joint Area Review of Children's Services, a multi-inspectorate review, led by the Office for Standards in Education and the service was rated 'Good'

within the 2007 Annual Performance Assessment. Similarly, it was noted after the death of Victoria Climbié, also within Haringey, that a joint inspection by the Audit Commission and the SSI had delivered a positive appraisal of social work services in the borough. In his report, Lord Laming (2003: 135) commented that:

> *Haringey's Joint Review concluded that the 'users of social services are generally well served'. In terms of children's services, the reviewers formed the impression 'of a working environment that was both challenging and rewarding for staff'. The report found, 'Overall, this is a service with a strong commitment to good practice, but also one that recognises that there are some inconsistencies that need to be addressed before further improvements can take place.' It went on to state that 'no single issue emerged during the Review that caused reviewers to have concern about the practice of child protection.'*

The disparity between the relatively positive findings of assessments based heavily upon indicators and the grave deficiencies in services which were identified in subsequent more detailed enquiries suggests the ineffectiveness of the performance management framework which lies at the very heart of a managerialist approach to the management of children's services. Laming (2009: 15) commented that 'it is undoubtedly not easy to find good measures of outcomes for safeguarding and child protection'. However, having clearly accepted the difficulties inherent in measuring outcomes, he nevertheless went on to suggest that 'all partners in Children's Trusts will need support from central government to develop a local performance framework and minimum data sets in order that their performance can be assessed against the identified needs of local children and young people.' (p16) and that 'the National Indicator Set should be revised with new national indicators for safeguarding and child protection developed for inclusion in Local Area Agreements for the next Comprehensive Spending Review'.

Each of Lord Laming's reports may be felt to give clear evidence of the shortcomings of a managerialist approach but, sadly, he seems to regard the problems as technical ones, and thus capable of correction by doing the same kind of things, but doing them better, rather than as fundamental and insuperable ones arising from the inherent limitations of managerialism in this context. Thus, even within his most recent report, he appears to seek to prescribe more of the same (Laming, 2009).

In a strong collective response to Lord Laming, the Association of Directors of Children's Services, London Councils, the Society of Local Authority Chief Executives, the Improvement and Development Agency and the Local Government Association noted that:

> *Effective inspection and regulation are important, but also have limitations. External challenge is useful but improvement, assurance and accountability at local level is more reliant on effective political leadership, good organisational leadership, and strong local governance. Without those elements in place regulation can have a limited effect on improvement. Effective regulation by Government as well as Ofsted requires **better and more balanced ways of assessing performance**. Statutory targets can be useful in terms of demonstrating strong systems and processes, but will understandably give little indication of the quality of services at the front door. Any additional national indicators must not result in a net increase to the national indicator set.*
>
> Original emphasis. Association of Directors of Children's Services et al., 2009: 2

This statement represents a clear recognition by leadership groups in local government of the shortcomings of targets and indicators, acknowledging that centralised performance management is unable to measure the one thing that really matters, the quality of the services actually delivered. It also suggests an emphasis on the role of local management in shaping the delivery of services which is antithetical to the centralised command and control model characteristic of managerialism.

Performance management systems driven by quantitative measurement inevitably impose substantial administrative burdens on the services in question. Because it is necessary to provide data on the meeting of targets, management information systems must be created to capture this, and substantial professional and administrative time must be devoted to data entry. Before the advent of computerised case recording systems, individual case data were recorded in a client file or files. These paper based systems formed the original basis for the specification of many of the IT systems that are now on the market. However the development or re-specification of these systems has come to be driven primarily by the need to provide data for statistical returns to government and to record case assessments in a standardised form which accords with nationally defined protocols. The consequences of this for front line

service delivery are explored by Wastell and White elsewhere in this book. Writing in the Guardian newspaper, White et al. (2008) noted that:

> *Practice is now configured through the integrated children's system (ICS), an electronic recording, performance management and data sharing system much lauded by government and senior managers as a valuable and time saving tool for social workers and ultimately the multi-agency safeguarding system. This is at odds with what we have seen. The onerous workflows, 'tasks' and forms associated with ICS compound difficulties in meeting timescales and targets imposed by government. Social workers are acutely concerned with performance targets, such as moving the cases flashing in red on their screens into the next phase of the workflow within timescale.*

Commenting on research undertaken into the impact of the Integrated Children's System in local authorities, they reported staff spending between 60 per cent and 80 per cent of their time at computer screens. They suggested that the pathways through the ICS system are very complex and that 'it remains difficult to find simple summaries of the current state of the case' (White et al., 2008). These issues are not peculiar to the ICS system. Having used a variety of computer systems in a range of different children's services departments, the authors of this chapter have experienced at first hand how hard it can be to gain a clear overview of a case from electronic case record systems, since these systems by their nature tend to fragment and disperse the social history of the child and the family. The relative inaccessibility of information adds substantially to the level of risk when decisions have to be made by workers and managers who lack a longstanding familiarity with the case. Auditing decision-making also becomes time consuming and problematical.

Ayre and Calder, discussing performance indicators and targets in Chapter 5, have argued that managerialist objectives have become so dominant over professional objectives that we are in danger of forgetting the primary purpose of our work. Much the same can be argued with respect to management information systems. The principal role of case recording is to aid effective work with a child and his or her family, but the research conducted by White et al. (2008) would seem to suggest that few children's service workers would recognise this as the primary function of the information systems within which their work is cast.

We have seen, then, that some of the problems inherent in a managerialist approach to the management of children's services stem from its ideological starting point. Whilst Taylorism and the view that scientific method can be applied to the management of human processes may have made sense at the start of the 20th century when applied in an American industrial context, this approach may be felt to have less to offer when applied to 21st century English children's social care, which is characterised by human processes and complex, multifaceted professional decision-making. The assumption that workers are fundamentally self-seeking and need to be motivated by extrinsic managerialist drivers may be felt to have limited validity in contexts in which professional values and an ideology of public service have traditionally played an important motivational role. Performance measures are likely to distort objectives and disrupt the delivery of high quality services because of their tendency to focus on process not practice.

This is not a time for more of the same; there is an urgent need to develop management processes and systems that empower and inspire professionals charged with the onerous responsibility of delivering services to vulnerable children and families. Instead of mimicking approaches borrowed from business and inspired by the profit motive and competition, we must start to promote management systems which are founded upon professional values and collaborative processes, and which, in consequence, are better fitted to harnessing the talents and energies of the children's workforce.

Beyond managerialism?

The concept of the competent workplace was developed in the early 1990s in response to a wave of demands being made of personal social services by the Conservative government (Evans and Pottage, 1992). The *Children Act 1989* and the *NHS and Community Care Act 1990* were accompanied by a 'new public management' approach to public service delivery (Langan, 2000: 158) with consequent far-reaching changes in service delivery. In such an environment, Pottage and Evans (1994: 11–2) found that many social workers 'felt disempowered and unable to operate within the value framework that they had used to guide their practice', that they 'saw

accountability as being met through prescriptive procedures and unrealistic measurements of competencies by performance indicators' and that 'the gap between expressed expectations and ability to provide was simply too great'. It would seem that little has changed.

The concept of the competent workplace relies significantly upon the idea of the 'learning organisation', a concept brought to prominence through the publication of *The Fifth Discipline* (Senge, 1990: 3). Senge focuses on the systemic nature of organisations and the need to set aside 'the illusion that the world is created of separate unrelated forces'. Giving up that illusion allows us to create 'organisations where people continually expand their capacity to create the results they truly desire . . . where people are continually learning how to learn together' (Senge, 1990: 3). In developing his concept of the learning organisation, Senge built upon the work of a number of other writers, including Donald Schön whose work on reflective practice is considered later (Schön 1971, 1978; 1983). The application of the concept of the learning organisation to social care has, in turn, been further developed by Gould and Baldwin (2004).

The use of the concept of the learning organisation in public services has been criticised because, like managerialism, its roots lie in industry and commerce. However, conceptually and ethically it sits much more easily than managerialism within the management of social care services. Baldwin (2004) draws on a framework for conceptualising organisational structure developed by Morgan and Burrell (1979). 'In this model bureaucratic or managerialist organisations are typecast as objective and status quo' whilst the learning organisation 'is a concept founded more within a social constructivist paradigm in which the organisation is conceptualised as constructed through relationships which hold the opportunity for change and development on a day to day basis' (Baldwin, 2004: 163).

Despite the apparently dominant position of managerialism in recent decades, the concept of the learning organisation has, from time to time, been promoted by the government. Taylor (2004: 76) suggests that this concept has, since the late 1990s, pervaded a broad range of government policy documents apparently 'embedded in the New Labour Modernisation Agenda'. However, citing as a prime example Investors in People, Baldwin (2004) concludes that, in reality, learning organisation concepts have been subverted and deployed in a tokenistic manner. Despite this, he notes that whilst 'there is no evidence that social care organisations have become fully functioning learning organisations . . . aspects of the learning organisation are appearing in some organisations' (Baldwin, 2004: 168). Having worked across a broad range of children's services, this analysis reflects the authors' ongoing experience. Whilst most children's services continue to be delivered within a managerialist framework, there is evidence of increasing dissatisfaction amongst managers and staff with the inherent limitations of this approach and there are some signs of the development of a range of activity which is more closely aligned with the concept of the learning organisation.

Developing the concept: the competent workplace

Central to the concept of the competent workplace is the assumption that the overall purpose of social care services is to offer an effective response to service user need through the maximum utilisation of the skills of the workforce. Key aspects of the required culture shift are the empowerment of the individual, the promotion of collective learning within the workplace and the effective use of information and intelligence held within the workplace to enhance service delivery. It is suggested that:

- The management, design and delivery of effective services must be founded upon practice experience and not simply upon preconfigured procedures and externally determined targets.
- Services must discover through a genuine engagement with service users the most appropriate methods of design and delivery.
- Service improvement is gained through learning from day to day experience within a partnership between managers and staff, a key role of management being to promote organisational learning.

Pottage and Evans, 1994

The competent workplace framework was developed and tested in a UK context by the National Institute for Social Work and the University of Manchester Mental Health Research and Staff Development Unit, with staff groups from a range of social care settings including mental health practitioners (Pottage and Evans, 1994).

Essential to the development of a competent workplace is the understanding that reality is socially constructed through interaction between individuals. 'There are portions of the real world, objective facts in the world, that are only facts by human agreement. In a sense there are things that only exist because we believe them to exist' (Searle, 1995: 1). Searle cites as one example money; the note in our pocket is only worth £5 because we all agree that it is. Consequent to this perspective is the recognition that our workplaces are socially constructed, and created and re-created by us on a moment by moment basis as communicative human beings. Through conversation we are continually constructing our realities, together with our colleagues and service users. In the early 1970s, Schön argued that:

> We must become able not only to transform our institutions, in response to changing situations and requirements; we must invent and develop institutions which are 'learning systems', that is to say, systems capable of bringing about their own continuing transformation.
> Schön, 1971: 30

Only those organisations which constitute themselves as 'learning systems', can successfully adapt and re-invent themselves within a context of continual change. The recognition that organisations are socially constructed creates the opportunity for participants to contribute collectively to the way in which they function, grow and develop. This approach contrasts sharply with the 'command and control' view of organisational management so closely associated with managerialism.

In this context, reflective practice must be regarded as central to organisational and personal professional development. Pottage and Evans (1994) like Senge (1990) drew upon the seminal work of Donald Schön, recognising that workplace learning is maximised by employing and valuing what Schön refers to as 'professional artistry' (Schön, 1983). This involves the ability to recognise when the required results are not being achieved and, in the moment, to try another approach, practising what Schön terms 'reflection in action' (Schön, 1987). In consequence, professional practice cannot be conducted and regulated solely by reference to preordained procedures and processes, 'breaking ''practice'' down into a series of tasks, and assessing a workers competence against these' (Pottage and Evans, 1994, p40). Baldwin (2004: 42) points out that:

> *Reflection-in-action and on-action (after the event) are key parts of professional practice in which the process by which we engage with others – colleagues and service users – constructs that practice and those relationships . . . Formal knowledge has a part to play, but so too does intuition, those tacit ways of understanding and action that become our strategies for making sense of the world.*

Judith Thomas, quoting Morrison (1996) contrasts retrospective reflecting-on-action with the immediacy of reflecting-in-action. 'Reflecting-on-action is a more distant, structured, logical analysis where the practitioner is "empowered through clarification, understanding and articulation of principles and theory, to develop greater professional autonomy through the conscious exercise of judgement"' (Thomas, 2004: 103).

Writing from the position of critically reflective practice, Robert Adams makes the point that 'it is not sufficient to be reflective. We need to use the understanding that we gain from reflection to achieve change' (Adams, 2002: 87). He goes on to argue that critical practitioners whilst 'deeply involved' need to develop the ability to be 'detached' from the situation with the ability to move between an 'insider' and an 'outsider' position. Adams, Dominelli and Payne (2002: 3) describe the cycle by which 'critical thinking leads to critical action, forming critical practice'. Workers are engaged in a process of reflexivity, 'thinking and acting with the people they are serving, so that their understandings and actions are inevitably changed by their experiences with others'.

Schön's (1987) thinking has also proved influential in distinguishing between the 'high-ground' of theory and the 'swampy lowlands' of practice, seeing theory as tidy and practice as messy. He suggests that 'in the varied topography of professional practice, there is the high, hard ground overlooking the swamp. On the high ground, manageable problems lend themselves to solution through the application of research-based theory and technique. In the swampy lowland, messy, confusing problems defy technical solution' (p 1). Johns (2004) helpfully develops this metaphor by arguing that the highlands and lowlands represents a dualism

of science and art and that we need to overcome this dualism to develop practical wisdom:

> *At the level of constructed knowing, the practitioner weaves the subjective and procedural voices into an informed, connected to self and others, passionate and assertive voice. There is no longer any dualistic thinking between art and science as they are woven into practical wisdom. From the perspective of constructed voice practitioners view all knowledge as contextual, experience themselves as creators of knowledge and value both subjective and objective strategies for knowing.*
>
> Johns, 2004: 11

Many of the challenges that workers and managers in children's services face are profoundly complex, including some which are beyond the ability or reach of any single agency to resolve. Such challenges are often referred to as 'wicked problems' or 'wicked issues' (Richards, 2001). Addleson (2003: 7) indicates that successful resolution of such issues involves 'a collaborative, participative, creative social process of sharing knowledge in order to make meaning, people engaging each other in conversations, saying what they think and know, telling their stories.'

The nature of the conversations we hold about practice are crucial. Senge (1990) illustrates this by distinguishing between dialogue and discussion. 'Dialogue' is drawn from the Greek word 'dialogos', which means a search for meaning or understanding. The word 'discussion', however, has the same root as the word 'percussion'. So when we are 'banging on', we are usually looking to win an argument, as if in competition with the other protagonists. However as Senge observes, 'a sustained emphasis on winning is not compatible . . . with giving first priority to coherence and truth (1990: 240)'. On the other hand, dialogue is characterised by the adoption of an open or reflective position, in which defensive routines are suspended and complex issues are considered from different viewpoints, in order that fresh meaning or understanding can emerge (Senge, 1990). When challenges are being considered on a one-to-one or team basis, a dialogical approach is much more likely to open up insights into the perspectives of others and to generate new ways forward than is an argument on the rights and wrongs of a particular position. When dialogue is adopted, the focus is no longer on winning or losing. Instead it shifts to finding the best way to move forward jointly. Senge (1990) acknowledges that both dialogue and discussion can be useful, but argues that many teams are unable to differentiate between the two.

In order to develop a competent organisation, we must understand how we develop professionally, both individually and collectively. Dreyfus and Dreyfus (1986) trace five stages in the development of professionals, suggesting that they grow from being novices dependent on explicit protocols that guide their action, to experts who are able to act intuitively on the basis of their knowledge and experience. Experts will often work without overt reference to individual theories, performing skilfully apparently without deliberation or focused attention. It may be argued that in seeking to direct the actions of practitioners by means of all-embracing sets of procedures and processes, we are currently ensuring that they remain forever novices. Instead, we need to create systems that safely encourage and enhance the development of expert practice.

Conclusion

The way in which we view organisations, and the metaphors we use to understand them, fundamentally affects how we try to run and manage them. If we view organisations as machines and the people within them as cogs, we begin to believe that we can pull levers and make things happen. If we view social work services as if they are factories then we may expect them to produce neatly packaged outcomes that we can measure easily.

In the latter part of the 20th century managerialism become deeply embedded in our political systems and consequently within both national and local approaches to managing public services. Early in the 21st century its efficacy as an approach to the management of local government, and particularly children's services, is beginning to be fundamentally challenged in a variety of arenas.

Strong and Prosperous Communities – The Local Government White Paper (DCLG, 2006a) introduced 'a radical simplification of the performance framework . . . Instead of the many hundreds of indicators currently required by central government there will be a single set of about 200 outcome based indicators' (DCLG, 2006b: 5). However, as Seddon (2008) observed, 'doing less of the wrong thing is not the same as

doing the right thing. It is not a matter of finding the "right targets"; this can only amount to doing the wrong things righter. The right thing to do is to use measures that help in understanding and improving the work. (p106). Nevertheless, insofar as the White Paper may be taken as suggesting a reduced reliance on statistical indicators, it may be felt to signal a dawning realisation on the part of central government that a target based approach to performance management of local government has failed to deliver.

Facing up to the Task (Social Work Task Force, 2009: 32) the interim report of the Social Work Task Force established in the wake of the Baby Peter case, makes a range of observations on 'performance management' in social work including:

- The impact of what social workers do is currently monitored at local level through a disparate group of performance indicators. We have encountered a widespread view among frontline social workers and line managers, several groups of other professionals, and some service users that these indicators are measuring such things as the rate at which processes are completed, rather than quality of service or outcomes for the service user.
- This is matched by a concern that local authority social workers are being managed, and their time is being deployed, in order to satisfy processes rather than provide quality.
- The overall effect of this appears to be a sense of a profession that is, in places, at risk of compliance rather than judgment. Social work is in need of a clearer account of how its effectiveness should be judged and how this could be incentivised in a new approach to performance indicators, inspection and evaluation.

Given that the Conservative Thatcher and Major administrations were responsible for the initial introduction of a managerialist approach to the regulation and management of local government services, there may be felt to be some irony in the fact that the Conservative party has become highly critical of 'Labour's culture of control'. In a paper entitled *Control Shift – Returning Power to Local Communities* (Conservative Party, 2009) it is suggested that:

> *Over the last century, Britain has become one of the most centralised countries in the developed world. Under*

Labour, this trend has accelerated. Top-down, central control is the hallmark of the current Government's approach – the last vestiges of a bureaucratic age, founded on the assumptions that Whitehall knows best and that only uniformity can guarantee fairness' (p 4).

The paper goes on to promise to 'abolish all process targets applied to local authorities' (p 2) as well as 'to end the micro-management of local government' and to 'liberate local authorities from intrusive central inspection regimes' (p 18).

The Conservative Party Commission on Social Workers (Chairman: Tim Loughton MP, Shadow Minister for Children and Young People) in its response to Lord Laming's latest report, comments unfavourably on the on the Integrated Children's System (ICS):

> *Social workers have said the template is too detailed and requires so much standard information that workers have to focus on completing the document rather than the assessment. There is a difficult balance to maintain between collecting all the information required and focusing on the key safeguarding factors and the analysis. If you imple-ment a tick-box approach to a case while at the same time you have a large caseload and are constrained by a strict timescale in which the assessment must be completed, you will get "tick-box assessments" rather the exercise of guided professional judgment. Reflection time is essential to enable professional social workers to exercise their skills.*
> Conservative Party Commission on
> Social Workers, 2009: 11

The Commission recommends the abolition of ICS.

We have also seen earlier in the chapter that a range of highly influential public bodies have called into question the efficacy of 'regulation' in improving the performance of children's services, recognising the importance of local political leadership and effective service management (Association of Directors of Children's Services et al., 2009).

It seems clear that the breadth and the depth of the concern felt about the impact of managerialism on social work has begun to increase exponentially. Only time will tell how close we are to the tipping point at which fundamental change becomes inevitable. As we contemplate how to repair and rebuild, we must make sure that we have maximised our learning from the errors of the last three decades. We must recognise and embrace the inherent complexity of the work in which we are engaged, and adopt systems of management which recognise that such complexity can only be addressed by

drawing upon and developing the skill and creativity of all those involved. Learning organisations providing their employees with competent workplaces offer us the best chance of meeting this challenge.

References

Adams, R. (2002) Developing Critical Practice in Social Work. In Adams, R. Dominelli, I. and Payne, P. (2002) *Critical Practice in Social Work*. Basingstoke: Palgrave Macmillan.

Adams, R. Dominelli, I. and Payne, P. (2002) *Critical Practice in Social Work*. Basingstoke: Palgrave Macmillan.

Addleson, M. (2003) *Perspectives on Organisational Change*. International Centre for Applied Studies in Information Technology. Available: www.icasit.org/km/kmrt/sept03/addleson_slides.ppt.

Association of Directors of Children's Services, London Councils, Society of Local Authority Chief Executives, Improvement and Development Agency for Local Government and Local Government Association. (2009) *Response to the Protection of Children in England: A Progress Report*. Association of Directors of Children's Services. http://www.adcs.org.uk/PressReleases/09%2004%2015%20ADCS%20LGA%20SOLACE%20Laming%20response.pdf.

Baldwin, M. (2004) Conclusions: Optimism and the Art of the Possible. In Gould, N. and Baldwin, M. (2004) *Social Work, Critical Reflection and the Learning Organisation*. Aldershot: Ashgate.

Burrell, G. and Morgan, G. (1979) *Sociological Paradigms and Organosational Analysis: Elements of the Sociology of Corporate Life*. London: Heinemann.

Clarke, J., Gerwitz, S. and McLaughlin. (2000) Reinventing the Welfare State. In Clarke, J., Gerwitz, S. and McLaughlin, E. *New Managerialism New Welfare?* London: Sage.

Conservative Party (2009) *Control Shift – Returning Power to Local Communities*. London: Conservative Party.

Conservative Party Commission on Social Workers (2009) *Response to Lord Laming's Inquiry*. London: Conservative Party.

DCLG (2006a) *Strong and Prosperous Communities: The Local Government White Paper*. Cmnd 6939–I. London: The Stationery Office

DCLG (2006b) *Strong and Prosperous Communities – The Local Government White Paper Summary.* DCLG. Available: http://www.communities.gov.uk/documents/localgovernment/pdf/153590.pdf.

Dillow, C. (2007) *The End of Politics: New Labour and the Folly of Managerialism.* Petersfield: Harriman House.

Dixon J., Kouzmin A. and Korac-Kakabadse N. (1998) Managerialism – Something Old, Something Borrowed, Little New. *International Journal of Public Sector Management*, 11, 164–87.

Dreyfus, H. and Dreyfus, L. (1986) *Mind Over Machine, the Power of Human Intuition and Expertise in the Era of the Computer.* New York: The Free Press.

Evans, M. and Pottage, D. (1992) *Workbased Stress; Prescription is not the Cure.* London: NISW.

Gould, N. and Baldwin, M. (2004) *Social Work, Critical Reflection and the Learning Organisation.* Aldershot: Ashgate.

Harris, J. (2003) *The Social Work Business.* London: Routledge.

HM Inspectorate of Probation (2007) *Criteria for the Inspection of Youth Offending Teams in England, Phase Four, Version 9.* London: HM Inspectorate of Probation.

HM Treasury (2002) *Opportunity and Security for All: Investing in an Enterprising, Fairer Britain: New Spending Plans 2003–2006*, Cm 5570. London: HMSO.

Hood, C. (1991) A Public Management for All Seasons. *Public Administration*, 69: 1, 3–19.

Johns, C. (2004) *Becoming a Reflective Practitioner.* 2nd Edition. Oxford: Blackwell.

Kolthoff, E., Huberts, L. and van den Heuvel, H. (2007) The Ethics of New Public Management: Is Integrity at Stake? *Public Administration Quarterly*, 30: 4, 399–439.

Lord Laming. (2003) *The Victoria Climbié Inquiry: Report of an Inquiry by Lord Laming*, Cmnd 5730. London: The Stationery Office.

Lord Laming. (2009) *The Protection of Children in England: A Progress Report.* London: HMSO.

Langan, M. (2000) Social Services: Managing the Third Way. In Clarke, J., Gerwitz, S. and McLaughlin, E. *New Managerialism New Welfare?* London: Sage

Munro, E. (2004) The Impact of Audit on Social Work Practice. *British Journal of Social Work*, 34: 8, 1073–4.

Osborne, D. and Gaebler, T. (1993) *Reinventing Government: How the Entrepreneurial Spirit is Transforming the Public Sector.* New York: Plume.

Pollitt, C. (1993) *Managerialism and the Public Services: Cuts or Cultural Change in the 1990s?* 2nd edn. Oxford: Blackwell.

Pollitt, C. et al. (1999) *Performance or Compliance? Performance Audit and Public Management in Five Countries.* Oxford: Oxford UP.

Pottage, D. and Evans, M. (1994) *The Competent Workplace: The View from Within.* London: NISW.

Richards, S. (2001) Four Types of Joined Up Government and the Problem of Accountability. In *Joining It Up to Improve Public Services 2001–2002.* Appendix 2. pp 61–70. Report no. HC383. (1971) *Beyond the Stable State: Public and Private Learning in a Changing Society.* London: Maurice Temple Smith.

Schön, D. (1983) *The Reflective Practitioner: How Professionals Think in Action.* New York: Basic Books.

Schön D. (1987) *Educating the Reflective Practitioner.* San Fransisco: Jossey Bass.

Searle, J. (1995) *The Construction of Social Reality.* London: Penguin.

Seddon, J. (2008) *Systems Thinking in the Public Sector: The Failure of the Reform Regime . . . and a Manifesto For a Better Way.* Axminster: Triarchy Press.

Sen, A. (2009) Pip Was Right: Nothing is so Finely Felt as Injustice. And There the Search Begins. *The Guardian (Comment and Debate)*, 14 July. 26.

Senge, P. (1990) *The Fifth Discipline: The Art and Practice of the Learning Organisation.* London: Random House.

Sim, J. (2000) One Thousand Days of Degradation: New Labour and Old Compromises at the Turn of the Century. *Social Justice*, 27: 2, 168–92.

Shotter, (2009a) *Notes Towards: Ontological Social Constructionism: The Corporeal Turn: On Coming to Know Our 'Way About' Inside the Relations Between Ourselves and Our World.* Unpublished.

Shotter, (2009b) René Bouwen, Relational Practices, and the Emergence of the Uniquely New. In Steyaert, C. and Van Looy, B. *Relational Organising.* In press.

Social Work Task Force (2009) *Facing Up to the Task: The Interim Report of the Social Work Task Force.* London: DCSF.

Taptiklis, T. (2008) *Unmanaging, Opening Up the Organisation to Its Own Unspoken Knowledge.* Basingstoke: Palgrave Macmillan.

Taylor, F. (1911) *The Principles of Scientific Management.* New York: Harper.

Taylor, I (2004) Multi-professional Teams and the Learning Organisation. In Gould, N. and

Baldwin, M. (2004) *Social Work, Critical Reflection and the Learning Organisation.* Aldershot: Ashgate.

Thomas, J. (2004) Using 'Critical Incident Analysis' to Promote Critical Reflection and Holistic Assessment. In Gould, N. and Baldwin, M. (2004) *Social Work, Critical Reflection and the Learning Organisation.* Aldershot: Ashgate.

White, S. et al. (2008) Repeating the same mistakes. *guardian.co.uk*, 19 November. Available: www.guardian.co.uk/society/joepublic/2008/nov/19/baby-p-mistakes.

Youth Justice Board (2005) *Youth Justice Plan 2005–2006 Guidance.* London: Youth Justice Board for England and Wales.

CHAPTER 11

Technology as Magic: Fetish and Folly in the IT-enabled Reform of Children's Services

David Wastell and Sue White

The transporting of the log is not an easy task ... the natives resort to a magical rite which makes the canoe lighter. A piece of dry banana is put on top of the log. The owner or builder beats the log with a bunch of dry lalang grass and utters the following spell: 'Come down defilement by contact with excrement! Come down, rot! Come down fungus ...' and so on, invoking a number of deteriorations to leave the log. In other words, the heaviness and slowness due to all these magical causes are thrown out of the log.

> Malinowski, Argonauts of the Western
> Pacific, 1922: 129

The Integrated Children's System will provide an assessment, planning, intervention and reviewing model for all children in need under the Children Act 1989. The Integrated Children's System is designed to ensure that assessment, planning and decision making leads to good outcomes for children. This approach reflects a holistic understanding of children's developmental needs and the capacities of their parents or carers ... [and] a coherent process which is focused on bringing about optimal outcomes for children.

> DoH, 2000

In this chapter, we draw attention to some serious design deficiencies in information and communication technologies currently in use in children's social care in England and Wales. Our enquiry, based on thorough empirical investigation, will seek to relate these problems to more deep-seated dysfunctions in the policy-making process itself. Taking a polemical aim, we will argue that New Labour's modernisation programme, rolled out across the public services, has been characterised by a talismanic faith in technology as a salve for a range of real practice problems. The policy dogma informing these 'IT-enabled' initiatives is powered, in our contention, by a form of magical thinking resulting in serious, pervasive and pernicious effects on practice.

A persistent theme of child abuse inquiries in the UK in the last 30 years has been deficiencies in inter-professional communication, recording and multi-agency intervention. The inquiry into the death of Victoria Climbié (Laming, 2003) was a pivotal catalyst in the reform agenda. Resulting legislative changes included the establishment of Local Safeguarding Children Boards, with the responsibility for safeguarding children and conducting reviews on all child deaths, increased regulation and audit of child protection 'services' and workforce and professional reform. In addition, measures have been identified to promote better information sharing, early identification responses and prescribed workflow processes, all powered by ICTs. Setting up databases, 'flagging' vulnerable children and coordinating interventions, aspire to provide a more differentiated (and cost effective) system of identification, assessment and intervention. Such projects seek to encourage professionals to identify early concerns and to take responsibility for acting on those concerns through a range of virtual interactions. Once observations are committed to electronic texts they become frozen, and appear to be authoritative representations of whatever they purport to describe.

In due course, we will describe the malevolent effects of these technological proxies, focusing particularly on the, now notorious, Integrated Children's System (ICS). But first, we must make the case for our 'technology as magic' trope, for here within lies the source of the devastating design errors meted out on practitioners in children's social care.

A magical mystery tour

Twenty first century government is enabled by technology – policy is inspired by it, business change is delivered by it . . . Moreover modern governments with serious transformational intent see technology as a strategic asset and not just a tactical tool. So this strategy's vision is about better using technology to deliver public services and policy outcomes that have an impact on citizens' daily lives: through greater choice and personalisation, delivering better public services, such as health, education and pensions; benefiting communities by reducing burdens on front line staff . . .

> Transformational Government: Enabled by
> Technology, Cabinet Office, 2005

The quote is worth dwelling on; its messianic zeal rings loud and clear. The reality, however, of this brave new world is somewhat out of joint with the techno-utopian rhetoric. In statutory children's services, the translation of professional practice into a range of standardised procedures, protocols and templates, all co-dependently mediated by ICT and subject to a 'performance management' regime based on defined targets and indicators, was aimed at enhancing child safety and welfare, ensuring that another Victoria Climbié could 'never happen'. But these systems also create new demands for institutional actors and it is far from clear how safety will be enhanced by the enthusiasm for standardisation and command-and-control management. Indeed, the empirical evidence is to the contrary as the public debate surrounding the death of Baby Peter has tragically shown. As we shall see shortly, there has been overwhelming evidence that there were very serious design faults with the Integrated Children's System from its very inception, but sustained by a vicious circle of 'magical thinking' it has nonetheless shown remarkable durability in the face of much resistance and negative evidence. We shall preface our reflections with a short discourse on magic itself, going back to the seminal work of Mauss (1950).

Although seeming opposites, technology and magic have much in common, as sociologists from Mauss (1950) to Stivers (2001) have noted. Both are instrumental, involving the deployment of a body of practical skill and knowledge to accomplish something of social value (Mauss, 1950). The difference would seem to lie in the link between cause and effect. Whereas magic is 'pure production, *ex nihilo*' (p 175) technology accomplishes through palpable labour and efficient causes. The image of the steam engine comes immediately to mind. There is nothing magical here about cause and effect (at least to us 'moderns'!). But for other forms of technology, extending the term to include non-material techniques, the distinction is more blurred, especially as the causal chain spreads out over time and space, and is mediated by links and levers that are social, not mechanical. We argue here that our faith in the instrumental efficacy of technology in an increasingly complex and technologically-mediated world has much the same magical character as the 'primitive' rituals of the Melanesian Waga-builder we opened with. They beat the log with a bunch of dry lalang grass

and utter a spell, we try to change the world by writing a software programme or a policy document which embodies an idealisation of how the world should be. If magic reflects the belief that the observance of certain rites, the muttering of incantations, the avoidance of taboos and so forth, will *in and of itself* produce desired effects, then magic is very much a feature of the mind-set of the modern world, especially the world of public policy and of business. We may not be so modern as we would like to think!

To assist in our task, let us commence by summarizing magic's 'key elements' from Mauss's seminal treatise, supported by a reference or two to Frazer's prior disquisition (Frazer, 1922). This will entail considerable simplification, but we will do our best. For Mauss, magic is first and foremost a social phenomenon. Magic needs believers! Magicians in all societies are creatures of public opinion, their power is not an intrinsic potency, but is 'socially constructed' by a credulous community in order to accomplish those 'outcomes' that the society seeks, bringing rain, curing illness, ensuring protection and safety. In crude terms, the magical way of 'problem-solving' is to fashion a magician with the power to solve the problems, give control to the problem solver, participate in the magical methodology, and 'hey presto'! Mauss (1950) stresses that magic is always practical, aimed at the achievement of change; it takes place in special often remote places, marked off physically, socially and psychologically too, in terms of the altered mental stages which are typically entailed (demonic possession, catalepsy etc.). The mechanical observance of rites, both non-verbal and verbal, is fundamental, as is the role of representations (e.g. effigies, arcane diagrams etc.) which may be abstract or concrete.

Verbal rites include spells and incantations, aimed at summoning up the required supernatural forces, or to tailor the rite, to achieve the desired effect. All is carefully prescribed. Mere performance of the routine is sufficient, as shown by the formulaic nature of the rites. That incantations can be quite inaudible and unintelligible does not detract from their magical potency: enactment is all. 'Between a wish and its fulfilment, in magic, there is no gap' (Mauss, 1950: 78). Magical causality works by the transfer of *properties* via 'secret sympathy . . . the impulse being transmitted from one to the other by what we may conceive of as an invisible ether' (Frazer, 1922). Any association of ideas would appear to suffice, even apparent opposites will do, e.g. the use by the Cherokee Indians of a yellow root to cure jaundice. This sympathy can be imitative (the law of similarity) e.g. symbolically enacting a cure effects that cure. Alternatively, the nexus may be contagious (the law of contact) exemplified by the widespread superstition that harm may be done to an individual through any severed element of that person (hair, nails etc.). A final and, for us, crucial characteristic of magic is its incorrigible nature and the unreflective behaviour of its adherents, practitioner and recipient alike.

> *Magic is a priori a belief . . . Magic has such authority that a contrary experience does not on the whole destroy a person's belief. Even the most unfavourable facts can be turned to magic's advantage, since they can always be held to be the work of counter-magic or to result from an error in performance of the ritual . . . Fortuitous coincidences are accepted as normal facts and all contradictory evidence is denied.*
>
> Mauss, 1950: 114–5

We shall see that these tendencies are writ large in the development of the ICS.

Paradise lost: the ICS

> *The result is a system that is bureaucratically perfect – literally, no one is to blame – and humanly a nightmare. It is characterised by harried workers managing and passing on 'cases', not caring for individual children. Of Baby P's 60 contacts with Haringey officials, very few were with the same people, yet social workers repeatedly told White's team of the impossibility of understanding uncertain, shifting human situations from a computer screen . . . As the LSE's Eileen Munro noted: 'Haringey had a beautiful paper trail of how they failed to protect this baby . . . The ICS fails on all counts. So, yes, heads should probably roll over the awful death of Baby P. It's just that they are not the ones most people think should roll.*
>
> Simon Caulkin, The Observer,
> Blame bureaucrats and systems for
> Baby P's fate, 23/11/08

In this section, we will turn to the ICS itself and reflect on the mayhem it has wrought in front line children's services. The above quote comes from an article by Simon Caulkin, the Observer Management Editor, written late in 2008, following the reporting of the death of a toddler known as Baby Peter. Baby Peter, aged 17 months, from the London Borough of Haringey, was killed in August 2007. He died as result of a blow to the head which knocked out one of his teeth, subsequently found in his stomach. He had a broken back and multiple rib fractures, numerous bruises and other lesions. His mother, her partner and the lodger were convicted in November 2008 of causing or allowing his death. The case received intense media coverage and sparked a further appraisal of child protection procedures and practices in England. The government asked Lord Laming, the architect of the post-Climbié reforms to appraise the extent of their adoption in England and a call for evidence was issued. The Government also appointed a Social Work Task Force, chaired by Moira Gibb, the Chief Executive of Camden Borough Council and an ex-social worker. Reflecting the pertinence of our research and the press attention it had gained, one of the authors of this paper (White) was appointed to the Task Force.

As the public debate swelled, the ICS began to be talked about in the vernacular vocabulary of practitioners and journalists, rather than the liturgies and incantations of policy makers and senior managers, as this submission to Laming by the public services union, Unison exemplifies:

> *UNISON wishes to draw attention to the seriousness of the problems being experienced by social work staff with the Integrated Children's System. The problems appear to be fundamental, widespread and consistent enough to call into question whether the ICS is fit for purpose . . . we have reports of a number of industrial disputes or collective grievances brewing . . . and in many more cases staff are voting with their feet and not using the system when they can get away with it.*
>
> Unison 2008: 8–9

The urgent need to review the design of ICS was identified as a priority by the Task Force. The need for such review has recently been accepted by the Government, and in the meantime its compliance criteria and prescriptive practice model have been significantly softened (DCSF, 2009). Yet, this relaxation comes some nine years after ICS was first conceived as a policy aim and five years after the start of the pilot phase of its implementation. Clear symptoms of its design malaise have been apparent throughout its life-course, and we will attend in due course to why it took so long for the cat to claw its way out of the bag. But first we must describe the profound impact that this dysmorphic system has had on practice. For this, we draw on data from a two year ethnographic study of the impact of performance management on everyday practice in five local authority children's services departments (for further detail on methods see Broadhurst et al., 2009) and also anonymised personal correspondence from social workers and managers following the media reporting of our study.

We will give just three quotes here, as the results of our ethnographic research have been extensively disseminated in recent papers (e.g. Broadhurst et al., 2009; Wastell et al., forthcoming). There are two major classes of 'fatal flaw' in the design of the ICS. One is the imposition of a rigid 'workflow' model of the professional task, decomposing it into a set of discrete activities to be performed in pre-defined sequence according to a set of non-negotiable time-scales. An initial assessment, for instance, must always be performed within seven working days irrespective of the complexities and contingencies of the case. Removing all discretion inevitably invites short-cuts and other workarounds in order to meet targets, meaning that errors thus become more not less likely. No techno-utopia this, the ICS has engendered an oppressive workplace characterised by rising levels of cynicism and alienation, with the best of workers, finding their professional discretion eroded and the work reduced to mindless form-filling, inevitably tempted to leave.

A much heard complaint relates to the overly complicated forms which are an integral part of the ICS's 'practice model'. To give a flavour, we give here two brief quotations:

It's much worse since ICS. Like when you've got a child in need and you need a conference, you can't get to the conference without going through strategy discussion and 'outcome of section 47' forms which populate from the strategy discussion forms. You used to just be able to write like half a side . . . but now you've got these terrible forms. You have to do one on each child, so if there are 5 children that's 10 forms and they are nothing to do with the work . . . they are just pointless and get in the way.

Team manager

I have certainly heard people say 'ok give me the youngest child's and the oldest child's and I will just read them. But because largely the issues are going to be the same and if there is anything for the individual child on the other children in that instant then you know to tell me about it but otherwise I am only going to read two of the reports'. And again that is quite disheartening because again I'm compelled to write 7 conference reports for quality assurance . . . I mean everybody tears their hair out with it I think.

Social worker

Here we quote extensively from a letter from a front line worker in Child Protection:

The system is simply not fit for purpose. I will give you precise examples.

Case one: A child was on a child protection plan. His circumstances changed dramatically between the first conference and the next review conference three months later. I was unable to change the child protection plan on the system. This is unacceptable. The registered plan no longer reflects the reality on the ground. This makes the system unsafe.

Case two: I have moved a child from its parents to his grandparents. The system would not allow me to change the child's placement because it will only register carers with a code number. Informal carers don't have one! Hence the child remains registered at the wrong address with the wrong carers.

Cases three and four: I have two babies now subject to Interim Care Orders. Both are still registered as being subject to child protection plans . . . I have spent a week in total of my valuable time trying to get the system to register the children's true circumstances, all to no avail. I constantly have red reminders of child protection meetings not called. It goes against my record as well as causing stress.

Magical thinking and the ICS

We have seen something of the disruption provoked by the implementation of the ICS, and of the resistance it has fomented. There is nothing new here. Looking back to the early days of the project, there was ample evidence that its design was flawed. It may seem tempting to blame the software companies for the malaise, but the more enlightened engineers know too well that technology is not magic and some have been making their own case for a more user-centred design process for some time, but to no avail. We must look elsewhere for the sources of the problems. The project began its life in the Department of Health, before moving to the Department for Children Schools and Families (DCSF) as a result of government restructuring. Its development has been spearheaded by a small cadre of senior civil servants and academics, who have remained integrally involved from conception onwards. As noted, there were unmistakable symptoms of practitioner disquiet even in the early pilot studies of the ICS, carried out by key members of the academic team involved in its design. But these adverse reactions, and subsequent negative feedback, have been consistently dismissed as 'teething problems' (see Cleaver and Walker, 2004; Cleaver et al., 2008) with problems invariably attributed to unreliable IT, inefficient local authorities, or 'confused practitioners'.

Oft-heard in our research are tales of requests to simplify the forms, for instance, going routinely ignored. The magic itself is never questioned: 'The Integrated Children's System is *designed to ensure* that assessment, planning and decision making leads to good outcomes for children' (DoH, 2000) and ensure it will! Indeed the faith of its proponents waxes ever stronger as the tide of resistance swells. In response to a very thorough evaluation by an independent academic team at the University of York, which damningly concluded that the ICS 'has not shown it is fit for purpose' (Bell, 2008) the DCSF responded:

> However, the design [of the evaluation] was based upon participating local authorities' commitment to implement the ICS fully within a seven-month period. There were, however, significant delays in the implementation process. By the conclusion of the evaluation the ICS had only been fully implemented in one of the sites. Despite attempts to revise the design and augment the data, it was not possible for all the aims and objectives of the evaluation to be achieved ... [therefore] the research does not provide a sound basis on which to judge the potential value of the ICS. Instead the study provides an informed assessment of the challenges which need to be overcome if this potential is to be realised.
>
> DCSF, 2008: 2–3

Nothing is ever wrong with the *design* of the ICS; all problems are attributed entirely to implementation, just as the failed spell is blamed not on the magic itself but on the way the ceremony was performed, or some other procedural flaw. The quote gives a strong, chilling sense of the indefeasible, circular reasoning so clearly associated by Mauss with the world of magic. Ingeniously, not only are the vicissitudes of the ICS reinterpreted as implementation challenges, but these same tribulations are invoked to undermine the evaluation itself; an incorrigible but fatally deluded position. Belief in the efficacy of the magic is strengthened, paradoxically, by its very failure.

A characteristic of magic, as we have noted, is the accomplishment of effects, typically remotely, by the automatic effect of the performance of the magical rite and the spell in particular. Magical language is typified by performative speech acts,

wherein the change-of-state (magic is always about changing the world) described or implied by the words and the symbolic, non-verbal actions of the rite is achieved directly by the performance of the rite. The phrase 'designed to ensure' has this incantatory character. There is no doubt in the minds of the ICS's architects that the implementation of their system will necessarily bring about the effects ('improved outcomes') which they seek. The policy discourse surrounding ICS has shown itself remarkably durable in terms of its core mantras. Fast forwarding 10 years to a recent document, we have a good summary of the credo which continues to inform ICS. Its opening paragraphs proclaim:

> The Integrated Children's System (ICS) has been developed in response to findings from inspections, research and inquiries which found that within children's social services there were failures to record, retrieve and understand the significance of information about children. These findings suggested the need for a more systematic approach to work with children in need. The ICS provides a method of practice and a business process which aims to support practitioners and managers in undertaking their key tasks of assessment, planning, intervention and review.
>
> DCSF, 2008: 1

What may one make of this discourse? At no point is there a carefully worked out, empirically-grounded, cause-effect argument for the benefits for ICS. Instead, we have a dogma founded on an unshakeable belief that, by setting targets, monitoring performance indicators and enforcing rigorous assessment procedures, policy objectives which are set out in the same terms, and which embody the same internal logic, will inevitably be achieved (Garrett, 2009). The evidence-base is ritually invoked but rigorous argument, critical analysis and robust research are conspicuous by their absence. In summary, we have a self-sealing belief system powered by magical thinking.

Technology figures prominently in this discourse, as it does throughout the whole of the New Labour modernisation project, as we have noted. Herein, the resonance with the sympathetic mechanisms of magic is especially striking. It is as if the material properties of technology to yield material effects through efficient causes are being magically transferred into the social realm through the spell-like incantations of policy and the sympathetic mechanisms of both similarity and contagion. The

ICS process model, presented as a flow chart with deterministic links, looks just like the blue print for a machine; magically, the software-mediated regime thus acquires the mechanical efficacy of its material counterpart. Or so the wishful thinking goes. The sympathetic effects of technology are doubled up by the actual physical presence of computers within the workplace. As a 'finite state machine', given certain inputs the computer guarantees prescribed outputs. Magically, these properties of perfect reliability will be passed on by contagion to the humans who also inhabit this world. The apparent belief of managers that the mere application of technology will solve problems and automatically enhance the performance of the organisations has been dubbed by Markus and Benjamin (1997) as the 'magic bullet theory of IT-enabled transformation'!

Stivers (2001) has dwelt at length on the relations between technology and magic in the contemporary world which he characterises as a 'technological milieu'. Technology is all-pervasive. Closer than nature, keeping us safe, sustaining all needs, mediating all relationships, it has become our 'chief sacred' (p 41) offering the promise of heaven on earth. In this techno-utopia, governance and leadership in all organisational contexts have been transformed into technology, in the form of managerialism. In the modern state, Stivers (2001) argues that people look more and more to government to solve all social ills, and as we saw with the magician, working this magic in return is what government sees as its primary role. The state becomes an increasingly technical phenomenon, using managerial means to solve all problems. That our faith in managerial technologies is essentially magic is confirmed by the juxtaposition of durable belief in the presence of objective failure. At the end of his analysis, Stivers concludes with the following quotation in which the policy resonances are only too obvious:

Management technique involves magical practices . . . [it] is faddish; theories have a brief shelf life, and old theories are constantly being re-packaged with new buzzwords and clichés. Obviously they don't work – they don't control uncertainty and predict the future. So why are we so susceptible to each new preposterous technique? Management technique promotes itself as a kind of technology; it clothes itself in the aura of technology. So if this management technique does not work, the next one to come along will.

Paradise regained?

Thus far we have painted a rather dystopian picture of the world of children's services blighted by ill-designed technology. There is, however, some cause for optimism, that an amelioration may arise through the operation of natural, dialectical forces, that the ICS will be undone through its own contradictions. There is a limit to the extent that manifest failure can be redefined as evidence of success even for those enchanted by the magic they have conjured up. The tragic death of Baby Peter has, as we have noted, produced just such a turning point, and there are opportunities now for a fundamental review of the design of ICS. There are messages here of more general import and we shall finish by exploring these wider implications. The problems we have noted are certainly not unique. Examples abound of other IT-enabled 'modernisation' projects, such as the gargantuan National Programme for Information Technology (NPfIT) in the UK health service. Eason (2007: 258) argues that NPfIT has generally followed a 'push strategy, thrusting new technology into the healthcare practices of the NHS', leaving little room for local design. Eason finds strikingly similar local adaptations (workarounds etc.) to those we have unveiled here, as well as equally concerning symptoms of stress and misuse.

The remedy for these ills lies, we believe, in a fundamental shift in the managerial mind-set, away from monitoring and control to design. Furthermore, a different approach to design itself is required, together with a change in our relationship with technology. Middle managers need to see their main business not as the brutal enforcers of targets but as the benign designers of the workplace. The idea of 'managing as designing' has gained some ground recently, although it is still rather an exotic notion. By design, we simply mean the creation of form, the translation of concepts and aspirations into concrete working realisations. In an organisational context, this means the design of systems made up of people, processes and technology in order to achieve the best possible performance. Finding the best way of organising the workplace, in more prosaic terms. If this is not the primary business of management, then what on earth is?

Doing design well depends on our attitude to technology. A magical attitude will no longer do. Hard work is required and authentic engagement; technology is too important to leave to others. Brown and Hagel (2003) contend that the productivity paradox (the dissociation between investments in technology and objective benefits) reflects the failure of many organisations to use technology to innovate in their business practices: 'Companies that mechanically insert IT into their businesses . . . will only destroy IT's economic value. Unfortunately, all too many companies do this'. Those organisations which stand out in terms of the business value generated by IT are those which emphasize its innovative potential, and have retained their in-house design capability, rather than relying on packed software or outsourcing (see for example Howcroft and Light, 2008). Sadly the opposite has been the trend in the UK public sector, not the least powered by government policies such as CCT (Lin et al. 2007). Tellingly, those LAs which have retained their in-house capability have produced successful examples of social work systems against the trend set by ICS. The London Borough of Kensington and Chelsea is one such breakaway authority. Expressly designed to support practice, rather than compliance with central dictat, their social work system has been widely acclaimed. The same Council minute (pp 2–3) which recorded their divorce from the national ICS project in 2008 runs as follows:

The system has been extremely well received by practitioners and many new social work recruits from other London boroughs have commented favourable on KCics in comparison with those systems used elsewhere . . . [which are] difficult to use, time consuming and overly prescriptive.

Royal Borough of Kensington and Chelsea, 2008

Design itself needs to be done non-magically. Techniques for design abound, and again we find the same tendency to see methodologies as magic solutions, which Wastell (1996) has dubbed the 'fetish of technique'. The antidote to mysticism is, as ever, a robust empiricism. Such a radically different approach to design, is not really so radical. What is required above all is to found the design of systems on the needs of users and a thorough understanding of their working practices. This insight applies to the design of any artefact, be it a form, a process or a database. The case for user-centred design [UCD] has been cogently made in many design contexts (Norman, 1998). Ethnographic studies have shown time and again that even work which seems highly routine

is a skilled accomplishment (Gasser, 1986), its orderliness is a product of the artful worker, not a property of the work-flow model. UCD is essential in order to gain reliable knowledge of how work is actually done for designing new tools and processes. And what may be said for IT design, may be said for policy too. Reform-as-learning (Hubbard et al., 2006) provides an alternative, design-informed approach to policy-making, based on co-construction and mutual learning, and has been shown to be efficacious in the educational domain where top-down methods have failed.

Technology is not some 'pixie dust . . . to be sprinkled over problems which then, hey presto, vanish!' (Dowty, 2008: 398). Dowty goes on to exhort that in 'child surveillance . . . the need to abandon magical thinking is long overdue'. Markus and Benjamin write of the enchantment of technology across all business sectors, and the need to break its spell. We may not find the business jargon congenial, but the sentiment is clear enough:

Many IT-enabled change projects fail, despite how much is known about ensuring success. In this article, we have argued that failure to employ best practices in IT-enabled change stems from mistaken belief about the causes of change – belief in IT as a magic bullet . . . IT is not a magic bullet. Change in human behaviour cannot take place at a distance but requires direct personal contact between change agents and targets . . . Successful change takes good ideas, skill, and plain hard work – but it does not need magic.

Dowty, 2008: 66–7

Acknowledgements

The research to which this paper refers was supported by the Economic and Social Research Council, Public Services Programme, Award Number RES-166-25-0048-A. The authors would like to acknowledge the vital contribution of other members of the research team, who are, Karen Broadhurst, University of Lancaster; Chris Hall and Sue Peckover, University of Huddersfield and Andy Pithouse and Dolores Davey, University of Cardiff.

References

Bell, M. (2008) Put on ICS: Research Finds Disquiet with ICS. *Community Care*. Available: http://www.communitycare.co.uk/Articles/

2008/06/05/108421/analysis-of-the-integrated-childrens-system-pilots.html.

Broadhurst, K. et al. (2009) Performing 'Initial Assessment': Identifying The Latent Conditions For Error at The Front-Door of Local Authority Children's Services. *British Journal of Social Work*, In Press.

Brown, J.S. and Hagel, J. (2003) Does IT matter? An HBR Debate. *Harvard Business Review*, June, 2–4.

Cabinet Office. (2005) *Transformational Government: Enabled by technology*, Available: http://www.cabinetoffice.gov.uk/media/141734/transgov-strategy.pdf.

Caulkin, S. (2008) Blame Bureaucrats and Systems for Baby P's Fate. *Observer*, 23 Nov.

Cleaver, H. and Walker, S. (2004) From Policy to Practice: The Implementation of a New Framework For Social Work Assessments of Children and Families. *Child and Family Social Work*, 9, 81–90.

Cleaver, H. et al. (2008) *The Integrated Children's System: Enhancing Social Work and Inter-Agency Practice*. London: Jessica Kingsley.

Department for Children, Schools and Families. (2008) *Integrated Children's System Evaluation: Summary of Key Findings*. London: DCSF.

Department for Children, Schools and Families. (2009) *Integrated Children's System: Changes to Policy Principles and Measures. LAC 1706090002.* London: DCSF.

Department of Health. (2000) *Learning the Lessons: Government's Response to Lost in Care*. London: The Stationery Office.

Dowty, T. (2008) Pixie-dust and Privacy: What's Happening to Children's Rights in England? *Children & Society*, 22, 393–9.

Eason, K. (2007) Local Socio-technical Development in the National Programme for Information Technology, *Journal of Information Technology*, 22, 257–64.

Frazer, J.G. (1922) *The Golden Bough: A Study in Magic and Religion*. London: Macmillan.

Garrett, P.M. (2009) 'Transforming' Children's Services? Social Work, Neoliberalism and the 'Modern' World. Maidenhead: McGraw Hill/Open University.

Gasser, L. (1986) The Integration of Computing and Routine Work. *ACM Transactions on Office Information Systems*, 4, 205–25.

Howcroft, D. and Light, B. (2008) IT Consultants, Salesmanship and The Challenges of Packaged Software Selection in SMEs. *Journal of Enterprise Information Management*, 21: 6, 597–615.

Hubbard, L., Mehan, H. and Stein, M.K. (2006) *Reform as Learning*. London: Routledge.

Laming (2003) The Victoria Climbié Inquiry: Report of an Inquiry by Lord Laming. Command 5730, Norwich: Stationery Office.

Lin, C., Pervan, G. and McDermid, D. (2007) Issues and Recommendations in Evaluating and Managing The Benefits of Public Sector IS/IT Outsourcing. *Information Technology & People*, 20: 2, 161–83.

Malinowski, B. (1922) *Argonauts of the Western Pacific*. London: Routledge.

Markus, L.M. and Benjamin, R. (1997) The Magic Bullet Theory in IT-Enabled Transformation. *Sloan Management Review*, Winter, 55–68.

Mauss, M. (1950) *A General Theory of Magic*. London: Routledge.

Norman, D.A. (1998) *The Design of Everyday Things*. Cambridge MA: MIT Press.

Royal Borough of Kensington and Chelsea. (2008) *Non-Acceptance of the Integrated Children's System (ICS) Capital Grant 2007–08*. Royal Borough of Kensington and Chelsea. Available: http://www.rbkc.gov.uk/howwegovern/keydecisions/Reports/Cabinet%20Member%20-%20Leader/KD02993R.pdf.

Stivers, R. (2001) *Technology As Magic: The Triumph of The Irrational*. New York: Continuum.

Unison (2008) *Unison Memorandum to Lord Laming: Progress Report on Safeguarding*. Unison. Available: www.unison.org.uk/acrobat/B4364a.pdf.

Wastell, D. et al. (forthcoming) Children's Services in The Iron Cage of Performance Management: Street Level Bureaucracy and The Spectre of Svejkism, paper accepted *International Journal of Social Welfare*.

Wastell, D.G. (1996) The Fetish of Technique: Methodology as a Social Defense. *Information Systems Journal*, 6, 25–40.

CHAPTER 12

Playing with Fire or Rediscovering Fire? The Perils and Potential for Evidence Based Practice in Child and Family Social Work

Donald Forrester

The arguments in this chapter are based on a belief that child and family social work is in profound crisis, and that there is an urgent need for radical change to address it. The report and media coverage following the death of Baby Peter are merely symptoms of a far more deep-seated malaise. Indeed, it is the failure of social work to be able to articulate what it does or provide evidence that it makes a difference in the face of the firestorm of media criticism in recent months that is the most concerning aspect of the situation. All the professionals involved with Baby Peter made mistakes, and several paid a steep price. But it is only in social work that the death of a child has (once again) seen attempts to reform the system and fundamentally change the profession. For the other professions involved with Baby Peter his death was seen as an example of individuals not achieving the expected professional standards; for social work it was taken as a condemnation of the entire profession.

This seems to be related to a more profound problem, namely can we – the social work profession – articulate and defend a vision of what we do and the contribution that it makes? It seems that at present the answer to this question is 'no'. Practice is now dominated by managerial and bureaucratic approaches (Social Work Task Force, 2009). Certainly there is a lack of a strong voice for social work. Our inability to develop and support a professional association is a condemnation of our lack of maturity as a profession. However, there is also a lack of a convincing and coherent vision for what social work is or should be. The dominant approaches in academic social work do not have a strong relationship to the realities of practice. All too often they seem to be taught to students and then left at the door of the first office in which the newly qualified worker is employed.

This chapter is not an attempt to delineate the manifest problems in child and family social work (though it may do so in passing). Rather it is an attempt to outline key elements of an alternative conceptualisation of social work in the United Kingdom. In doing so it has been influenced by my own experience of being a consultant for the Welsh Assembly Government [WAG]. For most of my professional career I have felt that I was able to articulate the many problems and limitations in the system. However, in 2007 – when meeting senior individuals within WAG – I was asked for the first time not what the problems were, but what should be done about them. This is a much harder question to answer! In this chapter I will attempt to argue that a better way of providing services involves three things. First, a *commitment* to using evidence based ways of working. Second, *investment* in developing an evidence base of what works for social work. Third, a focus on professional excellence in *developing and delivering* evidence based approaches (as opposed to a belief that evidence based approaches can be delivered as a cheap or simple option). Taken together these can be characterised as a vision of social work that focuses on *professional excellence in delivering evidence based practice.*

This is a controversial position within academic social work (and within a broader range of practice based disciplines, such as education and some areas of health); most academics would argue that the concept of what works should be put in inverted commas (to indicate that it is a contested term and that there are no universal interventions that work), or that we should use the term evidence informed practice (to denote the fact that evidence is only one of the things that should guide decision-making). Some go further. Holmes et al. (2006) in discussing evidence based practice in health settings, argue that as an approach it is 'outrageously exclusionary and dangerously normative with regards to scientific knowledge . . . a good example of microfacism at play in the contemporary scientific arena' (Holmes et al., 2006: 181).

In this chapter I argue that such thinking is part of the problem, indeed that it has led to an intellectually and politically weakened profession and has contributed to our inability to respond robustly and effectively to the current challenges. In order to make this argument the chapter first reviews (very briefly) the background to the current crisis in social work. It then considers the arguments against evidence based approaches within social work. In doing so, it suggests that evidence based approaches are like fire: a powerful tool but potentially dangerous if misused or misunderstood. Some of the criticisms of them are well founded, but properly understood none suggests that we should not be using evidence based approaches within social work. On the contrary, it is argued that evidence based approaches should provide a foundation for a reinvigorated social work and a focus for constructive debate within and across social work.

The final sections consider evidence based approaches and current initiatives within social work. Some recent initiatives in Wales and in Hackney are considered. Each places evidence based approaches at the heart of reform of children's services. It is concluded that what is needed is a profound and long-term reform of social services that places excellence in delivering evidence based practice at its heart. This truly would allow social work to rediscover the 'fire' that enthused and informed the first pioneers within the profession.

How did we get into this mess?

It would be misleading to suggest that there was a halcyon time when social work was perfect. Research and the evidence from government reports have been identifying serious problems within social work for decades. However, what appears to be true is that the bulk of the reforms of recent years have tended to make the system worse. There are various symptoms of this crisis. The amount of time that social workers spend filling in forms or at their computer – widely believed to be 70 to 80 per cent of their time – suggests a profession that has lost a vision of what it should be about. The domination of practice by performance indicators, forms and other bureaucratic and managerial ways of controlling practice is symptomatic of a profession that is not trusted to deliver services.

As a result, we now have a system whose arteries are so sclerotic that it is in need of radical surgery.

The government – particularly since 1997 – has been the key player in this infantilising and bureaucratising of social work. However, it is important to remember that the changes that they have made were all made with good intentions. For instance, the Looked After Children [LAC] materials, and subsequent developments from them, such as the forms accompanying the Assessment Framework or the Common Assessment Framework, were all attempts to improve practice. They were based on strong evidence that social work was not delivering the high quality services that children and families deserve and they attempted to formalise research findings and the views of experts on best practice (see for instance Cleaver et al, 2004; DoH, 1995; 2000a and b; 2001; Laming, 2003; Ward, 1995). As a practitioner, I greeted the LAC materials with great excitement, seeing them as a rational and convincing attempt to relate research to practice. Looking back I can see that the forms had a largely negative effect, with a great increase in time filling them in and a reduction of usability by professionals or service users. More importantly, forms cannot make up for poor professional practice. If social workers are not collecting and analysing information well, then a long form will not resolve that issue.

The example of the LAC materials, and subsequent developments, highlights one of the ways in which academic social work has been complicit in the de-professionalisation of social work. Key researchers closely involved with government have been genuinely trying to improve practice. However, their work has been undermined by a failure to understand and critique the ways in which policies are developed and put into practice. They, along with senior civil servants and government ministers, have conceptualised change as something that can be imposed and regulated from the centre. To a large extent the failure of this model for delivering public services is what has characterised a current broader loss of faith in New Labour. Certainly it has resulted in debasing the nature of social work services. The danger is that it may lead to a general mistrust of public services, and the challenge is therefore to identify and articulate more effective ways of delivering services in general – and social work in particular.

However, academic social work has been complicit in the failure of social work in a second way. There are many interesting approaches to social work articulated by academics. At the moment the 'three Rs' appear particularly popular: radical social work, reflective practice and relationship-based approaches. Each of these has strong arguments in favour of it; each emphasises elements of the core nature of social work. And yet these approaches seem highly unlikely to be put into practice by policy-makers or politicians. In some instances, this may be because they are unpalatable to senior managers (for instance, nobody is going to fund social workers to work to overthrow capitalism; such activities are generally best restricted to evenings and weekends). However, there are two more fundamental barriers to putting these approaches into practice. The most important is that they lack evidence that they would make a difference. Without such evidence why should policy-makers change things? Secondly, even if a policy-maker did want to move toward one of these approaches, they do not have a clear set of potential policy formulations. What would a system based on reflective practice, radical approaches or relationship based social work look like? How would it differ from current practice? The difficulty is not in answering these questions; it is answering them in a way that would convince policy-makers that the investment would generate real and measurable improvements in services.

The challenge for academic social work is therefore to articulate a vision of what social work should be that combines the best of current views of social work with a convincing rationale and set of policies for politicians and policy-makers. It needs to incorporate a commitment to individual and social justice, to humane and caring ways of working and to making a difference for individuals and for society. However, it also needs to involve evidence that it makes a difference and a convincing picture of how it might be put into practice.

This chapter attempts to argue for such a vision. At its heart is a commitment to evidence based practice [EBP]. EBP is argued to allow the development of a vision of what social work is and should be that can simultaneously inspire practitioners and convince policy-makers. The crucial reason for this is that any evidence based intervention has a focus on what happens when a professional meets a client and the difference that that makes. As such it is uniquely well-placed to allow a new and different vision for what social work should be about. This vision can incorporate the best of radical, reflective and relationship-based approaches, while remaining realistic and convincing.

This is a challenging goal. It is made all the more challenging by the fact that academic social work has traditionally been highly critical of EBP, and indeed by the fact that there are very good reasons for such scepticism – and many examples of the inappropriate use of 'evidence based' approaches. It is therefore necessary to review the criticisms of EBP before outlining a more nuanced and constructive vision of EBP and social work.

Evidence based practice and its discontents

First, what is EBP? EBP first developed in medicine, based on the idea that doctors should use the best evidence in deciding appropriate treatments. Similar ideas have been brought into social work and social care, however the original idea that interventions should be based on evidence has been tempered by the fact that each individual and family is unique and it is therefore difficult to specify approaches, that the circumstances and views of individuals must be taken into account and that other factors (such as ethical issues) also need to be considered. As a result there has been a move toward evidence *informed* practice, that is evidence as one of the factors that practitioners should take into account but not the only one.

In this chapter I argue for a narrower and more prescriptive definition of EBP: namely, the use of 'interventions' that are clearly defined and for which there is a strong evidence base. This evidence base requires the use of studies that compare the intervention with other interventions (including normal service). This type of evaluation is commonly called experimental evaluation and is particularly important as it rules out other reasons for changes. A good example of the need for experimental studies is research into Intensive Family Preservation Services (IFPS). These are crisis intervention services aimed at reducing the need for children to enter care. IFPS were believed to produce positive outcomes based on studies that found that between 80 and 100 per cent of children referred to the service did not enter care. However, when experimental studies randomly assigned families to either normal service or IFPS studies they found that children in each group were equally likely to improve and just as unlikely to enter care (see Forrester et al., 2008). There are complicated reasons for this finding, but the key point for our purposes is that it illustrates the unique power of experimental evaluations to identify whether a service is actually producing the changes that it appears to be creating, or whether these might have happened anyway. (Indeed, such an approach seems particularly important for social work, because so often after our interventions children and families still have significant problems; experimental methods would identify whether these problems would be worse with different interventions or none).

This is a relatively extreme form of EBP. It is loosely based on the interventions being analogous to specific medical interventions (such as surgery or a pill) and it is therefore worth considering in some depth the problems with such a position before looking at the arguments in favour of this approach.

There are four main arguments against this vision of EBP. First, there is an issue of generalisability. Science searches for and has been remarkably successful at finding generalisable laws. Thus if aspirin is found to reduce pain for lots of people in lots of different studies, it can be assumed that in general (and with some documented exceptions and risks) it reduces pain. The same is not true for psycho-social interventions. This is because the context within which interventions are delivered is crucial. Thus, a service delivering Cognitive Behavioural Therapy [CBT] in one locality may work very well, while one in another area seems not to work. Closer inspection may reveal that different clients are being referred to the service, that workers are delivering CBT in different ways or that social factors are influencing the effectiveness of the intervention. CBT – or other interventions – are not amenable to generalisable laws of effectiveness. Thus, many researchers in the UK now tend to agree with Pawson and Tilley in highlighting the importance of context in understanding impact and effectiveness; research cannot find out what 'works', only whether something works in a specific context at a particular time (Pawson and Tilley, 1997; Robson, 2002).

Second, EBP tends to individualise problems and it can fail to be critical of social and political factors involved in creating the issues being dealt with. Thus, for instance, CBT is an 'evidence based' way of helping people with depression, but it does not address the fact that depression is often created by social factors. Thus, people living in overcrowded houses, with limited income or without social support are far more likely to be depressed. Helping the individual to think differently does not address the social injustice that may be part of the reason that depression is on the increase in society. In practice, EBP rarely explores social factors because they are far harder to study; it is easy to compare the impact of receiving CBT with not receiving it, but very hard to compare the impact of a more equal society.

Third, this medical approach also fails to take a critical view of the definition of the issues being dealt with. Thus for instance, studies of Motivational Interviewing may show that it reduces 'problem' drinking but they rarely explore the way in which alcohol problems or alcoholism are defined and structured through social processes; CBT may reduce depression, but it rarely considers what depression is, who defines it and whether these processes individualise social problems. This can be crucial, as all the key issues that social workers deal with are open to challenge and need to be considered critically. EBP does not tend to do so.

Finally, a more pragmatic – but equally important – criticism of EBP is that it can all too easily be used as a tool of central managerial control. Thus for instance, in the youth justice field the government expressed great interest in CBT for young offenders. This was perhaps in part a way of standardising practice and allowing centralised control over what workers delivered. However, in practice this does not seem to have been particularly effective (Pitts, 2001).

These are very powerful arguments against EBP: how can I possibly be making it a central element in reconceptualising social work? Of course, there are also strong arguments in favour of EBP, but it is worth making a more general point at this stage. These criticisms are real and genuine limitations or problems for EBP. Central to my response is not an attempt to deny their importance, but rather to argue that it is precisely *because* social work takes these issues seriously that it is well placed to develop a vision of EBP which is better than the nature of EBP as currently practised. Or, looked at another way, if we do not wrestle with these issues and develop a form of evidence based social work we will increasingly find a highly individualistic, uncritical and managerial form of EBP imposed on us. It is therefore in a spirit of addressing these legitimate concerns and incorporating them into a new vision rather than refuting them that the following arguments in favour of EBP are made.

First, the issue of generalisability is often raised in a rather simplistic way. However, there are complex issues around generalisability even within the sciences and medicine. The example of aspirin was given earlier. However, in fact, the impact of aspirin is mediated by a wide range of factors. Age, diet, personal pain thresholds and a multitude of other issues can influence the impact of aspirin. In practice with this, or any other treatment, doctors might prescribe it and should then monitor whether it is working or producing unintended side-effects. Indeed, this is the heart of evidence based practice. Furthermore, there are serious arguments in favour of generalisability within social science. It is true that CBT, or many other evidence based interventions, do not always work. However, if an intervention has been found to work better than normal treatment in a large number of good studies, then it begins to seem naïve or stubborn to deny some level of generalisability. This is well illustrated in the following quote:

*An astronomer, a physicist, and a mathematician were holidaying in Scotland. Looking out from a train window, they saw a black sheep in the middle of a field. 'How interesting', said the astronomer, Scottish sheep are black'. 'No, no', said the physicist, 'some Scottish sheep are black'. The mathematician looked at them, looked out of the window and said, 'As a mathematician, I say that in Scotland there is at least one field, containing at least one sheep, **at least one side of which is black'**.*
Singh, 1997

Of course one can take the strict line of the mathematician, and argue that each study only shows that in that particular context a specific intervention worked, but in the real world if something has worked in a large number of similar contexts then it begins to seem unhelpfully obstinate to maintain that it should not be used. This is not to say issues around generalisability are not important (they are crucial – and are discussed further below) but it is to argue against a hardline rejection of generalisability as something that can be achieved to a level where it could (and should) inform practice. In practice pragmatic decisions need to be made about the quality of evidence, and issues around transfer and context are crucial in doing so. Admitting this is not the same as denying the possibility of developing broadly helpful knowledge about what works. At the very least, when developing an intervention for a new context it seems more appropriate to consider evidence about what has worked in other contexts than to treat that information as irrelevant.

Second, the key issues relating to critiquing the concepts being worked with and avoiding focusing on the individual are crucial if we are to develop a genuinely *social work* form of evidence based practice. The question is whether social work can develop evidence based approaches that are consistent with our central values. For instance, can we develop and evaluate ways of working that incorporate the views of clients, that intervene at social as well as individual or family levels and that can incorporate critical reflection on the goals of the intervention itself? It seems to me that there is no reason why this cannot be done, and indeed there is at least one example of such an intervention. Families and Schools Together (FAST] is a parenting intervention developed by a social worker (Lynn McDonald) and it seems to address many of these issues. For instance, FAST operates to help children and parents, but it also aims to build social capital and community involvement. It involves service users, not just in a tokenistic way but in defining the intervention for their community and in delivering it. The teams that deliver FAST are made-up of both professionals and service users. Furthermore issues of difference and discrimination are taken very seriously. The people delivering FAST need to be broadly representative of the communities they serve; it would not be acceptable for FAST to be delivered by white workers to a black or Native American audience (see for example Kratochwill et al., 2004 or FAST, 2009). Yet FAST has been experimentally evaluated and is accepted as an 'evidence based' approach (Harvard Family Research Project, 2007; Office of Juvenile Justice and Delinquency Prevention, 2009; Substance Abuse and Mental Health Services Administration, 2003). This is not to imply that FAST is perfect. However, it does contrast with most other parenting intervention programmes. Some of these are individualistic, though most are based on groupwork interventions, but all appear to share a tendency to individualise issues of parenting and to say comparatively little about issues of discrimination or broader social deprivation. The intriguing thing about FAST is that it successfully addresses many of the common criticisms of evidence based interventions, while remaining evidence based. This is a persuasive argument that these criticisms are of EBP as actually developed, primarily by psychologists and psychiatrists, rather than EBP as it might be. Indeed, it suggests that social workers should more enthusiastically and energetically be developing such approaches.

The final set of criticisms are of a rather different order. They are not theoretical criticisms of the nature or potential for EBP, but rather they focus on the politics of EBP and the ways in which it might be used (and sometimes has been used) inappropriately. A particularly good example of the misuse of 'evidence based' approaches is in the field of youth justice. Pitts (2001) reviews the experience of CBT as applied to young offenders. He notes that the initial research upon which the claims that CBT 'works' were founded were carried out in well resourced facilities in North America. This was then used as the basis for rolling CBT out across youth offending services in the United Kingdom. Perhaps unsurprisingly, CBT did not work nearly as well in these contexts The reasons for this are discussed further below. However, Pitts goes on to make a persuasive argument that EBP can be, and in this case was, used as a tool of central control by government of professional practice. For instance, specifying that practitioners must use CBT provides the opportunity for government to control in some detail what practitioners are meant to be delivering. Evidence based interventions are typically 'manualised', that is a book sets out in detail the nature of the work expected. Training and supervision are also often specified in some detail. In some instances, particularly research studies, this can even involve the number of sessions and the topics per session being specified. One can see why this might appeal to the desire for policy-makers to control and specify practice; it allows them to be very clear about what is being done and to be able to account for why it is being done by referring to the evidence base.

It is of course the ability of EBP to specify what is being done, why, and the evidence that it tends to make a difference that makes EBP a particularly powerful basis for policy-making. However, the youth justice experience indicates how easily these aspects of EBP can be misunderstood. To understand this better it is perhaps helpful to consider some recent research studies in the substance misuse field. Rather than considering these as if they were research studies, it is interesting to look upon them as policy projects. Researchers have a task: to make sure that practitioners deliver the intervention that has been specified, and to evaluate whether it makes a difference. In general a lot of attention is paid to the second element of this job, but in fact the former is just as important and perhaps more relevant to policy issues.

So, how do researchers get practitioners to deliver EBP? Practice obviously varies, and in what follows the focus is on the United Kingdom Alcohol Treatment Trial (UKATT) as it was the largest evaluation of alcohol treatment approaches in the UK and provides a very good example of issues in ensuring that an intervention is correctly delivered. There are a number of stages involved in ensuring that practitioners deliver an intervention within a research study. Within UKATT (Tober, 2007) these were broadly to:

1. Identify the approach that you want people to deliver.
2. Specify clearly the nature of the intervention (for example through a manual).
3. Select therapists who appear to have high levels of skill or potential.
4. Provide training (though in general not that much).
5. Provide supervision that focuses on actual practice and the skills used in real interviews, for example through tapes of practice (this in general lasted several months until practitioners achieved sufficient skill).
6. Only allow individuals to deliver practice when they are able to provide taped examples of actual practice that demonstrate they have adequate skill levels.
7. Periodically take tapes of actual practice and rate them to ensure that the intervention is still being delivered. Where a practitioner is not delivering the intervention then extra input can be provided to improve their skill level.

These steps have some things in common with the approach that Pitts criticised in youth justice. However, in UKATT they had two important differences. First, the practitioners reported very positively about the experience of having this input. Second, they produced very significant positive change in most people worked with. The two are perhaps not unrelated!

So, perhaps the key question is, why did the UKATT trial seem to work while the attempts to use CBT in youth justice broadly speaking failed? There are two key lessons for EBP. The first is that the approach identified for a particular issue needs to be appropriate. Central to Pitts' critique of CBT is that it provides an individualised approach to what is a social issue. This is a consideration that we should always be aware of in using evidence based approaches: is there evidence that they work, and do they seem to be the most appropriate approach for this issue?

The second lesson for EBP is at least as important. UKATT spent far more time and attention controlling the quality of the intervention that was delivered than Youth Justice services will have done in relation to CBT. This sort of focus on ensuring the quality of what is delivered is one of the key hallmarks of rigorous research studies. And the importance of this focus is highlighted by the frequency with which demonstration projects fail to replicate their findings when rolled out to other settings. There is even a name for this, it is called the issue of 'implementation fidelity'. Implementation fidelity is the extent to which replications of approaches tend to alter the intervention. There is strong evidence that when interventions are rolled out on a larger scale it usually results in a failure to reproduce all the elements of the intervention, and this tends to reduce the impact of the intervention.

There is a key issue here about standardisation and excellence in the delivery of services. Pitts' argument – and there are many who share this view – is that EBP is (or could be) used to standardise practice. There is a sense in which this is true; but a more profound sense in which this is a misunderstanding of EBP. To explore this further it is worth turning to consider more broadly the acquisition of high levels of skill in any field. This might be in any number of areas, from cooking to playing the trumpet, but because it is the area that I know most about I will use the example of learning a sport.

Being highly skilled in a sport (or cooking or the trumpet) allows one to improvise, to use one's skills flexibly (eclectically one might say) in order to meet the needs of the moment. Yet this is not how one *becomes* highly skilled. To become highly skilled almost the opposite is required. One needs to master the basic skills as set down by those who are already highly skilled. In sport one learns the basic techniques (for instance, passing, movement, shooting). In cooking one may follow recipes from a cookbook or be instructed by a chef.

Becoming highly skilled in any area therefore requires discipline. The core of the argument in this chapter is that a focus on delivering evidence based approaches provides the discipline that social workers need. Once one or more evidence based approaches are mastered, then the individual may be able to improvise and eclectically choose the appropriate approach for a specific situation. However, at the moment most social workers and social work students (and I was one of them!) who claim to be eclectic, in fact do not have any approach that they are skilled to deliver. It is rather like asking a musician what instrument they play and being told that there is no one instrument that can meet all their needs and that therefore they make each note in the way that seems best. We should be as suspicious of an eclectic approach in social work as we would of a 'musician' who cannot play any particular instrument.

There is a danger in such an argument, and the key issue here is that the problems and the potential of evidence based practice relate closely to the word 'discipline'. Pitts quite rightly highlights the danger that evidence based practice might be used as a way of disciplining workers; as a form of social control of professional practice. On the other hand, discipline is essential if one is to become highly skilled at any craft. And this discipline needs to be expected by those supporting the development of skill and accepted by those who wish to become proficient. This type of discipline, the discipline involved in learning to play music or make pottery, is related to, but conceptually different from, the sense in which discipline is a way of controlling and punishing. Crucially it is a form of discipline that requires the participant to wish to learn the discipline required.

There is a complex argument here about control and professional discretion. To what degree should the state be specifying the content and form of services and to what degree should this be left to professionals who deliver the services? In reality the days in which practitioners were trusted to deliver services are long gone. While criticisms of such approaches have perhaps over-played the extent to which services were run for the benefit of the practitioners rather than the users of services, it is nonetheless true that too often professionals running services resulted in services that were not responsive to the needs of those who use them (Le Grand, 2007). Furthermore, while critics such as Pitts rightly warn about the dangers of EBP, they would not presumably argue for a service in which there are no expectations or controls around the quality of the service that is delivered or the outcomes for the client. This would be an untenable position. The discussion therefore becomes not about whether what professionals do should be controlled, but about to what extent, in what ways and by whom should practice be controlled. For such a debate EBP is uniquely well placed to offer a way forward. There are several elements of EBP that make it particularly suited to an enlightened delivery of public services.

First, EBPs specify what they are delivering. For policy-makers and those using services this adds a level of transparency. This in turn means that those using services can be involved in evaluating whether the service as delivered is appropriate. Thus, for instance, evidence based parenting programmes have been reviewed by Native American groups and those that they felt particularly appropriate for Native American culture were identified (Kratochwill et al., 2004). This is possible because of the clarity over the nature of the intervention. It is not possible to do this for services that are delivered without this attention to the specific nature of the service.

Second, EBP by its nature opens itself up to evaluation. Because it specifies what is to be delivered, research can evaluate whether this was delivered and whether it tends to make a difference. This is of enormous practical help (how else can we find out whether what we do makes a difference?) but it is also surely an ethical imperative. If we do not evaluate whether what we do makes a difference, on what basis do we do it? If a doctor recommends a particular drug one would expect that they knew something of its likely effects. Surely we should expect the same of a social worker placing a child in care or referring a family to a service for family therapy?

Most importantly, EBP provides a refreshing way forward for those interested in developing excellence in practice. For in contrast to the dominant managerial approach, which focuses on bureaucratic collection of data on processes, EBP focuses on *what happens when a practitioner meets a client* and *what the outcome is*. This focus on practice is at the heart of the potential that EBP has for unlocking a better approach in social work. Instead of the collection of information on 'performance' indicators that measure processes that are only tangentially related (if they are related at all) to what is experienced by service users, EBP focuses on practice and the difference it makes.

However, it needs to be emphasised that delivering EBP is hard and poses challenges for practitioners and at a policy level. A crucial point for policy-makers to realise is that the research studies that achieve such impressive results invest huge quantities of time and effort in ensuring that practitioners are highly skilled and therefore able to deliver the intervention. As any coach or teacher knows, enabling people to reach the highest levels of performance requires an ability to harness and support the individual's motivation. It cannot be achieved by top-down diktat. Delivering EBP therefore requires a reorientation of services toward supporting practitioners in the very challenging process of delivering evidence based approaches. It is not an easy option; but it is an approach we should develop because such interventions tend to work.

EBP has often been set up as if it were in opposition to other approaches within social work, such as reflective practice, radical approaches or relationship-based work. However, this is a false opposition. There is insufficient space to explore these issues in depth in this chapter, however it should be obvious that there are substantial overlaps and commonalities between these different approaches. Where there are differences, they have the potential to be creative tensions rather than irreconcilable, provided that we are prepared to enter into debate across traditions. The potential for combining EBP with other approaches is most obviously true for reflective and relationship-based approaches to social work. EBP is almost always about relationship-based approaches in practice, and developing skilled ability to deliver evidence based approaches requires a reflective approach to one's own practice. However, the radical tradition has much to offer in highlighting the potential limitations of EBP and ensuring that EBP in social work is a more sophisticated, complex and genuinely psycho-social approach than that which often appears to be promulgated. EBP therefore seems to have great potential for promoting constructive debate across social work, but what are its implications for policy and practice?

Evidence based social work and new initiatives in social work

The widespread belief that social work is in crisis has led to several current initiatives designed to address problems within the profession. It is too early to judge some of these developments – and several are in the process of being evaluated. However, it is worth making some general observations and then discussing two current developments that place EBP at the heart of reforms to social work.

A key player in developing innovation within children's services on behalf of the government has been the Children's Workforce Development Council [CWDC]. The CWDC is currently running eleven projects aimed at developing new models for social work. These projects vary considerably, but common themes are creating teams or roles that improve interagency coordination, reduce the burden of bureaucracy and increase the time that social workers spend with clients. These developments are to be welcomed, and hopefully they are being rigorously evaluated. However, it is somewhat concerning that where pilots mention specific 'evidence based' approaches they either specify solution focused approaches (for which there is very little evidence) or intensive family preservation (which studies have tended to find does not work).

These errors are fairly symptomatic of two general problems within social work. The first is a widespread ignorance of research on what works. As a result, any approach that claims to work is treated as an 'evidence based' approach, regardless of the extent or nature of the evidence. However, the second problem is more profound, and that is a tendency to address perceived problems in practice through organisational change. All of the CWDC model programmes seem well intentioned, however few have much to say about what social work practice is or should be. Instead they focus on creating organisational structures that allow more contact with clients or greater interagency coordination. These are (probably) good things. However, there is a 40-year research tradition that shows that more counselling or social work does not

necessarily lead to better outcomes. It really is what you do as much as how much you do.

The same criticism can be made of another major initiative currently being carried out by the Department for Children Schools and Families, namely the piloting of 'Social Work Practices'. This initiative originated in the work of Le Grand and his belief in the superiority of market-based approaches to the delivery of public services (Le Grand, 2007). In essence, social work 'practices' involve a group of social workers, a private company or a charity contracting with a local authority to provide services for a certain number of looked after children. There are good reasons to be sceptical about this approach, though it seems unwise to prejudge the effectiveness of the service before the evaluation has been undertaken. But what is certainly true is that, once again, this is an innovation which focuses on the *structure* not the *content* of social work services; it is about *how we are organised* not *what we do*. This is perfectly reasonable: social work practices are a social policy response to perceived problems within local authorities. Social work practices may (or may not) be a good thing – but they have little to say about what social work is or should be.

In contrast, there are exciting initiatives which place the implementation of evidence based approaches at their heart. In Hackney and Wales, services are being or have been restructured in order to deliver approaches which are securely based on evidence. The crucial difference in these initiatives is that because they place evidence based practice at the heart of what they are proposing to do, they have much more to say about the nature of practice and how it should be improved. While both involve restructuring, the changes in organisation are designed to support specific models of practice excellence. Rather than assuming that more social work by itself will produce better outcomes, both focus on improving the quality of the social work practice itself.

In this respect Hackney have been national trail-blazers. Faced with an authority with multiple complex problems, the reform involved a radical change toward small teams, led by a consultant social worker and focussed on delivering evidence based approaches. The initial evaluation of the initiative is extremely promising. It found highly significant improvements in 'organisational culture' and 'social work practice' (as measured through a questionnaire developed for the study). Further research is under way, but these are encouraging initial findings (Cross et al., 2009).

This does not mean that there are not challenges for the Hackney initiative. A key one is that it has proved difficult to recruit consultant social workers. This is not for a lack of applicants. However, few have met the stringent criteria set by Hackney. Furthermore, most of those who have been appointed qualified abroad. This points to potentially very serious problems in the quality of social workers qualifying in the UK. In particular, very few have the knowledge or skills to deliver an evidence based intervention. This picks up on key themes from the recent Social Work Taskforce Report (2009) which highlighted systemic problems in the recruitment of social work students and a very low fail rate on social work courses.

The second major problem for the Hackney model is also broader, namely that there is in fact only a very limited evidence base for social work interventions. Hackney have based their services on using approaches found to be effective in other settings (namely Systemic Family Therapy and Social Learning Theory) (see London Borough of Hackney, 2008)). The process of developing skill in delivering these interventions seems to have produced very positive results, however we need far more evidence about which approaches tend to work with whom in social work settings and about the ways in which interventions need to be adapted or fundamentally changed to be compatible with social work.

The Welsh Assembly Government initiative, named Stronger Families, is currently being put in place (see documents on Welsh Assembly Government website (WAG, 2008)). In the pilot authorities' specialist teams delivering one or more evidence based interventions will work with families affected by parental substance misuse where there is a high level of need. Their role is not however confined to being simply another specialist team: their remit is to provide training and supervision to allow the delivery of evidence based approaches across the whole local authority. In tandem with this there are proposals to restructure the social work career, with levels all the way up to consultant social worker being closely tied to the ability to deliver and evaluate evidence based approaches. There are always challenges in putting new initiatives into place, however the most exciting element of Strengthening Families is the focus on defining what good practice is through using identified

evidence based approaches, and then supporting practitioners to deliver it in the belief that this will improve outcomes for children and families.

In England the report from the Social Work Taskforce (2009) outlines authoritatively the extent of the current problems for social work. Initial proposals to provide a more coherent voice for social work and to reduce the bureaucratic burden on social workers are most welcome. However, at present it has little to say about what social workers should be doing or the complex processes required to support them to do this. In this respect the missing element from the report is a thoroughgoing focus on developing and delivering evidence based approaches.

Conclusion

Entering into a new and more nuanced debate about EBP offers social work many opportunities. It allows us to engage with a way of researching and evaluating social work that we largely ignore at present. It offers the opportunity to develop a critical appreciation of the potential contribution that a critical and radical perspective can offer for evidence based ways of working. Furthermore, at the heart of EBP is a focus on developing the skills of social workers through direct supervision and support around practice. Most important of all, evidence based practice provides us with a compelling way of articulating what social workers do and whether it makes a difference. Indeed, if we cannot make a case for social work in the language of what works, we are unlikely to have our case heard at all.

Ultimately EBP offers the potential to redefine social work for the 21st Century. Yet its ability to do that is based on some very simple ideas, for EBP is fundamentally about carefully observing what practitioners do when they meet clients, measuring the impact of this and by doing so developing better practice. It is this that provides its opportunities to redefine social work and to reach across different traditions within social work. It is as simple and as complicated as that.

References

Cleaver, H. and Walker, S. with Meadows, P. (2004) *Assessing Children's Needs and Circumstances. The Impact of the Assessment Framework.* London: Jessica Kingsley.

Cross, S., Hubbard, A. and Munro, E. (2009) *Reclaiming Social Work: London Borough of Hackney Children and Young People's Services, Independent Evaluation – Summary*. London: Hackney Children's Services.

Department of Health (1995) *Child Protection: Messages from Research*. London: HMSO.

Department of Health (2000a) *Assessing Children in Need and Their Families: Practice Guidance*. London: The Stationery Office.

Department of Health (2000b) *Framework for the Assessment of Children in Need and their Families, Guidance Notes and Glossary for: Referral and Initial Information Record, Initial Assessment Record and Core Assessment Record*. London: The Stationery Office.

Department of Health (2001) *Studies Informing the Framework for the Assessment of Children in Need and their Families*. London: The Stationery Office.

Families and Schools Together (2009) *Families and Schools Together*. http://familiesandschools.org/.

Forrester, D. et al. (2008) *Final Report on the Evaluation of 'Option 2', Welsh Assembly Government*. http://www.option2.org/downloads/Option%202%20Final%20Report%20(pub%20web%20).pdf.

Harvard Family Research Project (2007) Family Involvement Makes a Difference: Evidence that Family Involvement Promotes School Success for Every Child of Every Age. In *Harvard Family Research Project Report, No 2*, Winter 2006/2007 Available: http://familiesandschools.org/media/family-involvement-makes-a-difference-hfrp.pdf.

Holmes, D. et al. (2006) Deconstructing the Evidence-Based Discourse in Health Sciences: Truth, Power and Fascism. *International Journal of Evidence-based Healthcare*, 4, 180–6.

Kratochwill, T.R. et al. (2004) Families and Schools Together: An Experimental Analysis of a Parent-Mediated Multi-Family Group Program For American Indian Children. *Journal of School Psychology*, 42(5), 359–383

Laming, H. (2003) *The Victoria Climbie Inquiry*. London: DoH.

Le Grand, J. (2007) *The Other Invisible Hand. Delivering Public Services through Choice and Competition*. Princeton and Oxford: Princeton University Press.

London Borough of Hackney (2008) *A Difference that Makes a Difference, Clinical Manual: The Role of Clinicians in the Social Work Unit*. London Borough of Hackney. http://www.hackney.gov.uk/reclaiming-clinical-manual.doc.

Office of Juvenile Justice and Delinquency Prevention (2009) *Listing for Families and Schools Together in Approved Programmes List*. http://www2.dsgonline.com/mpg/mpg_program_detail.aspx?ID=459&title=Families And Schools –Together (FAST).

Pawson, R. and Tilley, N. (1997) *Realistic Evaluation*. London: Sage.

Pitts, J. (2001) Korrectional Karaoke: New Labour and the Zombification of Youth Justice. *Youth Justice*, 1, 2, 3–16.

Robson, C. (2002) *Real World Research*. 2nd edn, Oxford: Blackwell.

Singh, S. (1997). *Fermat's Last Theorem*. London: Harper Collins.

Social Work Task Force (2009) *Facing up to the Task: The Interim Report of the Social Work Task Force (July 2009)*. London: DCSF. http://www.dcsf.gov.uk/swtf/.

Substance Abuse and Mental Health Services Administration (2003) Listing for Families and Schools Together in Evidence Based Programmes. http://www.modelprograms.samhsa.gov/pdfs/model/FAST.pdf.

Tober, G. (2007) Motivational Enhancement Therapy in the UK Alcohol Treatment Trial. In Tober, G. and Raistrick, D. (Eds.) *Motivational Dialogue*. London: Routledge.

Ward, H. (Ed.) (1995) *Looking After Children: Research into Practice, Second Report to the Department of Health on Assessing Outcomes in Child Care*. Norwich: HMSO.

Welsh Assembly Government (2008) *Consultation on: Stronger Families, Supporting Vulnerable Children and Families Through a New Approach to Integrated Family Support Services*. http://www.adjudicationpanelwales.org.uk/consultation/dhss/vulnerable/strongerfamiliese.pdf?lang=en&status=closed.

Conclusion

CHAPTER 13

For my Next Trick: Illusion in Children's Social Policy and Practice

Michael Preston-Shoot and Patrick Ayre

Let us take you into a magician's show. We have here a pack of picture cards with four suits: safeguarding professionals, children's outcomes, policy responses and community reactions. Looking closely, choose one card to represent each suit and place them in an envelope. Do not let the magician see the cards you have chosen but you may show the audience. Seal the envelope and hold onto it.

Magicians rely on the audience not being able to identify the illusions or to spot how the tricks are constructed. One illusion is to present a simple certainty. In children's social policy, the failure to safeguard Victoria Climbié and subsequently Baby Peter has been followed by the introduction of extensive legislative and structural changes in England to drive procedures and practice for safeguarding the most vulnerable children. The apparent certainty is that these structural and procedural changes are inevitable and that they will render vulnerable children safer. An inconvenient parallel is not held up for scrutiny, namely that children known to social workers have also been killed by family members elsewhere in the UK. There, however, the policy response has been different, as Butler and Drakeford in respect of Wales and Daniel and Baldwin for Scotland outline succinctly in their chapters. Welsh and Scottish policy and service structures are increasingly diverging from those in England, offering much by way of comparison. It would, of course, be to fall for the same illusion if one pretended that children known to social workers would always be safeguarded effectively in these countries. However, a pertinent question to answer is where the common lessons emerging from serious case reviews and inquiries into child deaths have best been learned. There have been sufficient overviews of inquiries and serious case reviews to map the findings and to compare which social services and inter-agency systems best correspond to and take forward the repetitive messages that they have delivered.

A second illusion derives from offering a false comparison. One such relates to the comparison drawn between teacher training and social work education. Trainee teachers are reported to be more satisfied than social work students with their professional education. So, the illusion goes, the professional formation of social workers should follow the model used in teacher training. Never mind if the knowledge and skills sets to be learned and practised are identical, nor whether the settings in which these are used are more or less likely to support or distort the learning acquired in training. It is enough to hold up a mirror and to see a clear reflection. Noteworthy, then, is the sidelining of the longitudinal study of social work degree outcomes (Evaluation of Social Work Degree Qualification in England Team, 2008) in favour of other, supposedly 'deep dive' but in reality more flawed reviews. Both the Social Work Taskforce (2009a; b) and Laming (2009a) selectively ignore much of the evidence for the outcomes of social work education. Equally, as yet, no one who has pronounced on the alleged deficiencies of the social work degree has yet to unpack the meaning behind whether social work students are sufficiently prepared for the social work tasks encountered in local authority settings, or interrogated the meaning of satisfaction with training.

Just as there is nothing inevitable about the policy direction taken in England, led by the Department of Children, Schools and Families, equally the evidence is at best equivocal for the outcomes of these changes and at worst deeply pessimistic about enhancing the capability of children's services to respond effectively to the complex challenges which they face. Laming (2009a) refers to the importance of supervision, manageable caseloads, resources, and the time needed to understand the circumstances of children and their families, all of which were known to be vulnerable to erosion long before the death of Victoria Climbié and none of which has been addressed effectively by subsequent reforms. The Social Work Taskforce (2009a; b) similarly has concluded that social workers are not getting the support they need to maintain high professional standards, which include strong supervision and continuing education, in order to develop reflective practice and sustain the knowledge and skills to make complex judgements. Rectifying such weaknesses in front line resources and guaranteeing standards for supervision and support will require investment and a commitment to engage with front line practitioners about their lived experience of work. Whilst the Taskforce (2009a) has recommended just such an engagement with the reality of practice, it appears to have avoided analysis of why longstanding lessons about what contributes to high quality services have still to be fully learned.

The policy-makers' trick, though, is through sleight of hand to offer just one apparent way of seeing the scene. Key themes in children's social policy and practice have become managerialism, the audit culture and over-reliance on quantitative key performance indicators. Ferguson identifies one impact of performance management and information technology, namely the loss of relationship time with children and their families. Pitts and Bateman also bemoan the paucity of professionals' contact with young people. Ayre and Calder highlight another impact, this time the elevation of timeframes and targets and the diminution of focus on quality of the work and its outcomes. Pitts and Bateman attack the same phenomenon, noting the conflation of targets and quality, and commenting that the evidence that matters has become not what works but what can be counted. Even then, as Brodie eloquently outlines, the performance assessment system does not meet the needs of the sector and the measures it prizes are inadequate. Chard and Ayre too provide a detailed critique of managerialism and the audit culture of quality assurance of performance, both in general and their inappropriateness for welfare services specifically. What is particularly disturbing, however, is not just the research-informed critique offered in these chapters but the absence of apparent recognition in official pronouncements. Laming (2009b) is critical of the distance that inspection has maintained from front line experience, its failure to focus on the work actually done by organisations, and its loss of a developmental function. The Taskforce (2009a) indicates that the priority given to ensuring the completion of processes should not be at the expense of a focus on service quality and outcomes for service users. Otherwise, there remains a remarkable acceptance of the current position.

The policy illusion for practice also includes proceduralisation, technicalisation and de-professionalisation of the social work task. Daniel and Baldwin point to the damage being done by social workers' loss of professional autonomy and by the volume of bureaucracy with which they have to contend. Ferguson, and Ayre and Calder similarly argue that the emphasis on, or faith in procedures to make child protection safe actually de-skills social workers, in part because it reduces the scope and space available for therapeutic practice, in part because it takes the emphasis away from staff developing sound professional judgements. Morris argues persuasively that mainstream services have, in the process, lost the capacity to support families. Pitts and Bateman present evidence of an intellectual de-skilling and estrangement from the professional task, created in part by the audit culture, that results in uncritical operatives who eschew debate about the policies being pursued. Perhaps this is one reason for the unlawful and unethical practice to which Preston-Shoot draws attention. Although the Social Work Taskforce (2009b) refers to the impact of bureaucracy, official pronouncements do not reflect serious engagement with this critique of how services to safeguard children are being constructed.

To perform an illusion requires confidence, in oneself and in the setting, as well as competence. Social workers too require confidence but, as Ayre and Calder capture, the climate in which they must practise is dominated by cultures of fear and blame. Brodie comments on the ambivalence in which the care system is held and offers evidence of the impact on job satisfaction and morale. Forrester too notes the condemnation of social work following the deaths of Baby Peter and Victoria Climbié, in marked contrast to the criticisms levelled against other professionals involved. The impact on social workers of such destructive emotions has been pictured in research-informed theory-building (for example, see Valentine, 1994). However, it is not a part of dominant meaning-making.

This stage on which social workers must perform also forms part of Preston-Shoot's argument, namely that the lived experience of practitioners, the organisational behaviour to which they are subjected, demonstrates that too many are not practising in benign environments. He questions, as does Forrester, what social work students and newly qualified practitioners actually learn in such settings, and what links they make between academic tuition and the realities of practice. He suggests that what is actually learned is something quite different from the formal academic and practice curricula in which may be prioritised the legal rules, social work values, and research informed knowledge about such concerns as child development. Both Chard and Ayre, and Wastell and White also take up the theme of oppressive workplaces and the need to have managers who will design competent organisational environments in order to maximise the likelihood of knowledge-driven, ethically-informed, skilfully applied practice. Disappointingly, as Forrester notes, research has been voicing concerns about the working environments in which social work is practised for some time. Preston-Shoot (2003) has provided one such review, analysing the evidence of harassment by managers, for shortcomings in supervision and support for front line staff, and for the impact of regulatory intrusion, bureaucracy, job insecurity and constrained service provision. He draws attention to repetitive lessons and subsequent non-learning from analyses of serious incidents. There have been serious problems for decades as the recurring themes from meta analyses of child protection inquiries (DHSS, 1982; Reder et al., 1993; James, 1994; Falkov, 1996; Brandon et al., 1999; Sinclair and Bullock, 2002; Brandon et al., 2008; Ofsted, 2008) will highlight.

Meanwhile, the link between training and better outcomes for children and their families remains uncertain, significantly because the lived reality of workplace activity does not connect meaningfully with academic and practice curricula envisaged by benchmarks (QAA, 2008) and occupational standards (TOPSS, 2002). Once again, current review and policy activity does not inspire confidence that lessons, both historical and more recent, will be learned. Laming (2009a) refers to the importance of a supportive learning environment for front line staff. He notes (Laming, 2009b) past employer reticence to release staff for continuing professional development but also assumes without apparent question that robust and consistent implementation of current policies will make children safer. The House of Commons select committee (2009) refers to the ridiculous levels of responsibility carried by early career social workers; notes that front line staff may find it difficult to practise what they know to be good practice, and cautions that employers may find it hard to support the Newly Qualified Social Worker programmes. The Taskforce (2009a) makes similar observations and pins its hopes on recommendations to improve working conditions, such as employers guaranteeing standards of support for staff. However, again there appears to be little meaningful engagement with long-standing research findings.

Some of the chapters in this book have illustrated the negative impact of these developments on how workers engaged in child care social work perceive themselves and their task. Others have charted the outcome for the recording, assessment and case management systems which underpin their work. All highlight what effective practice requires: research-informed, reflective, critically challenging staff supported by management systems which promote rather than undermine their effectiveness.

A further part of the magician's skill is to make the illusion or trick appear so easy and effortless. Laming (2009a) argues that knowledge is sufficiently advanced to be able to identify early children who are at risk of harm. The problem is simply that organisations employ thresholds that limit access to services and have insufficient skills to work across agency boundaries (Laming, 2009b). The illusion is that the children requiring safeguarding are always easy to spot. Pitts and Bateman name this as the risk factor paradigm, which suggests that one can prevent child protection tragedies by identifying high risk cases. However, as Reder and Duncan (2003) systematically rehearse, complexity and ambiguity cannot be magically erased from child protection practice. Organisational structures, agency and inter-agency procedures, individual belief systems, professional training, and the psychology of communication all impact upon how meaning is co-constructed and cases configured.

Of course, the magician has all the resources needed for the illusions to be performed. The same cannot be said for service providers working with children in need and young people requiring protection. Daniel and Baldwin, Chard and Ayre, Morris and Brodie all explore the impact of fixed budgets and limited resources, for instance on the decision-making process whereby cases are selected for intervention, on how procedures are used to justify rationing, on how prevention has become marginalised in mainstream services. The Select Committee (2009) calls for investment, whilst Laming (2009a) notes the necessity of adequate resources. The reality, currently, is of severe fiscal constraint in local authorities and other public sector organisations. This might mean social workers, and others, having to do more with less. More disturbingly, it could actually mean doing less with much less. Here, the impact could fall on preventive programmes, the wider safeguarding agenda, which in the guise of section 17 (*Children Act 1989*) has always been vulnerable to erosion (Braye and Preston-Shoot, 2009).

Magicians also weave spells to create an atmosphere in which the audience can choose to believe rather than question what they see before them. One such spell relates to measurement and inspection. Inspection of safeguarding services will now include unannounced visits but, as Ayre and Calder note, it will still not examine performance directly or, we could add, the lived experience of front line staff. Brodie is similarly sceptical, pointing out the reliance on monitoring to improve services rather than learning the lessons from critical engagement with research(ers). Daniel and Baldwin question the effectiveness of inspections, and it should be noted the positive evaluations which the London Borough of Haringey had received, arguing that they divert resources from practice and do not lead to improved outcomes. Chard and Ayre make a direct connection between inspection and the destructive culture of fear to which reference has already been made. Forrester suggests that the question that should really be asked is how best social work practice can be controlled and developed.

This faith in measurement and inspection is one example of how current policy activity misunderstands the process of achieving fundamental change. Managing change by ignoring or playing down the significance of the wider context, by using positional authority to force through procedures, by assuming that continual improvement is possible, by seeking quick fixes and by eschewing relationships with those individuals and groups on whom service delivery depends (Preston-Shoot, 2003) will ultimately prove less than effective.

One crucial component of belief is evidence but can this be trusted? This concluding chapter has already noted how some research evidence has been air-brushed out in current policy review. Morris points out, in respect of preventive services, the limited transfer of learning about effectiveness. Brodie too notes a paucity of research information and a lack of co-ordination in making professional expertise, including research findings, available. Wastell and White comment on how negative findings have been dismissed by government regarding information management systems on which they have placed such policy reliance. As well as commenting on the variable use of research in policy and practice, Forrester also suggests that social workers must develop their research skills. Both Forrester and Brodie argue for a more sophisticated development of evidence, to ensure that the research base is fit for purpose, understood and used.

What, of course, makes it harder to understand how the magician performs an illusion is that the onlooker does not see the whole system within which the trick is performed. What goes on hidden from view is as important, if not more so, than what the viewer actually sees. Ferguson draws attention to this phenomenon by calling for a whole network or systems approach. Part of that network must involve communities, as Daniel and Baldwin point out. Elsewhere, child protection researchers have identified missing domains which should comprise part of the assessment of children in need and children requiring protection (Horwath, 2007). This point about whole system focus refers back to the management of change and is illustrated by the now in vogue support for the creation of a social work college. This solution is looked to for professional leadership, advocacy of excellent practice standards and education, partnership working between employers and educators, and delivery of enhanced status and career progression for practitioners. However, without the authority to command resources and to hold organisations accountable it will be walking against the wind.

Each show offers a new illusion, a different trick. Leaving aside for the moment whether the proposed social work college offers the prospect of substantive rather than illusory change, both Morris and Brodie note this trend. Morris refers to policy churn, the speed of which actually cuts across evaluation and defeats the objective that change outcomes might possibly inform policy and practice. Brodie outlines how service development, having been initiative-led, has in some respects failed young people in care. Ayre and Calder suggest that the speed of change is such that neither practitioners nor managers can feel confident that they are aware of all the guidance relevant to their work.

The use of information technology has been presented as one such new solution although, as Chard and Ayre and Wastell and White argue, at significant cost to the time spent with families and without corresponding clarity about how IT systems will actually enhance the safety of vulnerable children. Another is integration. However, as both Brodie and Butler and Drakeford point out, England's approach to the integration of children's services has not benefited all young people and a critique may be long overdue. A corollary here is the advocacy in some quarters for greater specialisation in qualifying training. Daniel and Baldwin address this head-on by noting that specialisation can lead to the loss of a generic sense of responsibility for children. Indeed, in Scotland all students must consider the needs of children and have key capabilities in their care and protection. Equally, as all the chapters to a greater or lesser extent imply, what matters is how to ensure that qualifying training and continuing professional development influence the culture, shape and provision of service delivery organisations. One long-standing reality is that standards, whether relating to ethical, lawful and/or knowledge-informed practice, have been vulnerable to compromise, the result of underfunding and the knock-on effect on workloads and service provision (Marsh and Triseliotis, 1996; Braye and Preston-Shoot, 2009). Another is that policy-makers and employers, despite the rhetoric about staff development, have gradually allowed the erosion of professional formation in practice. It has stressed what practice is, not what it should be. It has reflected employer interests not those of service users and carers. It has encouraged conformity rather than critical reflection and has failed in basic sensitivity to front line staff without whom good practice is impossible. Therefore, when the Taskforce (2009a) calls for greater use of research and continuing professional development to inform practice, it might have been expected to have analysed why children's social work services, as currently configured, resourced and constructed, have often not been able to ensure high standards. Just such a systems analysis is

missing from the report, which makes it difficult to envision how the recommended changes to parts of the edifice surrounding the children's workforce will fundamentally realign services as a whole.

As these chapters demonstrate, it is far from clear how the lessons from child protection tragedies have been learned. Current analysis, as Preston-Shoot points out, appears remarkably ahistorical, with little reference back to previous recommendations from inquiries and critical exploration of the degree to which the learning offered has really been transferred into the resourcing and the configuring of practice. Although taking different facets of safeguarding policy-making or practice in England, chapters in this book have all punctured parts of the illusion that masquerades as learning the lessons from tragedy. They offer a detailed analysis of the strengths and weaknesses of the current social policy reform agenda, and outline both practical and conceptual changes which will represent substantive and substantial performance change. What ultimately these chapters outline is that there is an alternative. For Butler and Drakeford, the difference includes a clear relationship between children's welfare and the rights afforded them, and an identification of protective factors, support for which might help avoid future problem development. For others, such as Ferguson and Ayre and Calder, it is the quality of relationships between practitioners and families, underpinned by the same supportive but challenging relations between practitioners and their managers. The key message, as captured so graphically by Ayre and Calder, is that what finally counts, what really matters, is what social workers do with and on behalf of the people they work with. Equally, as Pitts and Bateman observe in relation to young offenders, policy and practice need to rediscover children. To paraphrase Bill Clinton, 'it's the people, stupid'.

Let's return to the envelope with which we began. Open it up. Take out and show us all the cards you chose. From the suit of safeguarding professionals you selected the social worker who is blamed. From children's outcomes, you selected a young person's death when known to social services. From the suit of policy responses, you selected the inquiry which recommends procedural changes. From the suit of community reactions you chose the card that demanded that named professionals took responsibility. Now the magician shows us another sealed envelope in which he placed four cards from a similar pack before the show. If we open it you will see that he chose the same four cards that you did, the same four that he always chooses. There they are inside. Now, that's magic! Unless we can make it different. This book points the direction.

References

Brandon M. et al. (2008) *Analysing Child Deaths and Serious Injury through Abuse and Neglect: What Can We Learn?* London: DCSF.

Brandon, M., Owers, M. and Black, J. (1999) *Learning How to Make Children Safer: An Analysis for the Welsh Office of Serious Child Abuse Cases in Wales.* Norwich: University of East Anglia/Welsh Office.

Braye, S. and Preston-Shoot, M. (2009) *Practising Social Work Law.* 3rd edn. Basingstoke: Palgrave Macmillan.

DHSS (1982) *Child Abuse: A Study of Inquiry Reports, 1973–1981.* London: HMSO.

Evaluation of Social Work Degree Qualification in England Team (2008) *Evaluation of the New Social Work Degree Qualification in England. Volume 1: Findings.* London: King's College London, Social Care Workforce Research Unit.

Falkov, A. (1996) A *Study of Working Together Part 8 Reports: Fatal Child Abuse and Parental Psychiatric Disorder.* London: DoH.

Horwath, J. (2007) The Missing Assessment Domain: Personal, Professional and Organizational Factors Influencing Professional Judgements When Identifying and Referring Child Neglect. *British Journal of Social Work,* 37: 8, 1285–303.

House of Commons Children, Schools and Families Committee (2009) *Training of Children and Families Social Workers. Seventh Report of Session 2008–09.* London: The Stationery Office.

James, G. (1994) *Study of Working Together Part 8 Reports.* London: DoH.

Laming, H. (2009a) *The Protection of Children in England: A Progress Report.* London: HMSO.

Laming, H. (2009b) *The Protection of Children in England: Lord Laming's Progress Report.* Evidence to the Children, Schools and Families Committee, House of Commons. London: The United Kingdom Parliament.

Marsh, P. and Triseliotis, J. (1996) *Ready to Practice? Social Workers and Probation Officers: Their Training and First Year in Work.* Aldershot: Averbury.

Ofsted (2008) *Learning Lessons, Taking Action.* London: Ofsted.

Preston-Shoot, M. (2003) Changing Learning and Learning Change: Making a Difference in Education, Policy and Practice. *Journal of Social Work Practice.* 17: 1, 9–23.

QAA (2008) *Subject Benchmark Statements: Social Work.* Gloucester: The Quality Assurance Agency for Higher Education.

Reder, P. and Duncan, S. (2003) Understanding Communication in Child Protection Networks. *Child Abuse Review,* 12, 82–100.

Reder, P., Duncan, S. and Gray, M. (1993) *Beyond Blame. Child Abuse Tragedies Revisited.* London: Routledge.

Sinclair, R. and Bullock, R. (2002) *Learning from Past Experience: A Review of Serious Case Reviews.* London: DoH.

Social Work Taskforce (2009a) *Building a Safe, Confident Future. The Final Report of the Social Work TaskForce.* London: DCSF.

Social Work Taskforce (2009b) *First Report of the Social Work Taskforce.* London: DCSF.

TOPSS (2002) *The National Occupational Standards for Social Work.* Leeds: TOPSS.

Valentine, M. (1994) The Social Worker as 'Bad Object'. *British Journal of Social Work,* 24: 1, 71–86.

Index